W9-BZT-180

GILES WHITTELL is a leader- and feature-writer for *The Times* and was previously the paper's correspondent in Los Angeles and Moscow. His other books include *Lambada Country* and *Extreme Continental*, describing his travels by bike and motorbike through Eastern Europe and Central Asia during the collapse of the Soviet Union. He lives in London with his wife and three sons.

From the reviews of *Spitfire Women of World War II*:

'Most engaging ... Whittell tells the story with suspense, perfect context and technical detail. It is quite impossible to read without emotional engagement ... one is all but overwhelmed by the sense of utter admiration' *The Times*

'A collection of stories of unusual young women living colourful lives and doing skilled, resourceful work, which cost sixteen of them their lives. Reading it is a bumpy flight as well as an exciting one ... the author's enthusiasm carries the day' *TLS*

'Impeccably researched and written'
The Times, Books of the Year

'An eye-opening and very moving illustration of the courage and sacrifice of women who deserve to be remembered alongside their more celebrated male counterparts'
Literary Review

'Extraordinary stories of women who had little fear and minimal concern for the enormous step they were taking'
Good Housekeeping

'Giles Whittell's affectionate book reads like a Boy's Own adventure turned on its head . . . and uncovers some exceptional tales' *Financial Times*

By the same author

Central Asia: The Practical Handbook
Extreme Continental
Lambada Country
Bridge of Spies
The Secret Life of Snow: The science and
the stories behind nature's greatest wonder

GILES WHITTELL

Spitfire Women of World War II

WILLIAM COLLINS

William Collins
An imprint of HarperCollins*Publishers*
1 London Bridge Street
London SE1 9GF

WilliamCollinsBooks.com

HarperCollins*Publishers*
1st Floor, Watermarque Building, Ringsend Road
Dublin 4, Ireland

This William Collins paperback edition published in 2021
First published in Great Britain by *HarperPress* in 2007

2

Copyright © Giles Whittell 2007
PS Section copyright © Travis Elborough 2008, except 'Of Pilots and Politics'
by Giles Whittell © Giles Whittell 2008

PS™ is a trademark of HarperCollins*Publishers* Ltd

Giles Whittell asserts the moral right to be identified as the author of this work
in accordance with the Copyright, Designs and Patents Act 1988

A catalogue record for this book is available from the British Library

ISBN 978-0-00-849060-7

Set in PostScript Giovanni Book with Photina display by Rowland
Phototypesetting Ltd, Bury St Edmunds, Suffolk

Printed and Bound in the UK using 100% Renewable Electricity
at CPI Group (UK) Ltd

All rights reserved. No part of this publication may be reproduced,
stored in a retrieval system, or transmitted, in any form or by any means,
electronic, mechanical, photocopying, recording or otherwise, without the
prior permission of the publishers.

This book is sold subject to the condition that it shall not, by way of trade
or otherwise, be lent, re-sold, hired out or otherwise circulated without the
publisher's prior consent in any form of binding or cover other than
that in which it is published and without a similar condition including
this condition being imposed on the subsequent purchaser.

MIX
Paper from
responsible sources
FSC® C007454

This book is produced from independently certified FSC™ paper
to ensure responsible forest management.

For more information visit: www.harpercollins.co.uk/green

For Karen

Contents

List of Illustrations

'Everyone is equal before the machine . . . There is no tradition in technology, no class-consciousness.'

Laszlo Moholy-Nagy

Prologue

'Indaba' is Zulu for 'conversation', and at the Indaba Hotel on the northern outskirts of Johannesburg a conversation is what I hoped for. If it materialised it would be with an elderly lady who had insisted several times on the telephone that she really had nothing to say. But we both knew this was not quite true, and now, as she walked carefully down the steps to the hotel entrance, with a grandson hovering at her shoulder, she looked up with a smile.

'You must be Betty,' I said.

She was easily recognisable from the one blurred picture I'd seen of her in a smart blue uniform, leaning on the wing of a Fairey Barracuda over sixty years earlier. Now she wore a gold-coloured woollen shawl and carried a stick. She was tall and alert, and gave the impression she might even be looking forward to our meeting. Her name was Betty Keith-Jopp.

Soon after that photograph was taken in late May 1945, Betty and a fellow pilot named Barbara Lankshear took off from Prestwick on the west coast of Scotland, the eastern terminus of the great Atlantic air bridge that had kept Britain supplied with bombers since before Pearl Harbor. They were both ferry pilots, unarmed and untrained to fly on instruments, with less than eighteen months' flying experience between them. Both were in Barracudas – lumpy, underpowered torpedo bombers with unusually large cockpits and a history of unexplained crashes. They were bound for Lossiemouth, 200 miles to the north on the rugged Moray Coast.

'Shall we sit outside?' Betty asked. She led the way through the hotel lobby and out onto a shaded terrace where we found a

1

table and talked briefly about the weather. Then she ordered a large glass of wine and returned to 1945.

She would never have taken off that day if there had been even a hint of menace in the weather report, she insisted, and initially the sunny forecast seemed to have been accurate. 'We were flying along perfectly happily. It was a lovely, lovely day.' But their route took them south of Glasgow, between Dunfermline and Edinburgh and into thick cloud over the northern edge of the Firth of Forth.

As ferry pilots, Third Officers Lankshear and Keith-Jopp had standing orders never to fly over the top of cloud as a way out of trouble. Barbara disobeyed those orders and was lucky to find a way down; she landed safely soon afterwards. But Betty decided discretion was the better part of valour and turned back. She knew there was rising ground behind the coast to her left, so began a slow turn to the right, unaware that she was losing height.

She saw the water a second before hitting it.

'I made a good landing, all things considered,' she told me, still quietly astonished at the memory. 'I just managed to get my nose up and the plane landed gently. It sat there on the surface for a few moments, then started sinking. I must have gone down quite decently, like in a lift.'

Still level, the aircraft settled on the bottom of the firth. Water began squirting into the cockpit from cracks between the canopy and fuselage. At first, not being a strong swimmer, Betty made little effort to get out. She thought of the life insurance payment that her death would trigger; of how her mother would be able to make good use of it caring for her brother, who had recently contracted polio. She thought of Amy Johnson, one of her heroes, dying in similar circumstances four years earlier despite vastly more experience in the air. 'I can't remember being frightened,' she said. 'I can remember more or less accepting it.'

Then instinct took over. She reached up, took a last breath and pulled the red canopy release lever above her head. A giant bubble from the Barracuda's oversized cockpit would then have headed for the surface. It could have taken her with it if she had unclipped her straps and parachute harness – but she hadn't. 'I wouldn't have had the intelligence to have worked those things out,' she said. 'I was working on reflexes. I was acting purely like an animal. I must have bashed the thing that released the harness once the water had come in. It took forever to get to the top.'

Even so, Betty was alive when she bobbed to the surface. There was a strong swell and the water was bitterly cold. She had no life jacket and the cloud that had engulfed her aeroplane now enveloped her. She had no way of knowing how far she was from the shore until a wave lifted her and she glimpsed it for an instant, too far to swim to but close enough to let her hope. She started to shout.

John Morris, skipper of the trawler *Providence* from the port of St Monans, would never have been anywhere near Betty had he not developed engine trouble earlier that morning. Nor would he have paid much attention to what sounded at first like a seal if it hadn't been so persistent. He altered course towards the barking, and Betty's head appeared out of the mist.

'All I can remember after that are the words "Hang on, laddie",' she said, sixty-one years later, sipping her chenin blanc on a cool South African afternoon. 'And everything going black, and tea being poured over my hands to warm them up.' She paused, blinking and smiling almost apologetically as if still unable to fathom her good fortune. 'Why that dear little fishing boat should have come chugging along just then . . . really and truly, it was a miracle.'

Yet it was not a miracle that she has often spoken about since. The stories of why Betty Keith-Jopp is so reluctant to talk about her escape from the bottom of the sea, and how she came to be flying into a cloudbank in a Barracuda in the first place, are among those this book tries to tell. They are part of the larger tale of a unique sisterhood of flying addicts – young, hopeful and ridiculously brave – who came to England from five continents to ferry combat aircraft for the Air Transport Auxiliary in the war. There were 164 of them in all, and they were the only women from among the Western Allies who flew in the war. (The Women's Auxiliary Air Force in Britain stayed firmly on the ground and in America the Women's Air Service Pilots – or WASPs – flew too, but never less than 3,000 miles from a war zone.) They flew torpedo bombers if they had to and Lancasters if they lasted long enough; but they had eyes mainly for the fastest aerial hot-rods of the age – Hurricanes, Mosquitoes and the plane that many of these ATA women came to feel had been designed especially for them, the Spitfire.

One of these pilots, Margaret Frost, lived for many years in an ancient half-timbered cottage on the far side of my grandmother's favourite flower bed in Sussex. I'd always known she flew Spitfires in the war, and occasionally she would appear on television on Remembrance Sunday in her best grey overcoat, dwarfed by Guards officers, laying a wreath at the Cenotaph. But I never asked about her flying – that might have been indelicate; and then she moved to Wales.

About twenty years later another ATA pilot, Ann Wood, walked up and introduced herself to me outside the old town hall in Newcastle, New Hampshire. She looked and talked like Katharine Hepburn in her septuagenarian prime, and the only reason I had her attention was that the occasion was my wedding. She had been my wife's neighbour in Massachusetts for twenty years, and a friend of Margaret Frost's since 1942.

In that absurd understatement of the war years, they had both 'done their bit'. Margaret would only venture that she had done her bit for England – and then only if pushed. But Ann was quite comfortable with the idea that she'd done hers for freedom; for a way of life she consciously held dear. She arrived in Liverpool in May 1942, one of twenty-five American women to join the ATA. She flew warplanes continuously until the end of 1945 and she told stories of craziness and courage that I had never heard from our side of the flower bed in Sussex; stories of upside-down engine failure and squeezing under bridges at high tide; of dodging

U-boats and romancing Earls and cooling beer down for the Atlantic ferry boys by flying it to 10,000 feet. It turned out that she had also kept a meticulous, clear-eyed diary that serves as a case study of fearlessness, and of mutual Anglo-American incomprehension.

Ann died as this book was being written, and it would have benefited from her criticism. But she and her fellow Spitfire women still deserve to be remembered for the quiet revolutionaries they were; I hope this helps.

1

Encounter

Monday, 22 September 1941 was a miserable day for flying. Low cloud covered England from Bristol to the Scottish borders. Where the overcast thinned an opaque autumn haze still blurred the horizon in every direction, and over the Midlands it mixed with smog from the munitions factories, turning the barrage balloons from a deterrent into an almighty trap. Even so, at about three in the afternoon, a lone Spitfire took off from Prestwick and headed south.

It climbed over the Ayrshire hills, then sped down the Nith valley to Dumfries and crossed the Solway Firth. It picked up the main west coast railway line at Carlisle and followed it past Oxenholme to Appleby, then headed east through the Pennines in search of clearer skies. Visibility did improve, but not by much. Reaching the London-to-Edinburgh line just south of Darlington, the plane turned south again and pressed on through the murk, England slipping beneath it as the enormous Merlin engine in its nose steadily drained its 90-gallon tanks.

The Spitfire was running almost on empty when, soon after 5 p.m., it descended towards Maidenhead and landed safely at what had been the peacetime home of the De Havilland School of Flying at White Waltham in the Berkshire countryside. It was now headquarters of the ATA. The figure who eased herself out of the cockpit once she had taxied to the dispersal area and cut the engine was perhaps the finest woman pilot then flying for the

Western Allies. There was no shortage of contenders in both Britain and America, and as Mother Russia fought for survival against the Nazi onslaught the following year her daughters excelled in the air, even in combat. But they had no-one quite like Lettice Curtis.

She was tall and slim, with angular features and a tentative smile. She was a triple Oxford blue (in tennis, swimming and lacrosse) with a degree in mathematics and a reputation, even at twenty-three, for extreme impatience with anyone she thought deserved it. Stepping off the wing of her Spitfire in the dark blue uniform of the Air Transport Auxiliary, she took her delivery chit to the operations room beside White Waltham's grass airstrip and handed it over with nothing much to report. No-one had been killed. No aircraft had been damaged. There had been no sightings of the enemy even though the entire route was within range of the Luftwaffe and bombing raids were still routine a year after the Battle of Britain. No-one had even tried a loop or a roll for the hell of it – and that was the point. No-one else had been flying.

For most pilots the day had been a washout. That meant unflyable; not worth the risk of ditching in the Wash or sudden death on the slopes of Black Cwm or Shap Fell. In particular, a group of American pilots based at White Waltham, all of them men, had tried taking off that morning. Every one of them turned back.

'It was many weeks later that I learned this, and of the consternation caused by the arrival of a female in a Spit',' Lettice Curtis wrote, and the sentence is laden with meaning. 'Consternation' is an exquisite understatement for the pique that a group of pilots apprenticed in barnstorming and crop-dusting across the American mid-west would actually have felt. And Curtis's satisfaction at having pulled off what the Yanks had balked at may simply have been too intense to put into words. For she was a remorseless competitor despite an expensive education in schools that valued refinement above all, and she had an unhappy knack of seeming less than cordial to Americans. Most of a lifetime later I sat down with another woman pilot in a retirement home in Oregon to talk about her wartime flying. On most subjects she was thoughtful and diplomatic, but when I mentioned Curtis her first words were: 'Lettice always looked on Americans as if they were a bad smell.' Which was unfortunate, because more were on their way.

The war by this time was two years old; two years in which tenacity in the air had saved Britain from an invasion across the Channel, and superiority in the air had become Churchill's obsession. On 12 July 1941 he had sent a note to Sir Charles Craven, Secretary of State for Air, under the command 'Action this day'. It ended with this peroration:

> We must aim at nothing less than having an Air Force twice as strong as the German Air Force by the end of 1942. This ought not to be impossible if a renewed vast effort is made now. It is the very least that can be contemplated, since no other way of winning the war has yet been proposed.

As a direct result of this memo, a gigantic chain of production was willed into being that would eventually rain fire on Dresden and give Eisenhower the air support without which D-Day would have been in vain. At one end of this chain were the bauxite mines of the British Empire and the Americas, from which the raw material for aluminium was dug in ever-increasing quantities. The next link was one of the great flukes of economic history – the astonishing potential for aluminium production created by the building of the huge Bonneville and Grand Coulee dams across the Columbia River in the American north-west in the depths of the Depression. Aluminium is produced by electrolysis; without the dams the Allies would have been hard-pressed to build the air force Churchill was demanding. As it was, from Everett in Washington state, now home town to the Boeing 747, to Castle Bromwich and Southampton, the miraculous silver metal, which in the nineteenth century had been as costly as gold, was banged and moulded into more aircraft in 1944 alone than Germany could produce in the entire war. Initially their cost was met from the Lend Lease loans signed by Roosevelt from October 1941 onwards as a way of aiding Britain without violating US neutrality. Then Pearl Harbor consigned that neutrality to history and rendered the whole question of payment secondary. Pilots were queuing up to fly the aircraft into combat. All that was missing were people to deliver them to the front line.

The first beneficiaries of this desperate need for ferry pilots were, inevitably, men. Thirty of them had been recruited in September 1939 on the initiative of Gerard 'Pop' d'Erlanger, an air-minded young merchant banker with an immaculate parting and a strong sense of duty. D'Erlanger was also a director of British Airways and a keen private pilot, and had been worrying for at least a year that hostilities in Europe would bring an acute pilot shortage if flyers like himself could not be used.

'Dear Balfour,' he had written in May 1938 to Harold Balfour, then Parliamentary Under Secretary for Air, 'I know how busy you must be and therefore have hesitated in worrying you, but there is a question which for some time has been puzzling me . . .'. Was there a reservists' Air Force in which people like him could enlist? The answer was no, and so, in August 1939, d'Erlanger suggested forming such a unit from holders of private licences with at least 250 hours in the air. The Director General of Civil Aviation, Sir Francis Shelmerdine, agreed, and put d'Erlanger in charge of it. One thousand licence-holders were contacted. One hundred of them replied, and thirty were selected after interviews and flight tests held at British Airways' wartime base at Whitchurch, outside Bristol. The first intake included a publican, a motorcycling champion and an animal lover who had recently flown back from Africa with two new pets – a cheetah and a chimpanzee.

D'Erlanger had envisaged the ATA as an aerial courier service for VIPs, medicines and the wounded, but even in the Phoney War his pilots were more in demand for ferrying. They called themselves the Ancient and Tattered Airmen because it was a more amusing explanation for their ATA badges than the official one, and because, to a great extent, it was true. In a rumpled sort of way, the ATA was the most exclusive flying outfit of the war. The name was an anomaly, *The Times*' aeronautical correspondent noted in 1941, and 'the body itself one of those curious, almost romantic improvisations which the special demands of war sometimes call into existence'.

To be eligible for membership you had to be ineligible for the RAF but still able to fly. That ruled out clear-eyed, coordinated, brave young men; but it ruled in a different sort of elite; one of oddballs, intellectuals, artists, bank managers, civil servants, wounded veterans and Francis 'Frankie' Francis – flying ace, backgammon ace, ex-Guards officer and raven-headed millionaire from the north shore of Lake Geneva. There, in peacetime, he had maintained his own Sikorsky biplane for joyrides over Gstaad and the Haute-Savoie. Come the war, he would have chafed at returning to a military hierarchy but among fellow civilians anxious only to fly, he was adored. It did his reputation no harm that he had the looks and torso of a film star and would strip to the waist for physical jerks whenever the sun came out.

For the winter of 1939–40 the men were seconded to existing RAF ferry 'pools' at Hucknall, near Nottingham, and Filton, east of Bristol – the future birthplace of Concorde. Here they got their hands on operational aircraft and were even permitted to ferry them to France. Women, by contrast, were considered by the RAF's top brass to be unworthy of either privilege, physically or temperamentally. They were never formally attached to RAF units and were based in their own all-civilian pools from the start, which came with the recruitment of the first eight pilots in January 1940. At first the only RAF machines they were allowed to fly were trainers – open cockpit De Havilland Moths, and, later, Miles Magisters (with a blistering top speed of just 132 mph).

The women had to struggle for nearly two years to be allowed in fighters, and five before they started flying them to Europe. Yet it was clear from the outset that despite their relative youth and their nickname (the 'Always Terrified Airwomen'), they were altogether more formidable than the Ancient and Tattered.

The simple fact of having learned to fly before the war made them an elite within an elite. Their eventual success in flying operational aircraft in the teeth of RAF resistance only compounded their kudos. They were marshalled by the daughter of a prominent Tory MP, championed by a powerful handful of 'pro-women men', and led through the air by the likes of Lettice Curtis. They were a close-knit group, barely twenty-strong. Many knew each other from Stag Lane, Heston and Brooklands – London's most famous pre-war flying clubs. Most were from monied backgrounds, with accents and assumptions to match. Those that were not were ruthlessly frugal. Some were well known, especially to the society editors of the *Daily Sketch* and the *Picture Post*. They were 'It Girls' doing their bit, but there was nothing remotely superficial about their courage or their motivation. On the contrary, their defining traits were inner steel and a fierce if usually unspoken patriotism.

Later ATA recruits found some of these pioneers downright imperious. Margaret Fairweather, the first woman to fly a Spitfire, was nicknamed the Cold Front. Lettice Curtis was known to everyone in the ATA but that did not mean she would talk to them. (One new arrival from South America remembers handing her a letter of introduction and being stunned when 'she read it, said nothing and turned away'.) Another relative novice who had to spend a week at the first all-women's ferry pool at Hamble, near Southampton, called it 'the loneliest time I've ever spent'.

But the exigencies of war – and especially the worsening shortage of pilots as the air war intensified – meant that all-comers would eventually have to be accepted by the pioneers, just as the pioneers had been accepted by the men.

And this was why, towards the end of April 1942 (and four months after Pearl Harbor) two young women in ATA uniform set off from London for Liverpool docks to meet a converted coal carrier called the *Beaver Hill*. These women were Pauline Gower and the Hon. Mrs Kitty Farrer. Gower, the high-achieving daughter of Sir Robert Gower, MP for Gillingham, had been appointed head of the women's section of the ATA in September 1939. Farrer was her adjutant. The ship they were meeting had had a rough and dangerous crossing from Montreal. The last convoy to have sailed this route had lost six of its ten vessels to U-boats, but the *Beaver Hill* somehow made it through both the German blockade and a ferocious three-day storm. On it were five unusual guests of the British government – the first five of twenty-five American women pilots to cross the Atlantic that year to join the ATA.

They cannot have been hard to pick out on the gangplank. In the tide of over a million Americans who came ashore at Liverpool to help Churchill reverse the catastrophe of Nazism only a few handfuls were women. Even so, Commander Gower and Executive Officer Farrer did not get to them first. As the ship's passengers disembarked, the Englishwomen were dismayed to see the captain and crew, formed up in a ragged line at the end of the gang-plank, surround their charges and smother them in what appeared to be drunken kisses. 'They grabbed each one of us and hugged us and kissed us on both cheeks,' one of those women remembered. 'Pauline Gower was so prim, I can just imagine her thinking, "Oh my god, what are these Americans doing?"'

Miss Gower and Mrs Farrer waited for the raucousness to end. Then they stepped forward to shake hands. By their own account they invited their visitors to dinner at the nearby Adelphi Hotel, and the new arrivals appeared to accept. In fact the Americans were exhausted and went off to sleep. Not one of them showed up at the appointed time, leaving Gower and Farrer to dine alone at a table for seven. They were so affronted that they left on the night train and suggested their American 'cousins' make their own way to London in the morning.

That suited Dorothy Furey perfectly.

Furey was the bewitching, violet-eyed daughter of a New Orleans banana importer, and she had already decided that Pauline Gower was uptight. Her father had lost a large fortune in the crash of 1929, and since then she had gained wide experience of the susceptibilities of men. She had also nearly killed herself looping over Lake Pontchartrain in an open cockpit Arrowsport biplane. She was twenty-four when the *Beaver Hill* docked in Liverpool, and the only one of the five women in her group to have packed an evening gown with her flying gear. She called it her *Gone With The Wind* dress. It was red and not especially long, and she would use it to spectacular effect before the war was out. Some of the other Americans called her the seductress. Not all were proud of her. For her own part, when Furey looked back on her fellow women pilots at the end of her life she stated quietly: 'There wasn't anybody to compare with me.'

Not that her hosts were quick to notice. On arriving in London, Furey and company were escorted directly to a meeting room near the Grosvenor House Hotel and – so she recalls – made to listen to a schoolmasterly talk by Pop d'Erlanger on 'ill-mannered Americans' and how not to be counted among them. Pop was popular, and, as it happens, an ardent admirer of Americans, but he seems to have irritated Furey no end.

'They called him the man with the runways on his shoulder because we all had stripes but he had gold, like an admiral,' she remembered. 'And he greeted us with a lecture on ill-mannered Americans. Yes he did. Because they had had some young men who had come over to help and they had, I guess, got drunk and behaved badly. So that was our greeting. I was so furious I nearly got up and walked out, except I didn't know where I was or where I would go.'

In the event the five Americans were taken to Austin Reed's on Regent Street to be measured for their uniforms. From there they went to Paddington to catch the train to White Waltham, thirty miles to the west. It was a journey that would become as familiar as ration coupons over the next three years, but it must have seemed unutterably strange that first time – to be trapped in the gaze of English fellow-passengers too war weary and curious to lower their eyes, to stare out at suburbs vast enough to swallow whole a New York borough, and then at 'countryside' too thick with roads and villages to count as countryside except on such a crowded island, as the aerodrome that was to be their gateway to a new life of heroic and unprecedented flying clanked closer by the minute.

Cars met the Americans at Maidenhead station. From here they were ferried to ATA headquarters, a flat-roofed, two-storey brick building next to the operations room. As the new arrivals clambered out they realised at once that the aerodrome's entire male pilot contingent had downed tools to size them up. Faces filled every window; they made a peculiar reception committee. Its members included the gruff and jowly Norman Shelley, an actor who would disappear without explanation for days at a time for what turned out to be stints impersonating Winston Churchill on the radio during the Prime Minister's secret absences abroad. There were also no fewer than three fully functioning one-armed pilots based there, among them the terrifying Stewart Keith-Jopp, Betty's uncle, who was also missing an eye. ('I was told he lost the arm on a bombing run in World War One,' Betty told me, miming the awkward business of hand-delivering high explosives from the cockpit of a Sopwith Camel. 'Apparently it went off in his hand, but he never talked about it.')

The other one-armed men were First Officer R. A. Corrie and the Honourable Charles Dutton, later Lord Sherborne, who was once interrupted by a woman pilot in the White Waltham common room arguing over which arm it was better for a pilot to be without. The answer was not clear, but Dutton did explain that he could take off in a Spitfire only with the control column clenched between his legs. And he could land only with the throttle pulled right back in advance. Every landing was effectively a forced one, with no second chances.

The most discerning judge of the new arrivals was probably Dr Arthur 'Doc' Barbour, White Waltham's chief medic. Barbour was Scottish, single, dedicated to his pilots' welfare and 'perfect for the ATA', according to a colleague who knew him well. He also had a fondness for grainy 16-mm 'adult films' that might have got him into trouble in another age, and he insisted that all new pilots, male or female, present themselves unclothed for their medical examinations. Barbour saw no reason to make an exception for the Americans on account of their gender or their nationality. In fact he seems to have relished forcing the issue, which is why one of the first orders given to the women of the *Beaver Hill* by their new employer was to strip. But by this time they had been joined in London by a mercurial millionairess from Manhattan's Upper East Side who considered herself their guardian angel – and she was having none of it.

Jacqueline Odlum Cochran, born Bessie Lee Pitman, had first delivered herself to Britain at the controls of a twin-engined Lockheed Hudson bomber the previous summer. Her many British critics called the trip a publicity stunt, which it was. Publicity had served Cochran well on her journey from shoeless orphan to cosmetics millionairess and daredevil air racer, and she was addicted to it. She was also married to an industrialist who was a friend of President and Mrs Roosevelt and a dependable donor to their Democratic Party. They in turn supported her idea of drawing attention to the work being done by women pilots in war-ravaged Britain. Hence the night crossing from Gander, Newfoundland, to Carlisle and on to Prestwick; nineteen hours in all, which she survived despite acts of sabotage by mutinous ground crews and mysterious tracer bullets fired up at her from the middle of the Atlantic.

Given only a little more luck, Jackie Cochran might have become a thoroughgoing megalomaniac. She had grand visions of an all-female US military flying force answering to none other than Jackie Cochran, and throughout the war she worked tirelessly to make this vision a reality. But first she had to settle for hiring twenty-five competent women pilots with at least 350 hours' flying experience to help ferry planes round Britain. By the time she started welcoming them to London she had travelled the length and breadth of North America to interview candidates whom she had canvassed in advance with long, excited telegrams.

'CONFIDENTIAL,' one of them began.

ON BEHALF OF BRITISH AIR TRANSPORT AUXILIARY I AM WIRING ALL THE WOMEN PILOTS WHOSE ADDRESSES AVAILABLE TO ASK IF YOU WOULD BE WILLING TO VOLUNTEER FOR SERVICE ... EVERY FRONT NOW OUR FRONT AND FOR THOSE DESIRING QUICK ACTIVE SERVICE SHORT OF ACTUAL COMBAT BUT INCLUDING FLIGHT EXPERIENCE WITH COMBAT PLANES THIS SERVICE ABROAD SEEMS IDEAL CHANCE ... WIRE ME 630 FIFTH AVENUE NEW YORK CITY AND YOU WILL RECEIVE LETTER WITH MORE DETAILS ... RELEASE NO PUBLICITY AS A RESULT OF THIS TELEGRAM.

When Cochran's gals started arriving in England she was ready for them, at the Savoy. White Waltham must have seemed terribly humdrum by comparison, but when she drove down there, at the wheel of a borrowed Daimler, it was not so much the shortage of glamour that irked her. It was 'Doc' Barbour's order to get undressed.

Cochran was livid. She was a bit of a prude, and she fancied herself as defender-in-chief of the good name of her handpicked representatives of dynamic American womanhood. 'There he is,' she wrote of Barbour, 'adamant about his damn procedures. There I am – not about to take off all my clothes or let the other American girls be subjected to such ridiculous procedures. Where was it stated that England needed its pilots to be examined in the buff?'

In the end it didn't matter. For both the British and the American governments, Cochran was an unclassifiable anomaly whose personal contacts and sheer force of will demanded attention. A pal of Roosevelt's – blonde, rich, short-fused, married but without her husband in attendance – had taken up residence at the Savoy. She could not be allowed to storm home firing off tirades to the

White House about British ingratitude. Instead, when she stormed back to London and started complaining to Pop d'Erlanger's paymasters at the Air Ministry, he caved in. The message was passed to Doc Barbour at White Waltham that he would have to satisfy himself with stethoscope and tongue depressor. Dorothy Furey and her fellow Americans entered the Air Transport Auxiliary with their clothes on.

Cochran had won her first pitched battle with England's 'damn procedures'. But she had lost any hope of being accepted by the British Establishment into which she had barged. According to the splendidly sober Lettice Curtis, Cochran had 'entirely misjudged the wartime mood of the British people'. And it was true. Ground down by rationing – of clothes as well as food – and with little first-hand experience of the United States, most Britons bought into the stereotype of American women as movie stars or gold diggers more readily than they let on. And Cochran's presence only reinforced it.

American men were not much more graciously received. When GIs started arriving in numbers later in 1942 they looked so healthy that Londoners started calling them 'pussies'. Margaret Fairweather was even blunter. 'What a strange, barbaric lot,' she sighed in a letter to her brother about the 'cousins'. 'So well up in bodily civilization and so dismally lacking in mind. They are really – the ones we contact at least – great over-grown wild adolescents.'

The disappointment was mutual. Ann Wood arrived in England as a twenty-four-year-old flying instructor infused with transatlantic solidarity by what she had seen in newsreels and heard in the CBS radio broadcasts of Edward R. Murrow. But the Brits and Britishness quickly drove her nuts. At first she gave them the benefit of the doubt. Landing in Liverpool a month after Dorothy Furey, she was impressed by the sight of 'fifty cheery little men' from HM Customs and Excise who came aboard her ship, a French Canadian freighter called the *Indochinois*. They were 'wonderful – didn't open a thing'. But once ashore she was immediately struck by 'the blackness and dirt . . . and then the poverty' of Britain.

She was unimpressed by the 'pretence' of the British labourer in his shirt and tie and 'inevitable tan raincoat which is black and shiny with grease'; by the 'puny moustaches' on so many supposedly stiff upper lips; by the lack of variety on the BBC, not just compared with back home but also with German radio, to which she also listened; by the 'utter and complete mess' of the White Waltham canteen; and above all by the unwarranted superiority complex of the British officer class, which was happy to blame America for anything and everything while its members blithely gamed the system for a few extra petrol coupons. As she wrote more than once during her first British summer, when rain and mandatory navigation classes kept her grounded for days at a time, 'sometimes I wonder about this war'.

The British, it seems, wondered less. (This, too, exasperated Wood. Her diary is peppered with pleas to her hard-pressed hosts to 'sacrifice less and THINK more'.) But then, for the British, the war was a much simpler matter of life and death.

A few weeks after Ann Wood disembarked at Liverpool, another smart young woman took off from White Waltham in a strong crosswind. She was flying a low-winged monoplane with an open cockpit called a Miles Magister, and her assignment was to familiarise herself with southern England. She was to land at Henlow, then fly over RAF Debden in Essex, head north towards Wattisham in Suffolk, land again at Sywell near Northampton and be back at White Waltham in time for tea. That day, she got no further than Debden.

Diana Barnato was an exceptional, intuitive pilot who once landed a Typhoon at 230 mph with a clear view of the runway beneath her feet because the underside of the plane had been torn off in mid-air. She was also lucky, and very rich. The daughter of British motor-racing champion Woolf Barnato, and granddaughter of a South African diamond tycoon who had provided amply for his descendants before being 'lost' over the side of the SS *Christiana* somewhere off Namibia, Diana felt just enough fear to survive. But not much more.

High over Debden that April morning the wind began to throw the Magister around as if preparing to snap its fabric wings in two. She decided to land, and made her way unannounced towards the aerodrome buildings.

Thanks to her parallel existence as a socialite it was rare for Miss Barnato to enter an RAF mess and not know a face or two, and Debden did not disappoint. She immediately recognised Sas de Mier, a Mexican air gunner then flying with the RAF in Bristol Blenheims over northern Germany. He introduced her over lunch to 'a well-built, thickset young man, dark with blue eyes [and] one of the worst haircuts I had ever seen'. This was Squadron Leader Humphrey Gilbert of the Humphrey Gilberts of Revesby Abbey in Lincolnshire. 'We got along fine,' Diana recalled.

Gilbert had the Magister's spark plugs removed and Diana was forced to spend three days at Debden, in which time she and Gilbert fell in love. Within three weeks they were engaged. Within a month, Gilbert was dead. He had survived the Battle of Britain to be killed giving a corpulent air traffic controller a lift in his Spitfire. As the ATA women were soon to learn, there was no spare room in a Spitfire cockpit even for the slimmest of them. Humphrey Gilbert, with a whole extra body in his lap, had found out too late that he couldn't pull the stick back. The aircraft barely left the ground.

Diana mourned Humphrey for many years, but not to the exclusion of pleasure or excitement or the company of other men. Life was too short – and too ethereal – for that, and the importance of filling every unforgiving minute with excitement was something on which all the early ATA women could agree. These included a willowy blonde ski champion called Audrey Sale-Barker (better known for most of her life as the Countess of Selkirk); the ice hockey international Mona Friedlander, whom the Fleet Street diarists quickly nicknamed 'the Mayfair Minx'; and Lois Butler, wife of the chairman of the De Havilland Aircraft Company, and former captain of the Canadian women's ski team.

Pauline Gower, who as Commander of the ATA women's section was queen bee of British women pilots in the war, had first excelled as the perfect schoolgirl at the Convent of the Sacred Heart in Tunbridge Wells. She was the Mother Superior's pet: bright, bouncy, diligent and fizzing with ideas. One of these, while still a teenager, was to follow her father into the Conservative party as an MP. But then an infection that required surgery almost killed her at seventeen, and permanently weakened her health. So she took up flying as 'the perfect sedentary occupation'. Mary de Bunsen, who was seldom photographed without thick glasses and a furrowed brow, found it a thrilling distraction from 'the ghastly importance of a good marriage'.

When these young ladies landed at stately homes and castles converted for use as Satellite Landing Grounds, they would often recognise the great lawns from weekend house parties. When they first flew Hurricanes, they celebrated with a sumptuous dinner at the Ecu de France in St James's – for who knew what tomorrow would bring?

The weather was always the decisive factor. When the sun shone at White Waltham, and the great Flight Captain Frankie Francis set hearts aflutter by removing his shirt and flexing his muscles, and the spire of the Collegial Church of St John the Baptist at Shottesbrooke could be seen beyond the trees at the western end of the runway, that meant good flying weather; at least two miles' visibility. The Shottesbrooke spire in plain view meant ferry chits at nine o'clock and long days in the air. It meant butterflies, because no good pilot ever assumed fog would not rear up out of a cloudless sky and grab her; but more than that it held the prospect of total gratification.

No women in Britain in the war were more admired for doing their bit – nor for their uniform – than those who flew with the ATA. But in doing so they partook of a very private pleasure. 'Our happiness was almost indecently visible in time of trouble and distress,' Mary de Bunsen fretted – unnecessarily. As Lettice Curtis knew, no-one ever saw these women at their happiest. To be airborne over the Pennines on a clear spring morning with a delivery to Colerne, Kirkbride or even Lossiemouth, jumping-off point for Scapa Flow and the murderous North Atlantic, was to be 'blissfully cut off from the rest of the world'. Alone in the cockpit, 'past and present would recede until existence became once more a pinpoint in time, concerned solely with the immediate present of gauges, weather, navigation and finding that next landmark'.

But when the cloud came down, so did the dreadful pall of death. Ferrying aircraft around well-defended Britain was, bizarrely, one of the most lethal activities on offer to either men or women in this war. Nearly one in ten of the ATA's women pilots died. None of them ever fired a shot in anger because they flew unarmed, so they were sitting ducks should the Luftwaffe happen on them. They could also be shot at by friendly ack-ack units, ensnared by barrage balloons and, at any moment, ambushed by the weather. They flew without radio, and this was tightrope-walking without a safety net: no weather 'actuals', no check calls to the nearest RAF or met station, no radio beam to home in on.

Immediately in front of their joysticks, on Spitfires and almost every other class of aircraft used by the RAF, was the same six-instrument panel: air speed indicator, altimeter, gyro compass, attitude indicator, turn-and-slip gauge and artificial horizon. ATA pilots knew what each instrument did and they used them separately every time they flew. But in the alchemic business of saving their own lives by using these instruments together to work out where they were going when the gloom outside their canopies was thick as concrete – in blind flying – they had no formal training at all. They were told this was to discourage going 'over the top' of cloud and generally ugly weather; and they were told this despite the fact that getting down through generally ugly weather is what instrument flying is for. The real reason seems to have been to save time and money, and the cost would be in lives.

When the Shottesbrooke spire was lost in cloud ATA pilots were not obliged to fly, but they still did. Out of boredom, rivalry, the pressure to deliver aircraft, or sometimes needling from operations officers who were themselves being needled by a chain of command that stretched directly to the Ministry of Aircraft Production and Churchill, they flew in all weathers, convincing themselves that holes would open up and let them down through the great blankets of condensation that kept England so green. They also flew every type of aircraft produced by the Allies. There were nearly 200 of them, from lumbering amphibian Supermarine Walruses to high-altitude reconnaissance Spitfires; from Blenheims and Beaufighters to Mitchells and Mosquitoes, from unsinkable old Tiger Moths to half-baked experiments like the Airacobra, with a rear-mounted engine and a transmission shaft that spun furiously between the pilot's legs.

What training the ATA pilots did have was thorough, and they were justly proud of it. It consisted of ground school in meteorology, map-reading, navigation and mechanics, with special classes on where to expect barrage balloons; then dual and solo flights in docile Moths to build confidence for the marginally faster Miles Magisters. In these, recruits were expected to complete no fewer than thirty long cross-country flights along fixed routes, intended to imprint on pilots' minds a giant aerial picture of England, with particular attention paid to railway lines and Roman roads since these were often the best guides out of trouble. Finally, pilots were assigned to ferry pools for 'Class I' ferrying, of light, single-engined planes. For promotion to faster Class II machines and above, all the way up to Class V four-engined bombers, conversion courses were eventually offered at the RAF's Central Flying School at Upavon in Wiltshire.

No training programme could familiarise every pilot with every type of plane in the sky. So they familiarised themselves, using a ring-bound set of handling notes prepared by Flight Engineer Bob Morgan of the British Overseas Airways Corporation. Twenty minutes with Morgan's notes was usually enough to work out what made a Walrus different from a Wellington, but not always, especially if the Walrus had been shot up or marked down as unserviceable. The ATA would still fly it to the wrecker's yard.

For combat pilots, the risks of flying varied from intense, in battle, to non-existent, on leave. For ferry pilots they were virtually constant. The weather never went away, and they (almost) never stopped flying. They worked thirteen days a fortnight and died steadily, on hillsides, in the Irish Sea, when their engines failed or blew up or their undercarriage refused to come down. The casualties' names were posted on the ferry pool notice board every morning, and everyone knew the dead as well as it was possible to get to know someone who might be gone at any moment. One notice at White Waltham read:

Accident Report. 12 September 1942. Hurricane JS346. Prince Chirasakti.
    Near Langholm 11.30 hours; aircraft flew into hill, the pilot having persisted too far into hilly country contrary to orders . . .

Thus perished the ATA's only Siamese royal. Diana Barnato remembered him fondly. 'Keen type,' she wrote. 'Pressed on too long. I shed a tear.'

By the time the Americans arrived, everyone who greeted them already understood what they had yet to learn. This flying lark was not a lark. The previous November Lettice Curtis had taken off from the Kirkbride (No. 16) Ferry Pool minutes before one of her most illustrious superiors, Captain Walter Handley of pre-war motorbike racing fame and the ferry pool at Hawarden, tried to do the same in a dreaded Airacobra. The engine over-revved and belched black smoke on the take-off run, but by that time Wally was committed. Seconds after leaving the ground his aircraft exploded.

Bridget Hill and Betty Sayer, the first women pilots to die, did not have the luxury of wondering in their final seconds what they could do to save themselves. They were passengers in a taxi plane that crashed through the roof of a house on the edge of the White Waltham aerodrome on 18 March 1942. Hill's closest friend from school was another ATA girl, Honor Salmon. She, too, was dead by summer.

When Diana Barnato's fiancé died, she cried briefly, in a phone box, until First Officer Corrie, one of the White Waltham one-armers, lost patience waiting for the phone and banged to be let in. But on the whole her compatriots conformed to stereotype. On hearing that a friend had died, they went quiet, pale, and after a while reached for the sherry.

This inordinate self-control impressed some of the visitors. Roberta Sandoz, one of the last Americans to arrive in 1942, eventually became friends with several of the earliest women recruits, including one who, she recalled, 'had already lost her first husband and while she was flying with me her son was killed in the air force. I think she missed two days' work. There was not a lot of embracing and sobbing and commiserating, and I admired that.'

Sandoz herself kept flying through the grief of losing her fiancé, a US Navy cadet who was killed in the Pacific shortly after her arrival in England. She was every bit as stoic as the British, but that did not stop the steely Lettice Curtis remarking that the Americans were much more outspoken than their European counterparts, 'and more emotional when their fellow pilots were killed'.

Whether the stiff upper lip extinguished fear or hid it was a personal thing, but there is evidence that the ATA's women may have coped better than its men with the imminence of death. There are repeated references in diaries and memoirs to men sitting around in common rooms on 'wash-out' days content to leave the verdict of the weather people unchallenged, while women took off into the murk on the off-chance of getting through. There was Betty Keith-Jopp, who remembered her lift-like descent to the bottom of the Firth of Forth six decades later with undimmed amazement – not so much at her escape as at thinking calmly of the insurance payment her mother would receive. There was Mary de Bunsen, lame from childhood polio and with a congenital heart defect that left her breathless every time she climbed into a Hurricane. 'You know,' she told a fellow pilot towards the end of the war, 'when I was in training pool I was so certain that I was going to be killed within the next few weeks that I didn't bother much.' By morbid contrast there was Flying Officer W. F. Castle, married with a son, from Birmingham. He had arrived at White Waltham in November 1941 with both arms and both eyes but precious little confidence – which the ATA training staff proceeded to undermine.

Castle brooded nightly in his diary:

November 8th. Our instructors are forever emphasizing the lethal nature of the forces which will soon be under our control if misused. This point is pressed home as every subject is taken.

November 19th. Now that I have started flying it is being brought home to me very clearly that this is not what you would call a particularly safe job . . . Although we are not required to fly in bad weather it often seems to happen that someone has flown into a hillside during bad visibility. Three deaths are reported this week, and there must have been two or three others besides since I have been here. I dread to think of leaving Peg and Daniel alone . . . the thought of Daniel, my son, being brought up without me chills my heart. I am determined to take every precaution possible.'

The next day, after stalling on take-off in a Magister, Castle was close to desperate:

It is being borne in on me more and more that if I am to preserve my skin I must quickly develop a sound flying sense and take no chances whatever . . . The sooner I can get away from the congested area of White Waltham the better it will suit me.

As long as the very human Castle pondered his mortality, and the ice cool Lettice Curtis flew in and out of White Waltham, rain or shine, as if on auto pilot, there could be no room for overt male chauvinism within the ranks of the ATA.

In the wider world, it was a different story. From the moment Pauline Gower had first talked to Sir Francis Shelmerdine about hiring women pilots at government expense to help mobilise for war, those who considered flying somehow intrinsically male began to vent. And no-one gave them more space to do so than C.G. Grey, editor of *Aeroplane* magazine and an old friend of Betty Keith-Jopp's uncle, Stewart. Early on, Grey weighed in himself. 'We quite agree that there are millions of women in the country who could do useful jobs in the war,' he wrote in reply to a letter Mary Bailey had sent in support of Gower. (Lady Bailey had flown from London to South Africa in a Tiger Moth in 1929, pausing only to attend a reception in her honour in Khartoum in a tweed flying suit.)

> But the trouble is that so many of them insist on wanting to do jobs which they are quite incapable of doing. The menace is the woman who thinks that she ought to be flying a high-speed bomber when she really has not the intelligence to scrub the floor of a hospital properly, or who wants to nose round as an Air Raid Warden and yet can't cook her husband's dinner.

Grey was right about the dinner, wrong about the menace. Lettice Curtis was a consummate flyer and completely uninterested in cooking. To be obsessive about flying and deliberately careless about anything conventionally 'female' was, in fact, the norm for ATA girls. This infuriated Harold Collings (*Aeroplane*, 5 January, 1940):

> Women are not seeking this job for the sake of doing something for their country . . . Women who are anxious to serve their country should take on work more befitting their sex

instead of encroaching on a man's occupation. Men have made aviation reach its present perfection.

Some of *Aeroplane*'s female readers agreed: 'I think the whole affair of engaging women pilots to fly aeroplanes when there are so many men fully qualified to do the work is disgusting!' one wrote. 'The women themselves are only doing it more or less as a hobby, and should be ashamed of themselves!'

She was not entirely wrong. Some of the women had taken up flying strictly for practical reasons. Lettice Curtis and Ann Wood, for instance, insisted that at first they saw it simply as a livelihood. But for most it was indeed a hobby, and one that often deepened into an obsession. And why not? What self-respecting pilot would not have grown obsessional about the prospect, however remote, of flying something as fast and glamorous and responsive – and as feminine – as a Spitfire?

Nothing parked these days on the grass apron at White Waltham comes close to the sheer power of a Spitfire. Even the Mark 1, with its bashful two-bladed propeller, had the thrust equivalent of six supercharged racing Bentleys crammed into its nose. At 16,000 feet its 27-litre Merlin II engine could generate more than 1,000 horsepower; enough to pull the pilot wedged behind it through the air at more than half the speed of sound.

Spitfires were so streamlined that when taxiing the heat produced by their engines had nowhere to go. Reginald Mitchell had removed the side-mounted radiators on the Supermarine seaplane on which he based his new design, replacing it with ineffectual slimline air intakes under the wings. If Spitfires weren't released quickly into the air, the glycol in their cooling systems would boil. They hated sitting around once started up, but once off the ground they made their pilots sing.

Even four-engined bombers proved easily handled by the tiniest women pilots. But the Spitfire, without exception, was their favourite. Mary de Bunsen would rejoice when let loose in one by humming fugues from Bach's B Minor Mass. Lettice Curtis warbled in prose: 'To sit in the cockpit of a Spitfire, barely wider than one's shoulders, with the power of the Merlin at one's fingertips, was a poetry of its own,' she wrote. 'The long, flat-topped cowling and the pop-popping stub exhausts gave an almost breathtaking feeling of power, and the exhilaration of throwing it around, chasing clouds or low flying – strictly unauthorised in our case – was something never to be forgotten by those who experienced it.'

And who would experience it? The arrival of the Americans risked dividing the women of the ATA. Would they all be as bumptious as Jackie Cochran? Could they fly? Were they really needed? But the yearning to fly Spitfires, and to a lesser extent Hurricanes, was something they all shared. This, no less than their desire to be involved in the war, was what accounted for their steady convergence on southern England, not just from across Britain and the United States but from Poland, Chile, Argentina and the Dominions.

Most of them believed passionately in the Allied cause, but all could have served it elsewhere and less dangerously had they not become smitten with the idea of flying the most thrilling aeroplane yet built. And verdant, crowded, hungry England was the only place in the world where they would be allowed to do it.

For the pilots, the war meant virtual parity of opportunity with men, eventual parity of pay, and all the flying they could handle. For their mentors, Pauline Gower and Jackie Cochran, it seemed to be a stepping-stone to an elevated yet egalitarian future. 'I would say that every woman should learn to fly,' Gower declared in an interview for the April 1942 issue of *Woman's Journal*. 'Psychologically, it is the best antidote to the manifold neuroses which beset modern women. The war has already accomplished much in this regard, but with the return of peace my advice to all women will still be – "Learn to fly".'

Jackie Cochran would have seconded that, but she wanted to do more than liberate modern women from their 'neuroses'. She wanted to change men's minds about women. The spring of 1942 found them both shuttling between White Waltham and London, politicking while their protégées hurtled round the skies above them. Their styles were diametrically opposite, but their goals were complementary. In a world turned upside-down, they even seemed achievable.

On the evening of 30 March that year, a rare joint appearance by Gower and Cochran set off an explosion of flashbulbs in Leicester Square. They had arrived together for the première of *They Flew Alone*, a hastily shot feature starring Anna Neagle about a woman pilot more famous than either of them would ever be. Her life had inspired many of the Spitfire women, but her death the previous year, at this point still shrouded in mystery, had prefigured many of their disappointments. Her name was Amy Johnson.

2

No Way Down

The film playing at Leicester Square that March night in 1942 depicted one of the most spectacular lives of the thirties, and one of the more mysterious deaths of the war. Towards the end of the film there is a scene set at Squire's Gate aerodrome outside Blackpool.

The date is 4 January 1941. The time is 11.45 a.m. Mist shrouds the aerodrome buildings, but within sight of them a bulky twin-engined Airspeed Oxford, both propellers spinning, sits on the concrete apron. In the cockpit is Amy Johnson, Hull fish merchant's daughter, ferry pilot and celebrity. Without her example of reckless daring over the previous ten years it is doubtful that the ATA would have had a pool of trained women pilots to call on, let alone an army of women volunteers hoping to be trained from scratch. As she waits she smokes a cigarette and chats to a refueller who has climbed into the co-pilot's seat to keep her company; she is hoping for better weather.

The scene unfolds on film as in life, except that in *They Flew Alone* Amy Johnson's face is Anna Neagle's – a thing of perfect skin and symmetry, and pluck shining from her very eyes. In real life the face was longer; a mournful-looking oval. Even so, despite a washed-out Christmas at Prestwick's Orangefield Hotel, with nothing to stare at for six days but fog, everyone Amy Johnson talked to over those last few days recalled that she seemed unusually content.

In the film she talks like Eliza Doolittle after Professor Higgins's ministrations. In life, a trace of a Hull accent lingered despite years of elocution lessons. In the film, when a third figure emerges from the mist to report that the weather's just as bad right down to Oxfordshire, she glances up at him and makes the only decision that was in fact imaginable for Amy Johnson. She says she will 'crack through and fly over the top'. In reality she said something very similar.

For most of the 164 women who ferried planes for the ATA during the war it was the pinnacle of their flying careers, unrepeatable after the war even as men went supersonic, into orbit and to the moon. For Amy Johnson it was something of a come-down, and a point of realisation that her celebrity could no longer cleave a path through Britain's hidebound bureaucracy. She had wanted a wartime role crafted specially for her, pioneering fast new airline routes to bind beleaguered Britain closer to her colonies, or swooping into northern France (before it fell) to keep young Tommy chipper. She offered to advise the Air Ministry – on what she wasn't sure. As it turned out, the Air Ministry had plenty of advisors.

Johnson had been overlooked for head of the ATA's women's section in favour of Pauline Gower, and even when Gower begged her to join she had to take a test. Once a ferry pilot, she had to leave her Astrakhan-collared flying coats in storage and wear navy worsted and a forage cap. And she had to share common rooms and taxi planes with the other girls even though, as she commented to her father, they practically worshipped her. Was this any way to treat the most famous woman pilot in the world?

Eleven years before that dank morning at Squire's Gate, Johnson had been sitting in another cockpit waiting for another weather window. This time the aircraft was a De Havilland Gipsy Moth, the Morris Traveller of the skies, a dope-and-canvas biplane built to cruise at 90 mph. Amy had named it *Jason*, which was the telegraphic address of her father's fish business. The venue was Croydon Airport. She had tried once already to take off but had failed to get the throttle forward fast enough to compensate for the weight of two extra fuel tanks and had pulled up a few feet from the perimeter fence. Now she tried again. Her father and a small group of friends watched from the tarmac in front of the aerodrome hotel. Jack Humphreys, her mentor and engineering tutor, had a sense of what she was getting into and was rigid with tension. William Johnson, down from Hull specially for this, had even less idea than his daughter of the risks she was running.

This time the Moth just cleared the fence. It staggered over the rows of houses beyond, its tiny engine (one tenth as powerful as the least powerful Spitfire's) hammering up into the westerly wind. Johnson climbed over Purley Rise and the Selsden Park golf course and levelled out over the waking villages of Kent. She set course for Vienna.

Virtually unknown, she was airborne thanks to her father's patronage and a modest fuel sponsorship arrangement with Charles 'Cheers' Wakefield, father of the Castrol brand of engine oil. But what made the combination combustible, and almost fatal, was her own searing ambition to be someone special. And three short weeks later she had realised that ambition. She was being mobbed by crowds of Australians wherever she put down, and bombarded with telegrams from Blériot, Einstein and King George V.

Amy Johnson was the first woman to fly solo to Australia. In the cockpit she wore leather when it was cold and cotton when it was hot, and she depended throughout her twenty-day flight on a four-cylinder, 110-horsepower engine pulling an aircraft with a spare propeller strapped to the outside of its fuselage. It was a breathtakingly modern thing to do. A handful of men had squeezed the 11,000 miles from Southampton to Sydney into a journey measured in days rather than weeks, but for a woman to attempt it – less than half a generation after being given the vote – was practically unthinkable. She had beaten Bert Hinkler's record as far as Delhi, but it was not for speed that Australia adored her. It was for having shrunk the world more vividly and definitively than a strutting male action hero could ever have. Here was the girl next door (sunburned and overtired, it was true), whose next door was in Hull. She had a toothy smile, a perpetually awed voice and actually seemed to like Australia. She also had the strange aura of someone who had cheated death.

Johnson's strategy for beating Hinkler's record rested on the idea of flying in a straight line. As far as she could tell from the primitive maps that were all Stanford's bookshop had for most of the journey, this would shave 700 miles off his route. Hinkler had looped south through Rome to Malta to maximise, he hoped, his number of nights on British imperial soil. Johnson headed straight for Constantinople via Austria. On the way, an overbearing crew of Viennese mechanics insisted on overhauling her engine but succeeded only in gumming up a spark plug. (This may never have come entirely ungummed; despite Johnson's hard-won engineering certificate and her meticulous filtering of all the fuel that entered *Jason*'s engine, one of the male pilots deputed to escort her on her victory lap of Australia wrote later, with ill-disguised satisfaction, that he had never seen 'an engine in such appalling condition' as hers.)

From Constantinople, Johnson had to find a way through Anatolia's forbidding Taurus Mountains, and this is where her straight line became sinuous. As she approached the mountains around lunchtime on 7 May, they were covered by cloud. She climbed to stay in clear air, as she would years later with much less reason to be scared. But at 11,000 feet her 'engine started an ominous coughing and spitting', she wrote afterwards:

I descended to 10,000 feet and decided to try to follow the railway through its winding gorges ... I had one very unpleasant moment when threading my way through an exceptionally narrow gorge with the mountains rising sheer on either side of me only a few feet from my wings and towering high above. Rounding a corner I ran straight into a bank of low clouds, and for an awful minute could see nothing at all. In desperation I pushed down the nose of the machine to try to dive below them, and in half a minute – which seemed to me an eternity – I emerged from the cloud at a speed of 120 with one wing down and aiming for a wall of rock. Once I could see where I was going it was easy to straighten the machine, but I was rather badly shaken.

Johnson's passage through the Taurus Mountains was undoubtedly terrifying and it marked her graduation from suburban dilettante to Shackletonian adventurer.

From Aleppo she flew to Baghdad, with only one forced landing in the desert, then down the Tigris, over Basra and on to Bandar Abbas at the eastern end of the Persian Gulf, her journey advanced across the Middle East like a line on a map in a movie. It was followed with quietly mounting interest in newsrooms the length of Fleet Street.

On 10 May, Johnson flew clear over Baluchistan and into aviation legend. Landing that evening at Drigh Road aerodrome outside Karachi, she had beaten Hinkler's Croydon-to-India record by two days and handed the papers an exquisitely constructed rolling news story. The tale of Britain's lone girl flyer had been germinating nicely ever since a reporter for the London *Evening News* had chanced on her at the Stag Lane Flying Club's hangar in North London five months earlier. He had written a prominent exclusive about a twenty-two-year-old blonde from the Midlands that was inaccurate in every detail except the headline: 'Girl To Fly Alone To Australia'. The scoop was widely followed up. Then interest slumped. It began to return when she took off, and when she smashed her first record she was considerate enough to do so a short drive from a major node of the British Empire. Karachi had reliable telegraphic links to London and a surfeit of hungry stringers. Best of all, it was at least ten days from Australia, even in a Gipsy Moth. If this Johnson lass could only keep flying, her story had legs.

She obliged. She pressed on despite crash-landing on a playing field near Rangoon, impaling her wings on bamboo shoots on a sugar plantation in Java, going missing for twenty-four hours over the shark-infested waters of the Balinese archipelago and shuddering to a halt in the half-light among six-foot anthills near the Portuguese colonial outpost of Atamboea. Every night she threw herself on the mercy of those she found. Every day she fought fatigue, rain, heat, volcanic dust storms and a private catalogue of terrors including, but not limited to, cannibals, engine failure and death by corkscrew dive into the sea.

It made terrific copy. The *News of the World* wanted exclusive rights and opened the bidding at £500 while Johnson was in the air between Calcutta and Rangoon. Before she took off again, the *Daily Mail* had won the auction (which was handled by her father) for four times as much.

When she landed in Darwin on Empire Day, solid servants of that empire cried with joy from Hull to Canberra. One who confessed to tears was a retired naval rating who wrote to Johnson's parents that 'in all a long, adventurous life' he'd seen nothing to compare with their daughter's flight. 'I was down the Java coast in 1858; you see I have been all that long journey myself and so have just a little idea of what it means. But then to do it alone, and in the air; it is more than wonderful, it is marvellous.'

The use of 'wonderful' was a reference to 'Wonderful Amy', an instant, cloying hit that played in music halls from Clapham to Llandudno all that summer. Not to be outdone, the pseudonymous Wilhelmina Stitch divided her 'Fragrant Minute' column in the *Daily Sketch* into four breathlessly worshipful stanzas, ending:

> *Amy! For ever more your name will stand synonymous with pluck;*
> *And when we weary of life's game, or when we whine and blame*
> *'our luck';*
> *We'll think of your immortal plane and spread our wings and try*
> *again.*

Johnson's flight to Australia was a singular achievement: pure in conception, pure in execution and perfectly encapsulating the escapist yearnings of a nation ground down by the Depression. But it was conjured from a complicated life.

As a teenager Amy had been a tomboy and a rebel. When she 'grew up', which she never really did, she combined soaring ambition with morbid self-doubt, vanity with shyness and outward prudishness with a serious libido. At the Boulevard School in Hull she was the only girl who could bowl overarm in cricket, and she led two mutinies. One of these involved wearing soft straw Panamas instead of hard straw boaters because she hated straw boaters and because her more vivacious sister, Irene, had moved to the more exclusive Hull High School – where they wore Panamas.

Constance Babington Smith, Johnson's first biographer, insists that the 'Revolt of the Straw Hat Brigade' ended up a humiliating solo effort. (The evidence from Johnson herself tends to support this: 'The majority of schoolgirls have no gumption at all,' she wrote later to her younger sister, Molly.) But there was no place for solitary gumption in *They Flew Alone*, shot in wartime as a propagandist piece. Everybody needed it. So everyone at the school shows up in Panamas and Amy is the Boulevard's Boadicea.

In fact she was a loner, quick to brood and slow to smile, especially after losing her two front teeth to a cricket ball and having them inexpertly replaced. As a teenager she may have been shy, though this was not the same as being afraid of boys – or men. On the contrary, by the time she was sixteen she was infatuated with one of the more exotic creatures to have graced Hull society before the war. Babington Smith, writing in the 1960s, spared his blushes by referring to him as 'Franz'. His real name was Hans Arreger. He was Swiss, sarcastic, rather squat, full in the lips and twenty-four years old. Johnson's aunt Evelyn had met him at her tennis club and invited them both to one of her parties. She was his ticket to better English and, eventually, to furtive encounters in London hotels. He was her Rudolph Valentino.

By later, wartime, standards their affair was not wildly adventurous. But for years it teetered on the brink of scandal, and it did not end happily. In the summer of 1928, seven years after the party at Aunt Evelyn's and almost as many since Johnson had made plain her wish to marry him, Arreger turned up unexpectedly at the London flat she was sharing with a girlfriend, to tell her he had married someone else – a BBC researcher based in Manchester. She flung herself on her bed and sobbed her heart out.

Part of her anguish was over having ceded the initiative at the last moment to someone she insisted she no longer loved. That spring she had sent him a devastating 2,000-word sign-off letter chiding him for stringing her along, chiding herself for her naivety and chiding men in general for their 'staring, desiring eyes'. 'I no longer want you, sexually or any other way,' she wrote. 'I don't believe we could for a single moment be happy together, and if you came to live in London I should probably leave . . .'. Just in case he concluded that she was seeing someone else, she added in a postscript: 'I do not want men and have no intention now of ever getting married.'

She would modify that position soon enough. In the meantime, reaching for something that might satisfy her yearning for excitement, and shock Arreger at the same time, she learned to fly.

To fly. Three quarters of a century later it is hard to think of any activity that comes close to the phenomenon of flying in the late 1920s in terms of danger, newness, glamour or the power to liberate and thrill. Pilots in 1928, like computer scientists in 1978, knew their machines were going to change the world. The difference was that every time the pilots went up in theirs they set themselves literally apart from the uninitiated throng, and risked their lives.

Johnson's first close encounter with this new world of daring and defiance came after a long bus ride to the London Aeroplane Club at the De Havilland aerodrome at Stag Lane, near Edgware. In April 1928 Stag Lane was London's launchpad to the skies, or at least to the clouds. Naturally inclined to push things until told to stop, Johnson walked onto the aerodrome without a membership card, found a deck chair and watched, enthralled, as the cream of the flying set practised circuits and bumps. Eventually she plucked up the courage to talk to one of them, who told her teaching could be had for 30 shillings an hour. That evening she wrote briskly to her parents: 'It is too good to be true . . . I'm going up one evening next week to sign the papers, and I'll probably have my first lesson next weekend.'

In twenty-five months she would be taking off for Australia with a thermos and a packet of sandwiches. The appearance of an epic journey accomplished on a whim was part of its extraordinary appeal, but in reality Johnson was fiercely driven – and not just by a desire to prove how much Arreger had underestimated her. She was also in search of powerful distractions from grief, for in the summer of 1929 her sister, Irene, had committed suicide by putting her head in the oven at her new marital home. Ultimately Amy was stubbornly convinced that whatever life threw at her she was destined for what came to be known as 'stardom'.

Not many women pilots in the ATA shared this conviction. Most considered it vulgar to court publicity or were actually scared of it (as some still are, in their late eighties, self-censoring at the sight of a tape recorder out of modesty and a lifelong allegiance to the Official Secrets Act). But all of them understood Johnson's love of flying as an escape from the wretched trap that faced adventurous young women in the 1930s. They had been handed the vote and a few seats in Parliament. They had won sullen recognition that a man's work could sometimes be done quite well by women (though not yet – Heaven forbid – for the same pay). Yet in practice almost as soon as they applied for work they were thrown back on the mercy of men.

In Johnson's case these men included Vernon Wood, partner in a City law firm. He gave this Sheffield University graduate, with her second-class degree in Economics, French and Latin, the best job she had before becoming famous – in his typing pool. There was also Jack Humphreys, sinewy chief mechanic at Stag Lane, who every evening after her day job taught her how to dissect and reassemble Tiger Moth engines. And there was her father, who sent regular envelopes of bank notes to his daughter, and boxed herrings to those who helped her.

For the women who followed Johnson into the air the war would give them a purpose. Johnson had to find her own. From the moment she first considered flying to Australia her best hope of sponsorship lay in persuading Lord Wakefield she could boost his sales of Castrol lubricants. She wondered about delivering an Irish setter to the Maharaja of Patula, since they both loved dogs, but eventually, less than a month before that misty Croydon take-off, Wakefield came through with a promise of petrol and £300 towards the cost of a plane.

The flight to Australia launched her into a new, blindingly public life that had the rhythm of a professional boxer's. Every few months, slackening gradually to every few years, she would hatch a new plan to risk her neck, grab some headlines and secure a fat purse with which to fund a lifestyle of sometimes prodigious extravagance. Her first goal after Darwin was Peking, but she got no further than Moscow after crash-landing in a snowbound field sixty miles north of Warsaw. (In Moscow, she found her fame transcended ideology and immunised her against internment: Lenin's widow hailed her as a model for Soviet womanhood.) She then flew to Tokyo and sat there for tea and photographs with General Nagaoka of the Japanese Imperial Aviation Society. In 1932 she smashed the London-Cape Town-London record in a De Havilland Puss Moth by taking a wild western route over the Sahara and Fernando Po. And the following year she made it 'backwards' over the Atlantic, against the prevailing westerlies, and joined the American aviatrix Amelia Earhart and the Roosevelts for tea.

Earhart apart, Johnson was the leading woman in an elite corps of aviation fanatics. Theirs was a golden age of record-breaking in which the right route, written up with the right sort of understatement and to deadline, could net a newspaper deal worth six figures in modern money. There was stiff competition for front-page treatment, but Johnson stayed in contention by means of the second most audacious stunt of her career. Over lunch at Quaglino's in Soho, on a spring Monday in 1932, she agreed to marry her most formidable and flamboyant rival.

This was Jim Mollison. More than anyone, Mollison drew Johnson into the 'Mayfair set' that epitomised 1930s style and superficiality, and from which the ATA eventually offered her relief. He was photogenic and knew all about the paralysing exhaustion of long-distance flying. Otherwise he wasn't her type. He was short-tempered and addicted to liquor and adrenalin. Scottish by birth, he had flown some of the earliest airliners to have entered service in Australia. It was there he met Johnson while escorting her to Sydney on her post-flight publicity tour in 1930. *They Flew Alone* depicts that meeting as the dreamy work of fate; an instant connection in a softly lit cockpit pushed through the night by four rumbling great piston engines. He asks for two dances at the Governor General's ball to which he is taking her, but when he seeks her out there the host himself, in cockaded hat and tails, declares her taken.

In reality, Mollison rates no mention in Johnson's diaries until 1932, when she met him in Cape Town and began to fall for him. Earlier that year she had had a hysterectomy, apparently to put an end to debilitating period pains that were interfering with her flying. At any rate, whoever married Amy Johnson would not have to be a model father, and when the press learned it was to be Mollison, this incomparably racy couple was adopted as story fodder with no sell-by date.

They lived together at once, not in a house or flat but in a succession of suites in the Grosvenor House Hotel. Their views were of Park Lane and the sky. Their public relations were handled by William Courtney's Aviation Publicity Services, which had a branch office in the lobby. Their shopping trips would often take in Selfridges – a short walk away on the far side of Oxford Street – which had its own aeroplane department.

Mollison was bad company. He was not quite a monomaniac: adulation and money interested him as much as flying. But he brought out the monomaniac in his new wife, and she drifted rapidly away from the emotional moorings her long-suffering father had provided. After years of regular correspondence in which she would trail her schemes, their costs and their potential returns and he would offer cautious encouragement and money, they fell out of touch. Will and Ciss Johnson would read of their daughter's flights and fancies in the papers, or hear of them from neighbours and have nothing to add.

On 22 July 1932 they received a rare letter from Amy posted from the Grosvenor House Hotel saying there was nothing to the printed rumours that her wedding to Mollison was imminent. But a week later a telegram arrived in Hull, at 9 p.m., also from Amy, to say the wedding was set for 10 o'clock the following morning and that she and Mollison were 'trying to keep it as quiet as possible'. Her parents were patently not invited. But something in the senior Johnsons snapped. They drove all night, left their car in Golders Green at 9.40 a.m. and took the tube and then a taxi to St George's Church in Hanover Square, arriving as the service ended. As the bride walked out in a black coat and white gloves, she failed to notice them. By the time she learned that her parents had made the trip they were inconsolable, and on their way back home.

Mollison's best man had been Sir Francis Shelmerdine, the Director of Civil Aviation, who managed to straddle the new world of Mayfair aviation crazies and the older ones of civil service and landed gentry. Yet when fate began to sour on Amy Johnson, even he couldn't help. Her marriage suffered from the start from Mollison's inability to resist other women – chief among them Beryl Markham, who had been seducing the Duke of Gloucester at the Grosvenor House Hotel even as Johnson was fêted there on her return from Australia. (Markham, who grew up drinking cow's blood and curdled milk on her father's Kenyan farm, later became the first person to fly non-stop from England – rather than Ireland – to North America. She was as fearless as Johnson, and, some say, a more natural pilot.)

Johnson, now being squeezed off the aviation pages by wilder, more glamorous upstarts, began a defiantly elegant descent from stardom. In 1934, she and her husband entered a race from Suffolk to Melbourne as favourites. They lost it to Charles Scott, a preening ex-RAF officer who, four years earlier as an envious escort pilot on her victory tour of Australia, had taunted her unsubtly about her dreadful period pains. The race ended for 'Jim and Johnnie' , as the Mollison pair were known to the press, with a seized-up engine and a furious, whisky-fuelled argument in their cockpit in Allahabad.

By this time they had in any case been eclipsed in the publicity stakes by none other than Jackie Cochran, the New York beautician and pilot who had hauled herself into the air by her proverbial bootstraps – and by marrying a multi-millionaire. In the race itself, she fared even worse than the Mollisons, running out of fuel over the Carpathians, but she had already beguiled reporters by emerging from her plane at Mildenhall wordlessly and in full make-up, with a printed press release drafted by her lawyer.

Two years later, Amy Johnson was back in the air to publicise a doomed business venture that she and a putative French backer (and lover) were calling Air Cruises. She climbed aboard a Percival Gull in a woollen suit and newsprint scarf designed for her by Elsa Schiaparelli, bound once again for Cape Town. She got there eventually, but only after botching a take-off in North Africa and restarting the whole flight a month later. Even then, far from being fêted at her refuelling stops in Italian-occupied East Africa, she 'could not shake off the feeling that I was a trespasser, and a nuisance at that'. She had been turned down by the *News of the World*, but a deal with the *Daily Express* let her pay off her overdraft and a debt to her father. It failed to rescue her marriage, though. She and Mollison were divorced in 1936, and the approach of war found her broke again and desperate for work. In June 1939, after a brief stint as editor of *The Lady Driver*, a decidedly earthbound new monthly, she accepted her first full-time flying job, shuttling day and night between Hampshire and the Isle of Wight for a local airline known as the Solent air ferry. The *Daily Mirror* considered it a story. 'Folks, you've got a chance of being flown by a world-famous air pilot for five bob a time,' it announced. It was honest work, but it ended abruptly with the outbreak of war and failed to serve as a springboard to the job she really wanted: the head of the ATA.

Johnson already knew and liked Pauline Gower. They had met at the London Aeroplane Club in 1931, when Gower was immersed there in the improvised sort of aero-engineering apprenticeship that Johnson had glamorised the year before.

Years later, she spent a weekend at the Gower family home near Tunbridge Wells, where Pauline and her friend Dorothy Spicer invited Amy to join their two-woman firm providing joy-rides in the sky to crowds who would queue up at fairgrounds across the country for a taste of the fad that was changing the world. Johnson considered them 'nice girls', but declined. Theirs was a raucous, retail sort of flying, taking off from new airfields for new crowds every day of the summer. Johnson considered it several steps beneath her. But as far as the aviation establishment was concerned, she was beneath them.

Francis Shelmerdine and Pop d'Erlanger favoured Gower for the ATA job on the grounds that she had never been an aviation record-seeker like Johnson, 'with all the publicity which is attached to that role'. This may have been sensible: the idea of putting women in RAF aircraft in wartime was an invitation to scarlet-faced apoplexy in the RAF's own high command, especially if they were to be led by the curious, chippy creature who had pioneered the heretical unisexing of the cockpit. But d'Erlanger's verdict was also a simply coded confirmation that Gower was 'One of Us'. Johnson, with her flat, Humberside vowels and undisguised need for recognition – not to mention money – clearly was not.

But Pauline Gower didn't forget about her. On the contrary, after she was appointed head of the ATA's women's section she sent Johnson a formal letter inviting her to apply to join up. Johnson did, and was put on a waiting list. In May 1940 she agreed to take a flying test that Gower assured her would be a formality, but Johnson appears to have been simultaneously revealed as a clumsy lander (which she was) and repelled by the idea of mucking in with the other hopefuls. She described one of them in a letter home as 'all dolled up in full Sidcot suit, fur-lined helmet and goggles, fluffing up her hair etc. – the typical Lyons waitress type . . . I suddenly realised I could not go in and sit in line with these girls (who all more or less look up to me as God!), so I turned tail and ran'.

It was true, or true enough. The younger pilots did revere her, but when Johnson eventually enrolled in the ATA in May 1940 she found she didn't mind. One of her admirers was Jackie Sorour, a tungsten-tipped South African who affected a ditzy innocence but would later pull off an extraordinary aerial hitch-hike to Pretoria and back. Sorour, a qualified instructor by the age of twenty despite her mother's dogged opposition to her flying, was interviewed by Gower at Hatfield in July 1940, and immediately admitted to the ATA. From Gower's office, she wrote later:

> I went to the crew room to find the pilot who was to give me a brief refresher on the Tiger Moth. There were four or five women lounging on chairs and tables. One was laughing as I entered. I looked at her dumbfounded as I recognised the face that had inspired me during my brief flying career and had flitted on the world's headlines for a decade. I rushed over to her and gushed: 'Miss Johnson, may I have your autograph?' She stared at me. There was a painful silence. Oh God, I wished the floor would open up and devour me. How could I have behaved so inanely? Suddenly she grinned: 'My dear child, I'll swap it for yours.'

There was something else that gradually endeared Johnson to the ATA besides the return of the old adulation – the prospect of flying Spitfires. For all her experience, Wonderful Amy had never flown anything faster than a De Havilland Comet, maximum speed 200 mph. The war was forcing up speeds. By the summer of 1940, when Fighter Command's precious Hurricanes and Spitfires were being tested daily to destruction by the Luftwaffe's formidable Messerschmitt 109s, the Vickers Supermarine factories in Southampton and Castle Bromwich were already turning out Mark V Spitfires capable of 400 mph when straight and level and no-one knew quite how fast in a dive.

Johnson never flew one. She died too soon. One reason for her death, oddly, was national security. Before the war the Lorenz company in Germany had devised a beautifully simple radio navigation system based on corridors of land-based transmitters. The transmitters on one side of the corridor would broadcast, continuously, only the Morse signal for A – a dot and then a dash. Those on the other side would broadcast only the signal for N – a dash, then a dot. Suitably equipped aircraft flying straight along the corridor would know they were on course because of antennae mounted at opposite ends of their fuselages: one tuned to the N signal and one to the A. As long as each antenna was the same distance from its signal's source, the dots and dashes would overlap into a continuous tone, dull but infinitely reassuring. If the plane drifted off this radio 'beam' in either direction, its antennae would slip in relation to their sources. The overlapping would become imperfect, the tone interrupted, and the pilot would be snapped out of her daydream or funk.

If you had an ordinary voice radio you could also call up the nearest radio-equipped aerodrome and ask it where you were. Eric 'Winkle' Brown, the finest test pilot Britain ever produced, once did this over a fogbound patch of Kent, and it probably saved his life. But in that Airspeed Oxford at Squire's Gate, with her chit for Kidlington in Oxfordshire, Johnson had no radio of any kind, and nor did any other ferry pilots. As the spliced-in newsreel puts it in *They Flew Alone*: 'No radio of course. Too useful for Jerry.'

The other reason Johnson would never fly a Spitfire was the

weather that was keeping her on the ground at an aerodrome near Blackpool on that miserable Sunday in January 1941; the weather that would have made the radio navigation option something of a life-saver; the sodden, all-pervading, bloody-minded British weather.

Johnson finally lost patience and took off at 11.49 a.m. Not many others ventured up that day, but Jackie Sorour did. 'That same afternoon I took off from South Wales in a twin-engined Oxford aircraft bound [like Johnson] for Kidlington,' she wrote in *Woman Pilot*.

The weather . . . lay like a blanket over the Southern Counties. Drizzle and low cloud was forecast for most of the route to Kidlington but with a promise of improvement. Reluctantly I headed into the curtain of rain and, a few hundred feet above the ground, searched for the promised improvement. It was non-existent. I should have turned back but valleys beckoned invitingly. I flew into one and peered ahead but the trap had sprung. The other end of the narrow valley was blocked with a wall of cloud. I rammed open the throttles, pulled the control column back and climbed steeply. With unnerving suddenness the ground vanished as the clouds swirled around the Oxford in a cold embrace and forced me to climb on instruments . . . I tried to keep the angle of climb constant. Suddenly at four thousand feet the clouds splintered into bright wintry sunshine; beneath me the clouds stretched to all horizons like a soft woollen blanket. Desperately lonely and frightened, I searched for a gap. There was none. Whilst I stayed above I was safe. Like a spotlight the sun cast a shadow of the Oxford on the top of the clouds and circled it with a halo of rainbow hue. I had the odd thought that I was the shadow and the shadow was me. Curiously I watched it to see what it was going to do next; silly thing, it was going round in circles.

The petrol gauge drooped inexorably. I had to go down . . . Reluctantly I throttled back and eased the nose down.

The clouds embraced me like water around a stone as I slowly descended. Two thousand feet. Fifteen hundred. One thousand. Six hundred. It's no good, prompted experience, get back. Ignoring the urgent warning I eased lower with the altimeter ticking off the altitude like a devilish clock. If I were lucky I would be over the hill-less sea. If not, I had not long to live. Suddenly the clouds broke, revealing, just beneath, the grey, sullen waters of the Bristol Channel. I pulled off my helmet and wiped the sweat from my face before turning towards the Somerset coast faintly visible to the east.

I looked at the petrol gauge. Twenty minutes left to find an aerodrome. Absently I worked out the little problem. Twenty times sixty. Two sixes are twelve. Add two noughts. That's it. One thousand two hundred seconds before I wrecked the aeroplane and paid the penalty for not turning back. But all the luck in the sky was with me that day. Soon after crossing the coast an aerodrome blossomed out of the ground like a flower from the desert. Pulling the Oxford round in a tight circuit I landed on the glistening, rain-soaked runway.

Next day on returning to Hatfield I learned that Amy Johnson was dead.

There is not much that can be said with any confidence about Johnson's last flight, though it must have droned on against an appalling crescendo of fear. For those left to reconstruct it over the years there is also the knowledge that, for all her fear, she had every reason to believe until the last second of her life that she would survive this scrape as she had so many others.

Did she, in fact, kill herself? She did once tell a friend that she was sure she'd finish up in the drink. And it was alleged by Jimmy Martin (later Sir James, an aircraft builder who never quite finished an aircraft for her to fly) that she told him her first impulse on learning years earlier that Hans Arreger had married someone else had been to end it all by finishing her flying training and then crashing. But the idea that her doomed run down to Kidlington was a suicide mission is even less plausible than the more popular conspiracy theory that she was carrying a mystery passenger on a clandestine or illicit trip (some speculated she was smuggling the faithless Arreger back to Switzerland, even though there is no evidence that she was still in contact with him) – and had to bale out because of a catastrophic malfunction or even after being hit by friendly fire.

The truth was almost certainly more prosaic, but just as deadly. She went 'over the top', as she said she would and as Sorour also did. But she couldn't 'crack on through' because there were no cracks in her swathe of sky: just deep, unrelenting cloud. Sorour had risked everything by descending through it. Johnson actually risked much less by summoning the courage to do what she had always dreaded and bale out– something, amazingly, that she had never had to do before. After three and a half hours the Oxford's second tank ran dry. As the two engines died, she feathered the propellers and levelled the plane at 3,000 feet, and falling. It was now gliding eastwards. She unstrapped herself from her seat, strapped on her parachute and walked a few steps back down the floating fuselage to the emergency exit door, which was not hinged. It had to be wrenched right out of its opening. Johnson managed this, and jumped. She would have experienced a considerable physical shock because the cabin had been heated but the cloud was nothing but freezing moisture; for anyone below, it was snowing gently.

When the parachute opened cleanly, and high enough for an orderly descent, Johnson would also have felt relief. At this point, still with no view of whatever part of England was beneath her but uninjured and alert, the only irreversible loss in her world that day was of one twin-engined Airspeed Oxford. Much else had gone wrong. There would be an accident investigation and report. She would have to answer questions. It would be a story. Pauline Gower, for one, would ask whatever had induced her to take off that morning, and in truth it would be difficult to tell her. Pride? Boredom? Sullen arrogance? A secret conviction of invincibility, annealed in the homicidal Taurus Mountains and somewhere over Nova Scotia one terrifying night in 1932?

When she descended through the cloud she saw for the first time that she was over water. Her parachuting nightmare was now coming true. The cold was about to intensify in a way she could not imagine, or endure for long. But even in the few seconds between appearing over the Thames estuary and plunging into it there were, suddenly, new reasons to hope. By pure chance there were ships everywhere, some close enough to help if only they spotted her and she could get clear of the parachute.

They had certainly spotted her. An entire convoy, numbered CE21, consisting of seventeen merchant ships, two destroyers, four minesweepers, four motor launches and five cross-Channel ferries converted to deploy barrage balloons, was steaming up the estuary. One of the balloon ships, HMS *Haslemere*, was closest to Johnson. From its bridge a Lieutenant Henry O'Dea actually saw her drop gently into the water at a distance of perhaps half a mile. His captain, Lieutenant Commander Walter Fletcher, ordered the *Haslemere* to head for her at full speed. Johnson was still alive when it reached her, and was heard to shout the words, 'Hurry, please hurry'. But she failed to grab hold of any of the lines thrown in her direction.

In its dash to pick her up, the *Haslemere* ran aground in mud beneath the shallow waters of the estuary's southern edge. Fletcher ordered the engines to slow astern but they took ten precious minutes to work the vessel free. By this time Johnson had drifted towards the ship's stern and was helpless with cold. As Captain Fletcher pulled off his outer clothes to dive in for her, a wave lifted the *Haslemere* and pushed Johnson under its propellers. As they fell, they crushed her. 'She did not come into view again,' seaman Nicholas Roberts, who was watching from the ship's bulwark, wrote later in an affidavit. Indeed, her body was never found.

Fourteen months later, *They Flew Alone* received its première at Leicester Square. In attendance, besides Pauline Gower, Jackie Cochran and Anna Neagle, was Lord Wakefield, Amy Johnson's faithful oiler. In the film, shaking his head in something like bewilderment, the Wakefield character tells a white-tied friend: 'She's driven a coach and four through centuries of custom and convention.'

'She's opened a great gap in the fence that's been surrounding our young women for generations,' the friend replies. 'And now the rest of the devils will come pouring through after her. I can't quite see the end of it.'

'There isn't any end to it. What that young woman has done is the sort of thing that goes on forever,' says Wakefield.

After a final image of Anna Neagle's character dissolving into a montage of uniformed women marching purposefully in all directions, the film ends with the dedication:

'To all the Amy Johnsons of today'.

3

Queen Bee

Could the ATA have managed without its women pilots? Sixty years after its demise I put the question to Sir Peter Mursell, the organisation's only surviving senior administrator. He replied without hesitation: 'Yes' – and there was certainly never a shortage of qualified male applicants eager to join the ATA.

Nor was there a shortage of female ones: Amy Johnson had inspired a generation of rich, or at least resourceful, women to follow her into the air. But they might never have flown in the war without the skilled and tireless lobbying of Pauline Gower.

Prominent progressives such as Captain Harold Balfour had offered enthusiastic predictions of a role for women pilots in the coming conflict as early as 1938. But the RAF's opposition was granite, and at that stage no-one had even thought of handing the job of ferrying military aircraft to civilians. Subsidised flying training in the Civil Air Guard – a belated effort to match Germany for 'air mindedness' – had helped to swell the ranks of civilian pilots and instructors, women as well as men, but when war was declared all civil aviation was grounded, and most of these new pilots melted away in search of other work.

It was on her own initiative that Gower requested meetings, first with Pop d'Erlanger and then with the Director General of Civil Aviation, Sir Francis Shelmerdine, in September 1939. D'Erlanger's instinctive answer to the question 'Why women?' was 'Why not?'. He accompanied Gower to the meeting with Shelmerdine on 21 September. It went well. Gower knew Shelmerdine through Amy Johnson, whose wedding he had attended as best man, and as a trailblazer in her own right. Gower came away with permission to recruit twelve women pilots and an understanding that she would be in charge of them.

There were hiccups. In late 1939 the RAF was still using its own pilots for most of its ferrying, and the whole plan to recruit women to the ATA had to be put on ice for three months while the RAF high command and its allies in the Air Ministry fought a rearguard action against the attachment of women to existing RAF ferry pools. Shelmerdine made several tactical retreats, assuring the RAF top brass that their men would never have to fly with women, insisting on a minimum of 500 hours solo experience for women candidates – far more than was required for men – and cutting Gower's initial quota, without explanation, from twelve pilots to eight.

There was also the Treasury's standard stipulation, uncontested at this point by Gower or anyone else, on women's pay. While they would be expected to perform exactly the same duties and work exactly the same hours as male ATA pilots, female ones would earn 20 per cent less. And there was one other thing, which may even have put a smile on the faces of the air vice marshals in their stalwart defence of gender apartheid. While their fighter boys would be arcing over Europe in sleek new Hurricanes and even sleeker newer Spitfires, these crazy women, initially at least, would be flying only Tiger Moths, with nothing to protect them from the elements except their clothing and a comical crescent of Perspex fixed to the front edge of the cockpit – and in the worst winter for almost fifty years.

As the *New York Times* reported two weeks after the first women pilots reported for duty at the Hatfield aerodrome north of London in January 1940 (and the time lapse is significant):

Now it can be told. For the first time since the war began, British censors today allowed that humdrum conversational topic, the weather, which has been a strict military secret in Britain, to be mentioned in news dispatches – providing the weather news is more than fifteen days old. The weather has been so unusually Arctic that by reaction the censors' hearts were thawed enough to permit disclosure of the fact that this region shivered since past several weeks in the coldest spell since 1894, with the mercury dropping almost to zero and a damp knife edge wind piercing the marrow.

The reference to zero was in Fahrenheit. It was the worst weather imaginable to be flying around in open planes. Small wonder that when the 'First Eight' attended a mid-winter photo shoot to mark their arrival at Hatfield, they looked happier in Sidcot suits than in their Austin Reed skirts.

Though not in Amy Johnson's league, Pauline Gower had been newsworthy in her own right for several years by the outbreak of war. Like Rosemary Rees she was the daughter of a senior Tory and smitten with flying. Unlike Rees, she had flown for a living. She started in 1931 as a freelance 'joyrider' flying from a field in Kent, and moved on to contract circus flying for the British Hospitals' Air Pageant. This was a less charitable outfit than the name implied, but the steady work helped make the payments on her £300, two-seater Simmonds Spartan, bought on an instalment plan. By 1936 she was operating a profitable air taxi service across the Wash from Hunstanton to Skegness. 'And now,' she told a BBC reporter at the start of 1940, 'I can claim to have carried over 30,000 passengers in the air.' Given that she had never flown anything bigger than a three-seater, it was no idle boast.

The flying had toughened her. Performing one summer evening in 1933 at Harrogate with the Hospitals' Air Pageant, Gower landed shortly before dusk to watch one of the show's most reliable crowd-pleasers with the rest of the spectators – the parachute jump. 'We had several parachutists, one of whom was named Evans,' she wrote. 'He was extremely clever at his job and could judge his descents so well that he often landed between two machines parked on the ground right in front of the public enclosure.'

There was a stiff breeze that evening, and plenty of visibility. Evans was taken up to 1,000 feet. He jumped and pulled his ripcord in the normal way, but he was drifting fast on account of the breeze. The performer in him still wanted to get down in front of the crowd, so he spilled air from the parachute by pulling on the shroud lines. The idea was to come down faster than usual to minimise the drift, releasing the shroud lines with a few seconds to go to allow the canopy to refill and soften his landing. Evans had done it scores of times before, but this time the parachute collapsed completely. The crowd watched, horror struck, as he accelerated into the ground unchecked by the twisted sausage of silk above him. He was killed instantly.

'Fortunately, the light was already beginning to fail,' Gower recalled. The performance was terminated immediately, and the shocked crowds went home. 'It was a blow for all of us. Evans was extremely popular ... but in the air circus business there is no time for sentiment.' Next day the Pageant moved on to Redcar. There, 'although the thoughts of many of us were at Harrogate with the still, dark form we had left crumpled up on the field the night before, the show went on as usual'.

Later, in the ATA ferry pools, the phrase adopted to describe the routine business of embroidering a close shave to make it sound closer still was to 'line-shoot'. It was used in the mess at the all-female No. 15 Ferry Pool at Hamble, in particular, to stop the chattier young pilots making fools of themselves. But no-one ever accused Gower of 'line-shooting'.

The toughening of this deceptively sunny convent girl with the bright laugh and a resolute smile had begun thirteen years earlier, on what her Mother Superior had feared would be her deathbed. Struck down in her late teens with a raging ear infection, together with complications of pneumonia and pleurisy, Gower was sedated for surgery that she was not expected to survive. A priest was summoned to her bedside and the other boarders at the Convent of the Sacred Heart at Tunbridge Wells prayed for her at evensong. She pulled through and emerged from her illness physically weakened and barred from team sports. But she was a bundle of nervous energy which she was determined to channel into that most daring and controversial of womanly pursuits, a 'career'. Whatever she chose would rile her father, a driven but illogical old paragon who set great store by education, including his daughter's, even though he would not allow her to go to university. So she set her sights on flying.

It was still two years before Amy Johnson ensured that flying eclipsed mere motoring as the fashionable expression of late adolescent rebellion for young women of means. But Gower was not interested in fashion. Nor was she one to hang about. She took her first flight, while still at school, with Captain Hubert S. Broad, who was visiting Tunbridge Wells as part of a national tour after competing in the Paris air races. She kept a diary and may have allowed herself a line or two of breathlessness in it about Kent from the air and the wind in her hair, and even about Captain Broad. But there is no such sappiness in anything she wrote for public consumption. She filed flying away as what she would do in the likely event that nothing else came along to satisfy both her need for excitement and her father's for respectability. And nothing did.

Dispatched to finishing school in Paris, she ran away. She wondered about earning a living playing her violin, but realised she wasn't good enough to perform and gave it up. Back home she was presented at court and 'did all the things expected of the debutante, and was bored to tears'. She dabbled in Tory politics, but the Tories were not ready for her. (Even Lady Astor, Britain's first woman MP, was only elected in 1919, and she was a Liberal.) So, on 25 June 1930, with Amy Johnson still on her delirious, nervewracking victory tour of Australia, Pauline Gower enrolled at the Phillips and Powis School of Flying at the Woodley airfield outside Reading. She did not tell her parents. For six hours' worth of flying lessons she managed to keep the reason for her trips to Reading secret. Then she told her father what she was up to, and he cut off her allowance.

Gower was a natural pilot, and did not have to wait long to go solo. But her novel idea of flying for a living (a regular living, as opposed to being paid large sums by newspapers for occasional death-defying epics in the manner of Amy Johnson), required a commercial licence and dozens more expensive hours of training. For a year she paid for them by teaching the violin. In that time she switched flying schools and moved to Stag Lane, and there she befriended the vulnerable Johnson just as Johnson was adjusting to her new life as a megastar. At the same time, Sir Robert Gower came round to the idea of having a pilot for a daughter. For her twenty-first birthday, to her 'unutterable joy', he made the down-payment on her first plane. It was a two-seater Spartan, about as cheap as aircraft came in 1931, 'but to me' she reflected, 'it was the finest aeroplane that had ever been built'.

Miss Pauline Mary de Peauly Gower became the world's third female commercial pilot, and Britain's first. She was already forming a grand world view centred on the notion of flying as a liberator of women and unifier of nations. Another of her new friends from Stag Lane, Dorothy Spicer, a pilot as well as an engineer, was more interested in engines than flying. Tall, blonde and very beautiful, she was a graduate of University College London and a qualified aeronautical engineer. She and Gower decided to go into business together.

Gower would later write an account of her time with Spicer as co-directors of the world's first all-female airborne business venture. Her publisher described it as 'a record of pioneer achievement in the air related with much humour and a cheerful philosophy'. The book was reviewed by the sniffy and none-too-progressive editor of *Aeroplane* magazine, C. G. Grey. Spicer, he wrote:

> looks more like the British working woman's idea of the idle rich, or alternatively a cinema star, than any girl I know . . .

[and] Pauline Gower does not give one exactly the notion of being one of the world's workers either. And yet for six years those two girls did a job of sheer manual labour, which would have been more than enough for half the British working men of the country.

Spicer kept the plane airworthy; Gower flew it. They started with a rented Gipsy Moth in a field near Sevenoaks, charging half a crown per flight and fifteen shillings for an aerobatic sequence consisting of two loops and a spin. When Gower's first aerobatics customer requested another loop she made him hand over another half crown in the air first. With Gower's Spartan, they flew from Wallingford in Berkshire, and spent the rest of that first summer flying for whoever would pay them, and playing host most evenings to friends from Stag Lane who would drive out to shoot the breeze (and rabbits).

They slept in a hut next to their beloved aeroplane, exhaustion competing with nightmares about a serial killer thought to be at large in that part of Berkshire. Besides joyriders, their customers included yacht race spectators from Cowes Week and a Gloucester-bound businessman who paid them a fat fee and then embarrassed them by telling a reporter that he was in 'lavatory deodorisation'. There were also two men pursued to the airfield by plainclothes detectives and arrested before Gower – with tank full and engine running – could fly them to France; and another who requested a moonlit flight over the royal residence at Sandringham. The directors of Air Trips turned him down.

There is no mention during this time, in anything written by them or about them, of boyfriends. 'It is only logical,' Gower mused, 'to suppose that matrimony will claim the majority of women pilots ultimately, just as it claims many other girls who have been trained at great expense for different professions.' It did claim them both, eventually. But as twentysomethings they had no time for whatever preceded matrimony. They were smitten with the thrill of flying, with being busy and with making money.

In 1933, in the course of six months with the Hospitals' Air Pageant, they flew from 185 airfields, moving from one to the next every day. For the next two seasons they stayed put in a field outside Hunstanton and let the holidaying public come to them. The following year, 1936, as Hitler hosted the Olympics and occupied the Rhineland, Gower and Spicer hit the touring trail again, this time with Tom Campbell Black's Air Display.

They had a miserable time. They witnessed another death, this time of a young and inexperienced member of the display team showing off in a new Drone monoplane near Hereford. He flew past the crowd at 400 feet, waving and smiling. Then he put the plane into a spin. 'At that height the result was a foregone conclusion,' Gower wrote briskly. 'Almost before the Drone hit the ground, the ambulance was on the spot. The pilot was extricated from the wreckage terribly smashed up and rushed to hospital. The show continued for another hour, then word was brought to us that he had died and the evening performance was abandoned.'

A few weeks later Gower herself was nearly killed, colliding on the ground with another plane while trying to take off from Coventry. She had been hit on the head by a wheel from the other plane; the wheel came off and Gower was off flying for a month. She saw out the rest of the season, but was badly shaken up and prone to unhelpful attacks of nerves.

This may have been one reason why the brave firm of Air Trips closed down for the season in September 1936, and never reopened. But another reason was undoubtedly the tragedy that befell the Gower family in November of that year. Pauline's mother, who was convinced, despite a lack of any symptoms, that she was suffering from terminal cancer, gassed herself in the kitchen at Tunbridge Wells. She left a note for her daughter: 'A very hurried line to send you my love, and all my wishes for your future happiness and peace . . . Again I say, you have nothing to blame yourself for. Try to forgive me. Your utterly bewildered and terrified but loving Ma.'

It was the sort of sign-off to crush a softer soul, but Pauline's had already been cauterized by six years of living one slip – one misjudgement – from death. She never spoke publicly about her mother's suicide; nor would it have occurred to her to. Instead, like Amy Johnson after her sister's suicide, she immersed herself in work with an almost manic vigour. Perhaps out of consideration for her father she made sure that more of her work was on the ground. In any case, by the time the war broke out her curriculum vitae was as full as her diary. She was a popular lecturer on aviation and women's role in it; a Civil Air Defence Commissioner for London; a district commissioner for the Girl Guides; a fellow of the Royal Meteorological Society; a King's appointee to the Venerable Order of St John of Jerusalem; and an active member of a new parliamentary subcommittee set up to review safety regulations concerning low-flying banner-pullers. She could surely cope with being head of the ATA women's section as well.

It was, in part, this zest for work that made Gower the obvious choice to lead the women pilots of the ATA. But she also had a natural gift for Whitehall diplomacy, and was superbly well-connected. Amy Johnson wrote gloomily to her father in late 1939 that 'had I played my cards right and cultivated the right people, I could have got the job that Pauline Gower has got'. Johnson was right that connections were invaluable for contenders in any hierarchy, and there were doubtless others who were aggrieved at having been passed over for the best women's job in aviation in the war. But the truth is they never stood a chance. Gower liked to say the world divided into two sorts of people: those who wanted to know and those you had to know. She knew them all.

4

The First Eight

On 9 January 1940, in the depths of a bitter winter and in the middle of the Phoney War, the office of Pop d'Erlanger contacted the news desks of the major Fleet Street titles, the BBC and most of the foreign newsreel companies represented in London to inform them of a 'photographic opportunity'. The following day, members of the Air Transport Auxiliary would be available for pictures and to answer reasonable questions at the Hatfield aerodrome north of London (recently relinquished to the ATA for the duration of hostilities by Geoffrey de Havilland and his aircraft company). There would be aeroplanes. There would be take-offs and landings. And there would be a bevy of interesting young women in uniform.

For this unusual and welcome photocall – the country may have been at war but there was no fighting – the press turned out in force. They were not disappointed. Rumours that women were to be allowed to ferry RAF aircraft, albeit only low-performance machines such as Tiger Moths, had first surfaced at the beginning of December 1939 and been widely reported. D'Erlanger rightly considered it a sensitive subject and had released no details except the name of the commanding officer of the women's section, Pauline Gower. Ever since, Fleet Street had been badgering him for more. Initially, there hadn't been much more to give. It was not until 16 December that Gower had even invited candidates to lunch and a flight test at Whitchurch, where the first male recruits had been assessed three months earlier. Twelve of the country's most experienced women pilots had attended, all with at least 500 hours in their logbooks, and from them eight were selected. Their names were kept under wraps over Christmas but come the New Year, d'Erlanger and Gower decided to relent.

Hatfield aerodrome had been owned and operated by De Havilland's until the war, and had been chosen as headquarters of the women's section because it was already home to many of the Moths they would be flying. The idea in inviting the press was to give them everything they wanted in one concentrated dose and hope they would be sated until something more momentous came along. In principle, it was a sound and modern strategy for managing the news. In practice it ignited a fascination with the women of the ATA that hardly faded throughout the war. To the chagrin of some of the male ATA pilots, who outnumbered the women by six to one, it also created an enduring public impression that this was an all-female outfit.

Luckily the First Eight had been well briefed and were cooperative. It was vital for both d'Erlanger and Gower that their new recruits struck the right balance between enthusiasm and seriousness – enthusiasm for a job that needed absolutely every hand on deck (including, as Gower later put it, 'the hand that rocks the cradle'), and seriousness because the slightest hint of frivolity would bring down an avalanche of harrumphing from the air vice marshals who considered their aircraft the sacred preserve of men.

That balance was duly struck. One of the pilot-mannequins on 9 January described the demands of the photographers:

They said, 'Pick up your parachutes and run to your aero-planes.'
We said, 'What, scramble? To Tiger Moths?'
They said, 'Yes.'
And so we did. We ran in our new creaking flying suits and our new stiff fur-lined flying boots carrying our 30 lb

parachutes. Then when we came panting back they said, 'We didn't get that very well, please do it again.'

They also wore their dress uniforms. The order of that day appears to have been an hour or two's gallivanting in oversized greatcoats and Sidcot flying suits, followed by a change into the navy worsted suits and forage caps for which these women were to become famous. They posed, exhausted, one final time on a stone patio outside the aerodrome's main building. In this picture, a classic of its kind, the pilots and the press reached a new and sullen equilibrium. In the background, the two propellers of a gawky De Havilland Flamingo point towards an opaque sky; a tractor nuzzles under its port wing. On the left, four of 'the Eight' sit demurely on a low wall. On the right, the remaining four, together with Gower, her adjutant and Lois Butler, sit in folding chairs round a trestle table laid with a white cloth and tea service. All but one of the group deign to look at the camera, but most of them do so with suspicion as well as weariness. If this is fame, they are determined not to look as if they care for it.

Only two raise anything like a smile. One of these is Joan Hughes: the youngest and least composed of the group, her hands next to her thighs on the wall. She is 5 foot 2 inches tall, 21 years old and has already been an instructor for three of them. In due course she will fly Lancasters to Lakenheath and a Tiger Moth under a bridge on the M40 as Lady Penelope's stunt double in a 1968 Thunderbirds film. For now, she looks as if she is about to push herself up from the wall and make a playful run for the camera. The other smiler sits at the tea table with her hands on her lap and her right shoulder raised in something like a shrug. She is Rosemary Rees, acrobat and daughter of Sir John Rees, Bt, MP. She has short, dark curly hair and a wit that one of her operations officers says could 'tear the husk of an argument or person with a very few words and leave the bare bones'.

Strictly speaking, Rees is more dancer than acrobat. Her only formal training to date, other than in the cockpit, has been at

Mme Astafieva's ballet studio in Chelsea. But unlike most of Mme Astafieva's pupils, Rees has put her endless hours at the barre to commercial use. She has hit the road, touring Britain in the early 1930s with a kitschy review ensemble called 'Catlin's Royal Pierrots'. She has been unmasked by her fellow performers as minor gentry, and nicknamed the 'Bloody Duchess' (mainly to give local reporters an angle). But even for toffs, membership of the Royal Pierrots requires acrobatics.

It was while dancing in Llandudno in the early summer of 1930 that Rose Rees became aware of Amy Johnson. 'Wonderful Amy' was the hit song of the season and it was played every night at high volume in the interval between the two halves of the Royal Pierrots' show. 'Amy, wonderful, Amy,' went the refrain, 'how can you blame me/For Loving you?/Believe me, Amy/You cannot blame me, Amy,/For falling in love with you.'

Eleven years later, Rees and Johnson were colleagues and comrades, both stuck in south-west Scotland in grim weather, waiting to fly south. Johnson was in Prestwick, at the Orangefield Hotel; Rees was in Dumfries. They had arranged that Johnson would pick Rees up if no taxi planes were moving from Dumfries, and apparently none was. So a call was booked to Prestwick to confirm that First Officer Mollison (Amy Johnson was still using her married name) would have to stop for a passenger en route to Kidlington as planned. But before the call went through the crew of an RAF Avro Anson walked into the watch office at Dumfries and offered Rees a lift.

'So I cancelled my call and went with them,' she told a stunned collection of women pilots later in the war. 'I wonder what would have happened if I had got through, and she had picked me up . . . Poor Amy! How she must have hated not finding that hole in the clouds.'

Datelined 'Somewhere in England', newspaper articles about the First Eight began appearing on 10 January 1940. They stressed accomplishment and lineage, not looks, and accomplishment is what marked these women out. They were doers par excellence; action ladies in the Johnson mould. They had to be. Even for those with money, to amass at least 500 hours flying time as a woman took dedication bordering on obsession.

When Joan Hughes had her first flying lesson at the age of fifteen she thought she would die of excitement. When the cost of further lessons went up to £2 and 10 shillings an hour, she told her father she was happy to go without food to help pay for them. And when the first of her many admirers asked her to marry him, and she realised he would expect her to give up flying, she 'ended it there and then'.

The ice hockey international and 'Mayfair Minx' Mona Friedlander told the journalist from the *Daily Mail* at the photocall that she had taken up flying in 1936 as a cure for boredom. Over the next three years, she gained a private and commercial pilot's licence, a navigator's licence and the staggering wage of £10 an hour towing targets for anti-aircraft gunnery units.

Winnie Crossley, 'party-minded' to her friends but poker-faced behind the tea table in the Hatfield photograph, had what was then a unique claim to fame. Her father, a Dr Harrison, had delivered the world's first surviving naturally conceived quadruplets in St Neots, Cambridgeshire, in 1935. Winnie had flown him there. She had also flown five seasons as a stunt pilot for C. W. A. Scott's air circus.

Next, but curiously absent in other photos of the First Eight, as if airbrushed out, or called away or gone to powder her nose, was Marion Wilberforce, daughter of the ninth Laird of Boyndlie, graduate of Somerville College, Oxford, mountaineer, ju jitsu enthusiast and all-round tomboy. This did not mean she was unable to attract members of the opposite sex, as a deportment teacher had once warned her. But before her fiancé would commit himself to marrying her in 1932, he spent six months in a monastery to be sure he did not want to go into the Catholic priesthood instead. Marion was waiting for him at the monastery gates when he came out.

By this time Marion was the proud owner of a De Havilland Cirrus Moth. She would later upgrade this to a Hornet and use it to carry livestock to and from her Essex farm at Nevendon Manor, and to explore Europe with friends or by herself, sometimes roaming as far as Budapest. She had logged 900 hours before joining the ATA.

Margaret Cunnison, the daughter of a Glasgow University professor, had earned her private licence at eighteen and worked before the war as an instructor at the Renfrew aerodrome on Clydeside. Gabrielle Patterson, too, was a flying instructor – the first British woman to earn an instructor's licence. She was married with a young son, and came from Walsall in the West Midlands.

All but one of the sitters for this portrait of uncommon womanhood survived the war. The one who didn't was the one who most obviously refuses to say cheese, sitting side-on to the camera and staring straight ahead.

This is Margaret Fairweather – the Cold Front – supremely capable, supremely self-effacing, and the epitome of what Pop d'Erlanger and Pauline Gower had been looking for in their First Eight. It did not hurt Margaret that she was born into the governing class. Not only was her father, Viscount Runciman of Doxford, a frontbench Liberal politician who had entered the House of Commons aged twenty-nine by defeating Winston Churchill for the constituency of Oldham; her mother also entered the Commons in 1928, making them the first husband-and-wife team of MPs in the history of Westminster. Her brother, Air Commodore the Hon. Leslie Runciman, and managing director of BOAC, was the person who had authorised d'Erlanger to set up the ATA. Even so, it seems that Margie preferred to get ahead the hard way. She had dropped out of Cambridge in order to study singing in Paris, but never sang professionally. She married at twenty-four and had a daughter, but later divorced. At thirty-five she was an upper-class single mum with means, motive and a serious case of wanderlust. What else could she do but learn to fly? Like Amy Johnson six years earlier, she even set her heart on soloing to Australia. But having divorced the son of one baronet, she married the son of another and altered her travel plans.

In the summer of 1938, by way of a honeymoon, Margie and Douglas Fairweather flew to Prague to meet her father, who was trying unsuccessfully to mediate between the German and Czech governments to forestall war. On the way back they gave themselves an extensive aerial tour of Germany, noting the locations of new airfields being built for the Luftwaffe in violation of the Treaty of Versailles, and hiding the details in jaunty letters home in a code of Margaret's own devising. The letters were addressed to her younger brother, the historian Steven Runciman, who gave them back to her on her return. He never found out what she did with them. 'It was of course pure espionage and entirely hush-hush,' he wrote, years later, in response to an inquiring letter from Margaret's daughter by her first husband, Ann. 'But I suppose they may have acquired some useful information.'

The amateur spies became professional pilots, instructing at an airfield outside Glasgow. Their personalities complemented each other. Douglas was eleven years older than Margie, and as ebullient as she was reserved. As a late convert to aviation he was also an ardent believer in its usefulness for his peacetime job as a patent agent. He would shuttle between client inventors in his own plane in double-breasted blue suits rendered light grey by a steady rain of cigarette ash. For a year or so, life at the Fairweather home in Stirlingshire, and in the skies above it, could not easily have been improved on. But then Ann had to start at boarding school in Oxford and a war that everybody knew was coming, came.

Perhaps the reason for the bleak look on Margie Fairweather's face at the Hatfield tea party was the prospect of a dangerous new life, apart from her beloved daughter and husband. But it might also have been the knowledge that a golden age of flying had passed into history, and so had the world that made it possible.

5

'All Over Europe the Air Was Free'

The transition from peace to war could be complicated as well as wrenching. For Rosemary Rees, a life of abundance became one of rationing. Her social status, which had been a security blanket, suddenly guaranteed neither security nor comfort. Flying, which had been pure adventure, was deadly serious. And Germans, who had been friends, were enemies.

Rees had given up professional performing after a couple of seasons. Then she circled the globe with an older brother (by accident: the Manchurian war had ruled out their planned return from Peking on the Trans-Siberian Express). She intended to resume dancing in 1932, but instead fell under the influence of an old Cambridge friend of her brother's, Gordon Selfridge Jr, who happened to be heir to London's biggest retail fortune.

'He had an aeroplane,' she wrote. 'He set out to persuade me that I wanted to fly. I thought "Whatever for? Who wants to fly?" But then he stood me a trial lesson with Baker at Heston and I was hooked.'

'Baker' was Captain Valentyne Baker, always charming, always immaculate, and one of the Mayfair set's most sought-after instructors. A softly-spoken Welshman, he had fought at Gallipoli and then taken up flying despite being gravely wounded there. (A bullet had lodged too close to his spine to be removed.) He was credited with shooting down fifteen German aircraft by the end of the First World War, and went on to become Amy Johnson's favourite teacher. He died test-piloting a prototype fighter that he had designed with James 'Jimmy' Martin and built with funds invested by the future ATA heartthrob Frankie Francis.

Rees sailed through her pilot's apprenticeship with barely a scratch. She then did as Gordon Selfridge told her; she bought herself a plane.

It was a handsome, two-seater Miles Hawk Major, one of the new, low-winged monoplanes that were puny by Spitfire standards but impressive for their time and enhanced by ultra-modern streamlining. For a girl from 'poor but honest parents' (poor, she explained, in that they were not among 'the rich'), it was the perfect European party plane.

Gordon Selfridge's rationale for urging Rees to buy her own aeroplane, as opposed to renting one, was that with a machine of one's own it was possible to enjoy extended continental air safaris without worrying about having to be back at Stag Lane by Sunday night. 'You won't have any fun without one,' he told his protégée. Rees would have had plenty of fun anywhere, but her Hawk lifted life onto a giddy new level. The aircraft that made this gallivanting possible were already being adapted to bomb Europe's industrial centres. This was clear enough to anyone who read the newspapers, but it only made these recreational pilots more determined to make the most of their peaceable versions while they could.

'All over Europe, the air was free,' the young Rees exalted, as she recalled the world opened to her by a private licence and a pair of wings:

> Wherever you went and however bad the weather you flew in, you were welcomed and congratulated on having got through ... All was freedom, welcome, and brotherhood, though it is true that towards 1939 the Germans, although still immensely hospitable, did become a bit touchy about where you landed ...

On her annual ski trips to Switzerland and Austria, Rees made friends with fellow skiers from throughout Europe. When they learned she was a flyer, they would invariably invite her to visit them in warmer weather.

Nearly all the European Aero Clubs gave parties during the summer. You were put up at hotels and taken to see the local sights in buses, unless you could fly there in your own aeroplane. The mayors wined and dined us. In France one was nearly always shown just how champagne was made and given plenty of it to sample. In Hungary we flew to the Hortobagy to see the horsemen, and in Sweden there was the opening of Stockholm's new airport. This was exhausting, because there seemed to be no darkness and nobody ever seemed to want any sleep.

Rees was a regular at the 'Magyar Pilots' Picnic', held annually at an airfield outside Budapest. She delivered Christmas presents to the Czechs in 1938, almost had her plane impounded in Berlin on her way home, and made frequent flying visits to the Adriatic 'because the Selfridges had bought a little island called Hvar there, off the coast'.

In Germany, the Nazis were not coy about proselytising; nor did the typical visiting British aviatrix go out of her way to avoid them. On the contrary, she seems, not unlike the Lindberghs at the same time, to have been fascinated. Rees describes an excursion laid on by the Düsseldorf Aero Club in a balloon:

We got into the basket and there were lots of brown-shirted young men about, holding onto ropes and being very busy. They pumped up the balloon full of gas and gradually it rose up above us and slowly the basket began to rise too. The brown shirts held onto the ropes until we were looking down into their upturned faces, then they let go and we were off.

It was lovely, whispering along with the wind, quite silently; you could hear the dogs barking down below and the pilot shouted out to a woman and she shouted back and waved. We coasted along. On the ground, the brown shirts were following in their cars.

The young Nazis were ardent evangelists, and there was no more lavish set-piece for their evangelising than the 1936 Olympics. Freydis Leaf, who went on to fly every class of aircraft except four-engined bombers with the ATA, travelled to Kiel that year as a teenager for the sailing events of the Olympics in which her father and her brother, John, were both medal prospects in the 6-metre class. While they were there the *Graf Spee* had pride of place in Kiel harbour – a silent, garlanded precursor of shock and awe – and three new U-boats were launched, which Leaf remembers thinking 'was a funny thing to do in the middle of the Olympics'. Even so, brother John, Aryan-looking and bilingual after a year in a German boarding school, became such fast friends with a group of young German naval officers that they made him a blood brother. And when the Führer himself came to host a rally, 'everyone said Heil Hitler and I terribly wanted to say Heil Hitler too because you got this sort of feeling with the whole crowd going . . .' (Leaf winces as she looks back across the decades from her Oxfordshire cottage); 'but my mother looked at me in fury, and my father was of course terribly anti-Hitler, and wouldn't go to Berlin to collect his medal.' (He won the gold.)

Hitler delighted in publicly tearing up the conditions imposed on Germany at Versailles. At the same time, he pretended to uphold them. Hence the brazen show of brand new naval steel at Kiel; hence also the German mania for gliding. It looked wholesome, poetic, and of course uplifting, this soaring exploitation of the stiff breezes and rounded hills of Thuringia and the Czech frontierlands. In reality it was a massively subsidised way of training pilots without putting them in banned fighter aircraft.

Rosemary Rees stuck to powered flight and in the winter of 1938/9 was advised to leave Berlin quickly, lest war be declared while she was there and she be impounded along with her beloved Hawk.

Naomi Heron-Maxwell, the granddaughter of the Earl of Macclesfield and sometime parachutist for the Alan Cobham Flying Circus, took up gliding in Hesselberg in 1935. She became friendly with Wolf Hirth, a one-legged German glider ace, and in due course became a regular at German gliding contests. When war broke out her initial reaction was to leave Europe for India, on foot. (She appears to have got no further than Egypt, where she spent the early part of the war before returning to England to join the ATA in February 1942.)

Ann Welch became so obsessed with gliding that she once drove 540 miles overnight in an MG Midget to get a spare part for her tailplane. At Dunstable in Bedfordshire in 1937 she met none other than Hanna Reitsch, Hitler's favourite pilot and one of the most deluded zealots of the Third Reich. Starting in 1943, Reitsch pleaded in vain with Hitler to let her set up an elite corps of kamikaze rocketplane pilots. But on her brief appearance at the Dunstable International Summer Gliding Camp six years earlier she seems to have been charm itself: 'Then Hanna Reitsch arrived,' Welch wrote by way of a caption to round off a strip cartoon she drew to commemorate the event. 'After an extremely good farewell party, the camp broke up. It was great fun. We hope the Germans enjoyed their stay with us, as much as we did having them.'

Welch also met Rudolf Hess, the Führer's deputy, in a ski hut above the Eagle's Nest at Berchtesgaden. She was on a skiing holiday arranged by a young German she had met at a party in London. This 'friend' – a Nazi PR functionary with a budget, she realised later – led her and the rest of a large Anglo-German group on foot up the snowbound alp from Hitler's eyrie to a Bavarian hut near the Austrian border. The plan had been to introduce them to the man himself, but this was January 1938, and Hitler was indisposed (presumably planning the annexation of the Sudetenland). Instead, Rudolf Hess wandered up to see them towards the end of their stay. Welch described the evening:

Wisely, perhaps, he said nothing political, but drank beer with us, talking about our skiing and gliding. He was like no other German I had met, having those slightly hooded far-away eyes of a dreamer ... After a few hours he left with a friendly farewell to ski down to Berchtesgaden before dark. We watched him go until he was a speck in the distance, as he seemed to be just as good as we were at falling over and making great craters in the snow.

Ann Welch died in 2002. Her daughter, a consultant at a London teaching hospital, told me her mother always reckoned the ATA's women were better pilots than its men. In Welch's case this was definitely true. She was a world-class glider pilot for many years after the war, and exuded an uncompromising, special forces-style rigour in everything she did.

The other ATA woman who glided before the war could neither rival Welch for warrior toughness, nor Naomi Heron-Maxwell for chutzpah. But she matched them both for inner steel. Mary de Bunsen, she of the polio-stricken leg, weak heart and poor eyesight, knew Germany well because she had relatives in Leipzig. Under her own steam – which was strictly limited: she would feel her heart strain walking up a gentle hill – she enrolled in a beginner's gliding course at Grunau in the Reisengebirge south of Dresden in the summer of 1939. By day she let her hosts hurl her into the air with giant catapults in 'Grunau baby' gliders with swastikas emblazoned on their tailplanes. In the evenings they would talk about the gathering storm 'without restraint, just as if we were going to be on the same side in it'.

'There was a certain amount of clicking of heels and heiling Hitler down in the village,' de Bunsen remembered, 'but most of it was shed like a cloak in the relaxed atmosphere on the hilltop. They didn't take Goebbels very seriously, but they were ready to follow to the bitter end a government which promised to restore, by whatever means, the greatness and independence of Germany.'

To her surprise and delight, de Bunsen won her elementary gliding certificate for a five-minute flight on the last day of the course. A mighty updraft sprang suddenly from the valley beneath the Reisengebirge, and the Germans insisted that the English Fräulein take full advantage of it. On her way home she called on her cousins in Leipzig, where they all drank champagne with whole peaches in each glass. But 'we knew that war was coming, and that it was the last time we should meet for many years,' de Bunsen wrote. 'It was a sad parting.'

Germany invaded Poland the following month. For Rosemary Rees, the party was over. For all those who had sampled German hospitality during the slide towards war, the strangeness of consorting with the future enemy was replaced by the business of preparing in earnest to fight him. But for Anna Leska, Barbara Wojtulanis and Jadwiga Pilsudska the invasion was an immediate catastrophe. Their country was being overrun by panzers advancing on Warsaw on three separate fronts. On 17 September 1939, Stalin invaded from the east. Poland's short-lived independence was being unmercifully strangled, and for any Pole hoping one day to help revive it there was only one rational course open – to escape.

6

Escape From Poland

In the autumn of 2006 the curator of the Museum of Polish Aviation, on the outskirts of Kraków, organised a modest exhibition of memorabilia. It was displayed in three glass cases in the middle of a hangar full of ageing aeroplanes. The captions were in Polish, but much of the contents consisted of yellowing sheets of British wartime paperwork: an ID card (ht: 5 foot 6 inches, bld: 'slight', eyes: grey, hair: brown); an Aviator's Certificate issued by the Royal Aero Club, 119 Piccadilly; a note dated July 1947 accompanying fifty-seven emergency clothing coupons – 'To enable you to buy civilian clothing on your resignation from the Polish Resettlement Section, Women's Auxiliary Air Force'; and an insistent letter from Colonel Mitkiewitcz-Zoltek of the Polish General HQ (London) to Flying Officer Cummings of the Air Ministry, written in November 1940:

> We hereby certify that Pilot Officers Leska, Anna and Wojtul-anis, Stefania . . . are both well known in the Polish General Headquarters and from the security point of vue [sic] are perfectly allright. They are right and proper persons for the nature of the work entailed by service with ATA.

There were also a couple of leather flying helmets, a pair of split-lens Protector brand goggles and, etched with the initials RAF, something that looked like a silver powder compact.

Each of the Misses Leska, Wojtulanis and Pilsudska were

allocated one glass case in the exhibition, but nothing in them explained how they had made their way from Poland to Piccadilly despite the best efforts of the Gestapo. The only real clue to this was an unremarkable three-seater single-engined Polish-built RWD 13 monoplane parked next to the exhibit cases. This was not the exact plane in which Anna Leska escaped, but it was identical in everything except livery and markings. Leska's call sign, SP-WDL, was in the blue and grey colours of the Wedel Chocolate factory of Warsaw. It had scratchy beige elephant-cord upholstery and, for joysticks, two aluminium prongs, unadorned except for a black Bakelite knob on top of each – not much against the Luftwaffe, but it served a purpose.

Anna Leska's experiences of the first months of the war were to leave her, as one American friend put it, 'deeply and permanently upset'. She told parts of her story to various people but it is quite possible that she never told all of it to anyone. She could be famously short-tempered. On 'wash-out' days at Hamble ferry pool she would chain smoke through bridge hands, cursing her lousy cards. She scowled even when telling jokes in her bad English, and she pursued a feud with one of her fellow pilots that had to be settled by the commanding officer before it ended in a mid-air collision.

In September 1939 Leska was twenty-nine, the daughter of an army colonel and a doyenne of the Warsaw Aero Club. Stefania Wojtulanis – known to her friends as Barbara – was two years younger and popular as an air racer. She was also Poland's first female parachutist and licensed balloonist. As women, both had been turned down by the Polish Air Force, but the war changed that. Within days of the invasion they were attached as couriers to the personal flight of General Jozef Zajac, Commander-in-Chief of the Polish Air Force. This did not make them Air Force pilots – women in armed aircraft was still a step too far – but it did enable them to commandeer unarmed planes to keep ahead of the advancing Wehrmacht, hiding them under the cover of trees each night to prevent them being bombed by the morning.

In one incident that Leska described later to Alison King, her favourite confidante at Hamble, she could see German troops destroying a bridge barely a mile away as she wheeled her plane out of the woods and unfolded its wings. She took off down a sloping potato field, potato plants tugging at her undercarriage, as a column of panzers swept into plain view along a road at the bottom of the field.

The Polish army surrendered on 27 September – but the air force did not. General Zajac ordered his staff to rendezvous outside Czernowice in Poland's extreme south-eastern corner (now in the Ukraine). It was from here, at the foot of the northern slopes of the Carpathians, that Leska flew to freedom with four passengers crammed into the Wedel Chocolate Company's tiny grey three-seater. But it was a strange sort of freedom that awaited them.

Pouring south over the mountains, by air or bullock cart if they were lucky but otherwise on foot, were tens of thousands of Europe's most motivated enemies of Nazism. Hitler made it clear to the Romanian government that if it wanted to avoid Poland's fate it should intern its Polish refugees. Romania obliged. Leska landed at an aerodrome where her compatriots were sleeping head-to-toe in the hangars and all other available space was occupied by Polish aircraft. These would be confiscated. The luckier Polish officers found refuge in Romanian homes, sparing them the internment camps where perhaps 100,000 refugees spent that winter, many of them dying of a combination of malaria, cold and malnutrition. Leska was eventually taken in by a local police chief and his wife.

Britain's 'guarantee' of Poland's territorial integrity turned out, in the face of blitzkrieg, to have been more of an open-dated IOU. But certain individual Britons had the wit and compassion to advocate swift action to help those Poles stuck in Romania. One of these was Group Captain A. P. Davidson, former air attaché to the British Embassy in Warsaw, where he had been impressed by the Polish Air Force's professionalism. Hurriedly evacuated to London, Davidson urged the French and British legations in

Bucharest to help General Zajac spring his people from Romania on the grounds that they were a key strategic asset. He knew that extricating them would not be easy. There was no question of enlisting Stalin's help; those Polish officers who had fled east had been shipped to the Gulag or executed in the forests of Katyn. Nor was there any hope of an amnesty from Hitler. He might still have been hoping to avoid war with Britain, but his chosen method of dealing with the Polish military – to crush it – had served him well so far and he saw no reason to change it.

Romania was thoroughly infiltrated by the Gestapo and its informers. In the mountains, where unauthorised possession of skis was punishable by death, refugees were liable to be hunted like animals and shot on sight. In homes like the one where Leska found herself a lodger, who was she to know which side her hosts were on?

After a week she received a message from her squadron leader. She was to meet him at seven that evening at a crossroads near the house. There would be a car, and she was to wear a skirt. It took them a week to reach Bucharest and once there seven months to get visas for France.

By the time she arrived in the south of France in May 1940, Anna Leska had had no contact with her family since her escape from Poland. Her mother and sisters, as far as she knew, had stayed behind. Her father might have tried to escape, like her, to join the Polish forces gathering in exile, but by what route and with what success? Dozens of routes were being tried, some via South Africa to avoid the North African war, some ending in the gold mines of Kolyma, in the Soviet Far East.

As she checked into a hotel in Menton her own family name, in familiar handwriting, jumped out at her from the guests' register. Her father had stayed there two days earlier on his way to England. Rather than follow him, she continued to Paris, where the Polish Air Force was still technically headquartered, and where Wojtulanis and two other Polish women pilots had already arrived by different escape routes. For a few weeks, these four became much admired oddities. They would be the only women from the Western allies to wear full air force pilots' uniforms in the entire war. It was General Sikorski's idea, and militarily inconsequential since the fall of France was imminent and the Polish Air Force was in no position to prevent it. 'All four women were commissioned as pilot officers,' Wojtulanis wrote of her group. 'In steel-blue uniforms with a single star on each epaulette, they became a sensation on the streets of Paris.'

When Pétain capitulated in June 1940, Leska was bundled onto a boat from St Jean de Luz to Plymouth. From there, she went immediately to London and the Polish General Staff building on Buckingham Palace Road. A Polish officer whom she happened to know saw her as she was waiting, exhausted and more rootless than ever, in the lobby. He advised her to report to Room 303, without explaining why. She set off up several flights of stairs and then followed a series of dimly lit corridors, eventually knocking on door 303. It was opened by her father.

In the late summer of 2006, I took an evening train up the West Bank of the Vistula from Kraków to Warsaw to meet the last surviving Polish woman pilot of the ATA, Jadwiga Pilsudska. I asked her what she knew of Anna Leska's journey from the Warsaw Aero Club to Buckingham Palace Road. She thought for a while, then said apologetically that 'there were so many stories, things that happened that you were interested in, that somehow either she told me and I can't remember, or we never talked about it'.

Had Leska been reluctant to talk about it?

'No, it just didn't happen.'

Pilsudska and Leska had kept in touch in England after the war and lived close to each other in Warsaw for ten years after the fall of communism. Not for the first time I got the sense of memories carefully compartmentalised to prevent one set contaminating another.

For Jadwiga Pilsudska herself, the process of reaching England after the invasion had been accelerated by the fact that she was the daughter of the founder of modern Poland. Her father, Marshal

Jozef Pilsudski, had conceived a new Polish nationalism for the twentieth century and used it to weld together the Greater Poland bequeathed to Europe by the First World War. He had died in 1935, but his spirit, the spirit of Poland, seemed to live on in his daughter. The press would turn out to watch her glide at weekends at Sokola Gora. Here was the new-model Pilsudski, as brave as the Marshal; and as air-minded as she was beautiful. She was modest, yet self-assured, youthful, yet somehow wise.

When Colonel General Heinz Guderian and the XIX Army Corps rolled in to Poland Jadwiga and her family fled with her father's uniform in a black leather suitcase.

> I went with my family – my mother and my sister – when Warsaw was evacuated. We stayed in the country for a few days in a farmhouse belonging to my cousin, and then went to Vilno [Vilnius, now the Lithuanian capital]. Vilno was our family place and we had relatives there. And then of course the Russians crossed the frontier on 17 September.
>
> When the Russians came my mother decided to go to Lithuania, and then there was a plane to Riga, and we were advised to go via Stockholm. My mother was urged to go to Paris, where most of the Polish who had escaped were gathering, but the plane was going to England. And that's how we arrived.

While those of her uncles who had stayed in Warsaw were arrested and thrown in the Lyubianka, Pilsudska and her mother and sisters stayed with the Polish ambassador in London. They did what they could for less fortunate children of the diaspora. One, a medical student and friend of Jadwiga's, had been an intern on a cruise ship bound for South America when the country was overrun. She returned to Southampton instead of Gdansk and started a new life with nothing but the trunk she had taken on the cruise.

It was not impossible to go back, not if you had the desire and a purpose and the right connections in the underground.

Pilsudska wanted to, she told me, but it seems she was dissuaded from doing so partly because the loss of Marshal Pilsudski's daughter would have been too great a blow for the morale of the Home Army and the government and armed forces in exile. But she would sooner not talk about it. The explanation is the compartment wall across her memory: 'My life stopped on the 17th of September,' she told me with sudden clarity. 'I left everything behind and had to start something completely fresh.'

That something would be flying, but she did not know it yet.

7

'None of Us Is Snobbish'

> 'Now, none of us is snobbish, but somehow we do object
> to writing our names on bits of toilet paper.'
>
> *Pauline Gower, on the tendency of young boys at pre-war flying
> displays to request pilots' autographs on scraps of paper picked up
> after the popular trick of cutting streamers into thousands of small
> pieces with one's propeller.*

Gower was right. The early ATA women were not snobs. Far from it; they were ardent meritocrats. They just happened to be meritocrats in a discipline for which one hour's instruction cost roughly what the average shop worker could expect to earn in a fortnight. This made them a self-selecting elite in terms of daring to risk their necks and ignore social conventions, but first of all in terms of money. Rose Rees's idea of 'poor' was most people's rich. Amy Johnson was practically blue-collar by ATA women's standards, because she was from Hull and her father was in trade – but he was still one of the city's most prominent businessmen.

So it surprised no one that the ninth recruit to the ATA women's section was Lois Butler, wife of the chairman of De Havilland; nor that the tenth was Lady Bailey, the daughter of an Irish peer and wife of Sir Abe Bailey, an indulgent South African millionaire.

In 1929 Lady Bailey had won the admiration of millions, and the Britannia Trophy for the year's most outstanding air performance, by flying solo to Cape Town and back on the pretext of meeting her husband. It took her ten months. Unlike her friend and rival, Lady Heath, who had taken off from Pretoria for London the previous year with a shotgun, fifty rounds of ammunition, a tennis racquet, high-heeled satin shoes, a black silk evening dress and a fur coat, Lady Bailey travelled light. In addition to undergarments and a tweed flying suit she carried only a pair of mosquito-proof boots, some tinted goggles and a flying helmet. She crashed on both legs of the trip: outbound, she turned her plane over on landing in Tanganyika and had to wait there while Abe replaced it. Apologising to him for her late arrival at the Cape, she said she had got 'muddled in the mountains'. On her return she landed heavily soon after leaving Cape Town and had to wait four months for spares and repairs. Geoffrey de Havilland, who knew her from Stag Lane, said she 'knew much more about the technique of navigation under almost impossible conditions than most people were prepared to credit'. But Amy Johnson said she never seemed to plan her flights or even to have any clear idea where she was going.

That apart, the trouble with Lady Bailey's appointment to the ATA was that she was aged fifty. Even by the standards of the 'Ancient and Tattered' this was pushing it. The National Men's Defence League and readers of *Aeroplane* resumed their eruptions about women encroaching on men's work, and rather than endure public accusations of pulling rank, Lady Bailey resigned within a week.

For a few days she had epitomised the ATA's defining ethos: quietly brave, deceptively casual, defiantly eccentric. But any void she left was quickly filled by a stream of new recruits infused not just with Bailey's limitless enthusiasm for flying but also with the energy of youth. And few combined these quite so strikingly as Audrey Sale-Barker.

When the Sale-Barker name began appearing in aeronautical dispatches in the summer of 1940, it had a certain resonance. Skiers would have remembered her as captain of the British women's team at the 1936 Winter Olympics in Garmisch-Partenkirchen in Bavaria, and the winner before that of a string of alpine trophies as fabulous as their names – the Lady Denman Challenge, the Kandahar Ladies Ski Club Championship, the Donna Isabella Orsini Cup – all fought for on the precipitous east face of the Schilthorn above Mürren (which Ian Fleming would later rename the Piz Gloria for the purposes of James Bond's imprisonment by that most unscrupulous brainwasher of young women, Ernst Stavro Blofeld).

Society types would have known of Sale-Barker as an elegant fixture of the London season and its satellite events in Paris and Le Touquet. They would have recognised her delicate features and slightly upturned nose. They might have heard her charming lisp at parties, and they might even have heard her name linked with the impossibly dashing Lord Knebworth (who would later die in an air crash).

Hardcore aviation buffs would have recalled her winning free flying lessons in a competition sponsored by National Aviation Services at the 1929 Aero Exhibition, Olympia, for her performance on a 'Reid pilot indicator'. This was an elaborate contraption that supposedly measured pilot aptitude with coloured discs connected by a maze of push-rods to pedals and a joystick. Sale-Barker scored higher on it than all other competitors, male or female, and having won those flying lessons she shone from her first touch of the control column. Then nineteen, she earned her private 'A' licence after just seven hours of instruction at the new Hanworth aerodrome near Twickenham. And on her first solo, spectators – including a man from the *Daily Express* – were surprised to see this 'pretty, dark haired society girl' climb to nearly 3,000 feet and loop the loop, then plunge into a spinning dive.

Like Rosemary Rees, Sale-Barker was not 'rich', but neither was she 'poor'. She was the daughter of a doctor and an actress and lived in one of the smart new mansion blocks behind Sloane Square. As a teenager she was such a fine and fearless skier that her winters in the Bernese Oberland were sponsored by the

Amy Johnson, pictured after crash-landing near Rangoon en route to Australia in 1930.

Above and below The department store heir Gordon Selfridge gave Rosemary Rees a flight in his De Havilland Dragonfly and urged her to buy her own plane to improve her social life in the early 1930s. She duly purchased a sleek new Miles Hawk Major.

Left Audrey Sale-Barker, animal lover, natural pilot, Olympic skier and occasional model.

Below Sale-Barker and her friend Joan Page flew to Cape Town in a Gipsy Moth in 1932. Their crash on the way back set off an international media frenzy.

Left Gerard d'Erlanger, founder of the ATA, was groomed at Eton, Oxford and in the City.

Below Pauline Gower, founder of the women's section of the ATA, was a reluctant debutante and avid pre-war flyer, but she hardly flew in the war, which irritated some of her subordinates.

Lt.Col. J.T. Moore-Brabazon, Minister of Aircraft Production, with d'Erlanger (*left*), Gower and Chief Operations Officer A.K. Smith, at White Waltham. 'Brab' smoothed the way for women to fly Hurricanes and Spitfires.

A classic portrait of the 'First Eight' taking tea at Hatfield, 1940, together with Lois Butler (*4th from right*) and Henrietta Stapleton-Bretherton (*3rd from left*). The others (*left to right*) are: Joan Hughes, Margaret Cunnison, Mona Friedlander, Gabrielle Patterson, Rosemary Rees, Marion Wilberforce, Pauline Gower and the Hon. Mrs Margaret Fairweather.

The men of the ATA regarded the women with amiable curiosity, then simply as comrades. Here Keith-Jopp (with cigarette on far right) sits next to d'Erlanger for tea at White Waltham.

Lettice Curtis, seen climbing into a Spitfire, was the first woman cleared to fly four-engined bombers. 'To me,' she said, 'second place at anything was a failure.'

Curtis (*left*) and Gower in the cockpit of an Anson. As their body language suggests, they did not always see eye to eye.

Gabrielle Patterson climbs out of an Airspeed Oxford to join (*left to right*) Lettice Curtis, Jenny Broad, Audrey Sale-Barker and Pauline Gower. Weapons were removed from the Ansons' gun turrets to end the anomaly of civilian crew flying armed aircraft.

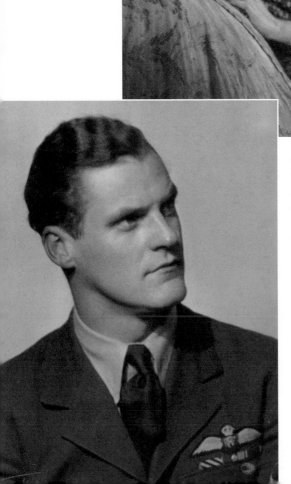

Above Daughter of a motor-racing millionaire, Diana Barnato Walker became the first woman to fly a Spitfire to France.

Left Derek Walker was Diana Barnato Walker's first and only husband. He was killed in a Mustang six months after the end of the war in Europe.

Kandahar Ski Club (of which Lord Knebworth was president). Since she did not have to pay to learn to fly either, the question of whether she would have been able to afford to on her own did not arise. As the diarist for the *Daily Sketch* put it after a visit to Hanworth aerodrome, she simply 'excels in all manly sports'. She could not quite love them all equally, however. After that first solo loop and spin she confessed to finding flying even more exciting than skiing, which might have dulled her competitive edge on snow. In 1931, after years as the dominant women's racer in the Alps, she lost the women's downhill at Mürren. And when she came into an inheritance at the age of twenty-one, she spent it on a Gipsy Moth.

Friends started calling her Wendy, after Wendy in Peter Pan, who learns to fly. For her own part she started whispering about South Africa. She told her mother she planned to spend Christmas in Cape Town with their friends Lord and Lady Clarendon – not to make any headlines, but as a holiday. Her mother forbade it unless she could find a chaperone. Audrey produced one in the form of Miss Joan Page, fellow pilot and daughter of Sir Arthur Page, Chief Justice of Burma.

When the two young pilots realised that Sir Arthur and Lady Page would be passing the South of France in late October 1932 in a steamer bound for Rangoon, they had the makings of a plan: a surprise call on Joan's parents in Marseille, a stimulating aerial potter down the Nile in the cool of the Egyptian autumn, and a warm African Christmas in relative comfort (Lord Clarendon was South Africa's Governor General). If the skiing season still held any appeal after all that, there would, thanks to the invigorating miracle of private aviation, be plenty of time to get back for it.

Audrey and Joan told Mrs Sale-Barker not to breathe a word of their plan to anyone. They told the chaps from the *Express*, the *Mail* and the *Mirror* to keep quiet too. The whole thing was secret, they insisted. It was a holiday, after all. No records would be broken and in any case they loathed publicity. Even so, someone managed to persuade them to pose for a cheerful-looking pre-flight portrait in front of Audrey's new machine at Heston, and the papers entirely misunderstood their intentions with regard to coverage. Their 'secret' trip, less ambitious and ostensibly less newsworthy than those of Amy Johnson, Lady Bailey, Lady Heath and others before them – except, of course, in being secret – was extensively reported from day one.

Even the *Tatler* columnist known as 'Eve' betrayed them: 'I was sworn to secrecy,' she wrote as the agencies flashed back the news of their safe departure from Marseille for Corsica: '[Miss Sale-Barker] particularly dislikes the publicity given to women, just because they happen to be women, for attempting or accomplishing feats which would be quite ordinary for a man.' But Eve could not resist plugging someone so 'eminently paragraph-worthy', and added that Sale-Barker was 'an extremely attractive person with a lovely figure' who 'happens to be one of the best ski runners in the world'. The *Tatler* added that Sale-Barker hoped to be back in time for the season at Mürren.

But she didn't make it. All went well as far as Benghazi. The women put in an 800-mile day worthy of Johnson herself, following the Libyan coast and descending, tired and after dark, towards Cairo's Almaza aerodrome. The runway was unlit. Sale-Barker was at the controls in the Moth's rear seat. According to one report, the ground crew heard the engine and scrambled to create a make-shift flarepath with car headlights. Sale-Barker skilfully swerved to avoid a house seconds before landing but came to rest against a windsock pole, which put the aircraft out of action for at least four days.

The Cairo press corps picked up the story. They reported – or concocted – a rumour that the RAF had agreed in advance to escort the defenceless young aviators across the Sudanese desert to Khartoum, and had then reneged on the plan. True to their professed abhorrence of publicity, Page and Sale-Barker never explained how they got to Khartoum. At Malakal, Nairobi and Bulawayo they had no comment for reporters. (Even on her return to England six months later, all Sale-Barker would tell *Aeroplane* magazine was that the question of RAF desert escorts was never discussed.) Into this news vacuum an increasingly intrigued and desperate Fleet Street inserted at least three male chaperones, among them a mysterious American pickle salesman who took Page's seat from Wadi Halfa on the upper Nile to Khartoum; a second passenger for Audrey from Khartoum to Juba; and a third man to accompany Miss Page upriver by boat.

When they reached Cape Town the 'Air Girls' continued their stonewalling. In the absence of usable quotes, one paper printed a quite pitiful fictional transcript of the encounter that ended with:

Fifth Reporter: 'Don't you really like reporters?'
Miss Sale-Barker and Miss Page (together): 'We certainly do not.'
Chorus of Reporters: 'But we like people who don't like publicity.'
And the newspaper reporters of Cape Town have decided that the two girls' 'go-as-you-please' flight was a good effort.

But it was not quite over. The press left Page and Sale-Barker alone for Christmas at the Governor General's Cape Town residence, then picked up the story again as they began their homeward journey. For 1,200 miles it was uneventful. The first indication that something was wrong reached London in time for the evening papers on 16 January 1933 in an excited Reuters cable datelined Nairobi and with almost limitless scope for embellishment.

BRITISH AIRWOMEN MISSING!

Planes Searching in Lion Country

Two young Englishwomen who left Moshi (at the foot of Mount Kilimanjaro) on Saturday afternoon at 5.15 are missing . . . Three aeroplanes are searching an area of 100 square miles . . . they decided to follow the local East African mail plane . . . heavy rain . . . gusty winds . . . the male pilot decided to turn back . . .

In this version, from the *Birmingham Mail*, the lead pilot then hurtled past the dauntless women, forty yards from their wingtip but heading already in the opposite direction and waving frantically at them to follow him,

> but on arrival at Moshi he found they had not done so. Since then, nothing ... search is taking place in a wide area of plain ... Jungle infested with big game ... country that swarms with lions, elephants and buffalo ... every Government post and railway station warned ... appeals broadcast from Nairobi wireless.

Overnight, in Fleet Street, Nairobi and along the thousands of miles of fizzing telegraph wires between them, all hell broke loose. For any 'special correspondent' brave enough to head out into the bush south of Nairobi, or, better, to pretend he had, there would be scoops aplenty. By the morning of the 17th, the *Daily Mail* had the stricken Moth upside down, a complete wreck and definitely 'Among Lions' – the aircraft having been spotted in 'desolate wilds' just forty miles from Nairobi by a Captain Tanner of the Rhodesian Aviation Company. That night, the London *Evening Standard* put the pilots – almost anticlimactically – in a Nairobi nursing home where they were said to be 'very cheerful'.

At least Sale-Barker had a badly gashed head. Page, with a compound fracture to the leg, had been carried by her rescuers through two miles of rough scrub to a waiting aircraft on a stretcher improvised from a section of the wrecked plane's wing. The rescue plane had flown her to Nairobi and landed 'by the light of flares'.

The *Express* had been biding its time – but not wasting it. The following morning it surpassed itself, and the competition, with an eyewitness exclusive that occupied most of the inside front page. It was the pilots' 'Own Story of Their Jungle Ordeal'; it told of 'Food and Water Exhausted' and a 'Poison Arrow Threat'; of the Moth flying smack into a hillside and somersaulting to a halt in the dark; of the 'notorious Lions' only a mile away. And above it all, the headline: 'Injured Girl Flyers Send lipstick SOS.'

According to the *Express*, after two hideously painful nights without food, water or human contact, Miss Sale-Barker spotted a Masai herdsman who was so alarmed by this pale apparition that he stopped her approach by threatening to use his bow and arrow.

> Eventually by signs Miss Barker made him understand their plight, and by the gift of a flying coat, which he afterwards wore in the rescue operations, she induced him to agree to walk 50 miles to Nairobi with her appeal for help, which she wrote with a lipstick.

There followed detailed descriptions purportedly from Sale-Barker herself of trying frantically to fly on instruments alone through thickening mist, of being frightened to death, sleepless from pain and terror and 'thrilled by the sight of the native', only to have her joy snatched away when, 'at the sound of our cries, he threatened me with his bow and poisoned arrow, then turned on his heels and fled'.

'Desperately,' she was quoted as saying, 'I leaped in pursuit . . .'.

Afterwards, Sale-Barker disavowed almost every detail of the *Express*'s 'scoop'. There had been no interview, she told *Aeroplane* magazine, no somersault, no about-turn by a mail plane, no poison arrow threat and no 'notorious Lions'. Puffed up by its own mini-scoop six months after the event, the *Aeroplane* concluded that 'the British press at home and in Africa behaved disgracefully over the whole affair. Apparently the newspaper people were unable to understand that two young English gentlewomen might like to make a tour by air without publicity or self-advertisement.'

Perhaps. And yet the disavowal itself does not ring quite true. Page and Sale-Barker did crash, in the dark, in zero visibility, having lost sight of another plane they had been following. They did suffer grave injuries and a grim night in the bush. There may even have been lions around. On waking, they did meet a Masai herdsman, and Sale-Barker did write out for him, in bright red lipstick, the SOS that saved their lives. 'Please come and fetch us,' it implored whoever read it. 'We have had an air crash AND ARE HURT.' It hangs today in the family home of Lord James Douglas-Hamilton, Sale-Barker's nephew, a few miles east of Edinburgh.

The pilots recuperated in Nairobi. On their return to Europe by boat the racing at Schilthorn was over. But the snow was still worth a visit – the giant cliffs separating Lauterbrunnen in the valley floor from Mürren on the alp above provided some protection from the press. Sale-Barker went there to readjust to society and to mourn Lord Knebworth, who had been killed in her absence. Her eventual return to England in May 1933 was written up by the 'Talk of London' columnist in the *Daily Express*:

> She is slender. Her face is ethereal. She has a quiet voice. She looks unadventurous. She is extremely modest about her achievements . . . Yet she is physically one of the most courageous women I know. It is worth going to Switzerland simply to see her choose the most direct line down a steep hill and 'take it straight'.

Wendy was a 'name', whether she liked it or not. She also had style, and a marked preference for plus-fours and puttees over a full-length trousers on the slopes. Inevitably, the build-up to the next ski season found her featured in full-page advertisements in the *Tatler* for Fortnum & Mason's latest skiwear: Sale-Barker is pictured standing on artificial snow, most of her face in a shadow cast by her thick blonde hair.

Her sartorial flair never left her. When the time came to be measured for her ATA uniform, in June 1940, Sale-Barker shunned Austin Reed, went to her own tailor in Savile Row and stipulated a scarlet satin lining for her jacket. It was a characteristic flash of colour, wisely hidden. For the women of the ATA still had to prove to the RAF, and men in general, that they were serious about flying.

8

'We LIKE You In Your Harness!'

The spring of 1940 was bitterly cold, which made it an ordeal for the First Eight in their Tiger Moths. It was also a particularly anxious time for Pauline Gower, because by no means all the publicity generated by the Hatfield photo opportunity of 10 January had been as helpful as she had hoped.

It made no difference that the women pilots were not, at this point, to be allowed anywhere near frontline operational aircraft. The Moths were RAF machines, and the news that women would be flying them spread fast. It spread outward from the Hatfield aerodrome, then started bouncing back again. On 17 January 1940, a week after the chilly photocall, the Nazi propagandist William Joyce, better known as Lord Haw-Haw, read out the gist of the *Daily Express*'s report on the day over the wireless from Hamburg. He was still trying to dissuade the British from fighting at all, and he picked up on the money angle. He quoted an envious RAF man as saying the ATA girls would be getting £8 a week, and mocked this as 'a novel plan for getting back some of the money the fathers and husbands of these young ladies have paid, and will pay as taxpayers to the Government for this war'. Nor did he let the young ladies off the hook. He called them unnatural and decadent, and Goebbels himself pitched in, calling them 'perverted'.

To begin with, plenty of Brits were inclined to agree. Taking their cue from *Aeroplane*'s flatulent editorial blast against women who fancied themselves as bomber pilots when they lacked 'the intelligence to scrub the floor', readers let rip in numbers. 'Someone has erred grievously . . . The present ATA is nothing more than a tea party – yess'r and they are getting paid for drinking tea.' 'I am absolutely disgusted . . . When will the RAF realise that all the good work they are doing is being spoiled by this contemptible lot of women?' They were 'overpaid show-offs', mere imitators of the true titans of aviation. The National Men's Defence League agitated for the question of women pilots encroaching on men's work to be discussed in Parliament.

It did not make Pauline Gower's life any easier that her brave young flyers were, in fact, earning substantially more than many RAF pilots. Junior flying officers conducting operational sorties over northern France were earning the princely sum of £4, 7 shillings and sixpence a week. The ATA women were on £6. This was less than Lord Haw-Haw claimed, 20 per cent less than their own male colleagues were paid – as per Treasury rules – and less than Americans of either gender would receive as of 1942. But it still seemed an awful lot to new RAF recruits and to middle-aged men casting about in vain for moderately exciting war work, especially when most of the women to whom it was being paid seemed to be the type who received aeroplanes from their fathers as gifts.

Gower appeared to understand this. 'You never know,' she told one reporter, 'it might cause ill-feeling with men in the RAF or other services if how much we receive is made public.' But of course it *was* made public, and in the meantime the initial headlines after the Hatfield event seemed to have been calculated to irritate the air force. They had enthused about 'Ace Girl Pilots' and fantasised about girls 'out to show the RAF' in '350 mph fighters'. To top them all there was a photograph taken from behind one of the Eight, a parachute swinging against her bottom as she walked away, captioned: 'How d'ye like the togs, girls?'

The *Sketch*'s answer was: 'We LIKE you in your harness, and the bustle which is a parachute. We like your air. In fact, we LIKE you flighty!'

With coverage like this there was, for a few months, a real risk of the RAF running out of patience with the whole idea of women in their planes. Never mind that the aircraft these women had been assigned to fly could barely manage 80 mph and that their pilots were under intense pressure to make every last landing perfect. 'We carried an appalling burden of responsibility,' said Rosemary Rees. 'If one of the men broke an aeroplane it was a black [mark], of course, and much to be deplored, but after all people *do* occasionally break aeroplanes, don't they? But if one of us had broken one it would immediately have been, "There, you see, we always said they couldn't do it and they can't." . . . We dared not put a foot wrong.'

For months none of them did. Their task was to deliver Tiger Moths from the De Havilland factory at Hatfield to RAF training stations and storage hangars. The snow did not start melting that year until April, and the delivery destinations were mainly in Scotland and Wales. Sometimes the women – and those men handed the short straw of an open cockpit – had to be lifted bodily from the aircraft, catatonic with cold after three hours in minus thirty degrees' windchill. At No. 4 Ferry Pool at Prestwick, not yet the swaggering transatlantic terminus it would become, they would 'warm up' in the derelict carcass of a motor bus. In Whitchurch they used a converted wooden crate. Later there would be clever people at White Waltham and in an RAF hut on Salisbury plain to crunch the air movements data for 800 airfields and tens of thousands of planes, and provide taxi aircraft to bring the ferry pilots home at the end of a day's work. But that numbing winter, and for most of the following one, standard procedure was to trundle south on the freezing night sleeper to St Pancras in time to do it all again next day. Occasionally berths were available in the sleeper carriages, in which case the ATA would foot the bill. But just as often ferry pilots would spend their nights sitting on their parachutes in the corridor. When the trains were that full, Lettice Curtis preferred to climb up and stretch out in the luggage rack.

The women were, at least, allowed to dress appropriately. D'Erlanger had initially argued that they should fly in their official uniform of jackets, skirts and black silk stockings. (According to Rees, he simply disliked the sight of women in trousers.) Gower pointed out that this would not only be unbearably cold in winter, but immodest. Pop relented. As long as they changed immediately on landing, the women could fly in trousers or Sidcot suits, depending on the weather. Rees felt the cold particularly badly and kept it at bay with multiple layers of shawls, blankets and furs. The requirement to change on landing was eventually relaxed – though d'Erlanger continued to insist that skirts be worn on leave and in London, and women pilots continued to stuff them into their overnight bags wherever they were flying.

For months, the First Eight performed with epic stoicism and an unblemished accident record. Pauline Gower ensured that d'Erlanger and Sir Francis Shelmerdine at the Air Ministry knew this, and they never resisted her efforts to get her pilots into newer, more powerful planes. They knew, apart from anything, that the pilots' logbooks never lied. They were masterworks of disinterested data in old-fashioned pen and ink; the incontrovertible core evidence in the women's case to the male maharajas of the flying establishment. If their 500-plus hard-earned hours were more than enough to put a man in a Spitfire, why could they not do the same for a woman?

In the end there would be no answer to that. But in the summer of 1940 there were still plenty of officials, civilian as well as military, who believed, as Rees put it, that '"Women can't fly fast, complicated, heavy, fighter aircraft. They are not built or conditioned for it".' And then, as if to prove them right, Mona Friedlander landed heavily in a Lysander.

The Lysander was a high-winged monoplane with a 50-foot wingspan and an exceptionally low stalling speed, designed for dropping spies behind enemy lines, and, if necessary, picking them up. With a strong enough headwind it could take off in 250 yards.

When Friedlander bounced in one and burst a tyre, a dark cloud descended over Hatfield. As the women's perfect safety record had extended into the summer of 1940, Gower's softly-softly approach had begun to yield dividends. Her pilots were given chits for Miles Magisters and Masters, then Percival Proctors and, eventually, low-performance operational types including the Lysander. Now one of them had been 'bent'. Here was the told-you-so moment that they had all dreaded and the harrumphers had been waiting for. Before the women were allowed to resume flying anything heavier than a Tiger Moth, a full inquest was held into their leg strength, powers of concentration and reaction times when hit by windshear.

The Mayfair Minx had come dangerously close to jeopardising the whole insanely daring project, the one that consumed the daydreams of every one of the pioneers, even though they spoke of it only *sotto voce* for fear of hexing it. Mona, alone among them, had actually dared breathe a word of it to a reporter. 'Oh,' she'd said airily when the *Daily Mail* had asked what she hoped to achieve in the ATA. 'We're all waiting to fly a Hurricane.' Even she did not yet dare say 'Spitfire'. Women in Spitfires? Given that they were still officially restricted to trainers, and then only on their best behaviour, the idea would have invited ridicule. Before women would be allowed to fly fighters of any kind, the world would have to change

9

'Brab's Beauties'

So much changed so quickly in 1940 that the world seemed to have surrendered to a monstrous experiment in time-lapse photography. Holland and Belgium succumbed to the blitzkrieg in six days. Italy sided with Germany. France and the Channel Islands fell. Chamberlain resigned as Prime Minister and Churchill replaced him. Half a million British and French troops were evacuated from Dunkirk, and, under Emergency Regulation 18B, 763 members of the British Union of Fascists were interned.

It was the human cost of the Battle of Britain, however, that brought forward the day when women would fly aircraft worth bragging about. In the two weeks between 20 August and 6 September 1940, Fighter Command lost 103 pilots killed and 128 seriously wounded. By mid-September its total pilot strength of 1,000 pilots at the start of the battle had been cut by a quarter, and Churchill was deeply worried that those being scrambled to replace them were 'ardent but inexperienced pilots drawn from training units, in many cases before their full courses were complete'.

On 15 September Churchill woke at Chequers. It was a clear morning, 'suitable for the enemy'. He had had a special train fitted out with a bath, bed, office, radio telephone and staff quarters to enable him to visit the busiest fighter stations in Kent and Sussex on a couple of afternoons a week 'to see for myself what was happening' (and to raise morale). But on this particular day – a

Sunday, he noted, like the day of the Battle of Waterloo – he asked to be driven to RAF Number 11 Group Headquarters at Uxbridge on account of the weather, which held the promise of unusually intense action. He was not disappointed.

The nerve centre from which Luftwaffe movements were monitored and the RAF's response for the whole of south-east England directed comprised just a small amphitheatre, two storeys high, arranged round a giant blackboard divided into six columns, one for each of London's main defensive fighter stations. A swarm of officers fielding incoming intelligence and issuing orders to the squadrons filled the 'stalls'. Churchill sat in the 'dress circle', enthralled. The day started quietly, but by mid-morning all twenty-five squadrons under Number 11 Group's immediate command were in the air, most for the second time after refuelling, and three more squadrons had been scrambled from Number 12 Group, based at RAF Stanmore. Wave after wave of German aircraft showed up in the Uxbridge amphitheatre as signals representing groups of 20-plus, 40-plus, 60-plus and even 80-plus aircraft.

'Hitherto, I had watched in silence,' Churchill wrote. 'I now asked: "What other reserves had we?" "There are none," said Air Vice Marshal Park. In an account which he wrote about it afterwards, he said that at this I "looked grave". Well I might . . . the odds were great; our margins small; the stakes infinite.'

In such circumstances, no RAF pilot could be spared for anything but combat. And no RAF commander who objected to women ferrying his aircraft could look anything but foolish, which was just as well for Pauline Gower.

By the beginning of June 1940, a letter from Gower had lain unanswered on Pop d'Erlanger's desk for three weeks. In it she asked what she should do with suitable women applicants whom she had turned down on orders from above but who would surely be useful if the RAF's pilot shortage worsened any further. It is possible that the ever-chipper Gower was getting on d'Erlanger's nerves, pushing the women thing again after her ill-advised hiring of Lady Bailey earlier in the year. More likely, Pop simply had other things on his mind as his main client, the RAF, geared up for its epic defence of the realm.

Gower did not take his non-responsiveness personally. She just went 'around the blockage', as she put it in her diary. She sent an ostensibly innocent request for advice to her friend Leslie Runciman, Margie Fairweather's brother and director general of BOAC, who happened to be d'Erlanger's boss. And she requested a meeting with Air Marshal Sir Christopher Courtney, who was on secondment from the RAF to take charge of supply and organisation at the Air Ministry.

Results came swiftly. Runciman had words with d'Erlanger and Gower had dinner with Courtney. The two seem to have hit it off famously. The meal was the perfect chance for Gower to explain to someone in power the frustration for a highly experienced woman pilot – such as those on her waiting list – of watching raw male recruits reach for the sky in state-of-the art aircraft when all they wanted to do was help, but rules prevented them from flying anything at all. For Courtney, the meal presented an opportunity to be seen to be acting on the Prime Minister's most urgent priorities: a few days earlier, Churchill had lit a firework under the Air Ministry, demanding to know why it had failed to ratchet up pilot supply when his friend, Lord Beaverbrook, had worked such miracles with the supply of aircraft. 'It will be lamentable indeed if we have machines standing idle for want of pilots to fly them,' Churchill concluded.

The morning after his meal with Gower, Courtney informed d'Erlanger that he had authorised her to double her number of pilots, take over all ferrying of the RAF's new Percival Proctors (a low-wing, three-seater monoplane with a closed cockpit). Further, Gower had been told she could now select five of her best pilots for training on bigger, faster aircraft.

By the standards of world events in 1940 it was small beer. Yet something significant had happened. A dam on a tiny tributary

of a mammoth war effort had been breached by a perfect combination of reason, timing, charm, cajolery and the discreet use
of those people whom one 'had to know'. It was vintage Gower.
It wouldn't have happened in peacetime; nor would it have
happened without her.

News of Gower's modest British coup spread quickly through
the ranks of the ATA, and Amy Johnson, who had joined in May,
wrote to her parents showing her first real enthusiasm for her new
work. A chosen few would very shortly be training 'on Masters,
Hurricanes and things like that!' she told them, clearly assuming
she would be one of them. 'I am very thrilled at the prospect.'

Veronica Volkersz was thrilled, too. Hers became a name that
flyers conjured with. The first British woman in a jet, she was
considered 'vague' on the ground but brilliant in the air. She
loathed England after the dizzying colour and astringent air of
Srinagar high in Kashmir, where she spent some of her teenage
summers as the daughter of a major in the Royal Scots Fusiliers.
But she forgave the old country at least some of its slate skies and
girls' boarding schools when furnished by her father (now retired),
with a 17-hand Irish jumper called Killarney and an Aston Martin
sports car. She always drove it with the hood down, and sometimes sported a white leather helmet.

Volkersz craved excitement. Cars and horses went some way
to satisfy this craving, but not so far that she could resist learning
to fly when subsidised lessons were offered in 1938. Her enrol-
ment was covered in her local Windsor paper under the headline:
'Beauty Queen Joins the Civil Air Guard'.

The Civil Air Guard (CAG) had been set up in October 1938
with Lord Londonderry as its Chief Commissioner and the aim of
deepening the country's pool of pilots in the event of war. But the
entire organisation had been grounded, along with the rest of the
country's civil aviation, at the outbreak of war. So Volkersz became
an ambulance driver in the Blitz. The news that the ATA were
recruiting women as pilots had left her 'wildly excited' to the point
of leaping from buses to chase anyone she thought might be

wearing their uniform. When finally summoned for a flight test she made the grade but was only offered a place on a waiting list.

Veronica shared a small flat on Hyde Park with her father, who had come out of retirement to work for MI5. She spent the winter of 1940–41 attending West End bombsites in her Volunteer Aid Detachment uniform and parties at the Brasserie Universelle on Piccadilly in cocktail dresses. 'On February 1st, 1941,' she wrote later, 'tottering home after night duty, I opened the door of the flat to see a long brown envelope lying on the floor.' It bore a Hatfield postmark. 'My fingers trembled with excitement as I tore the flap open. I knew at once what it would say.'

Eight months later she would be back in London, celebrating after flying her first Hurricane.

For Mary de Bunsen the progression from earthbound suppliant to queen of the skies was less straightforward. The fourth daughter of the Rt Hon. Sir Maurice de Bunsen – Bt, GCMG, GCVO, CB and British ambassador to Vienna – at the age of four she contracted polio. This resulted in her right leg being two inches shorter than her left and of limited use below the knee. She had to wear an orthotic boot for most of her childhood. Her heart, they told her later, was 'rather an odd shape for a Mosquito pilot' – and weakened from birth by a hole in the wall between its two main chambers. Had de Bunsen been male and healthy, her eyes alone, barely visible behind her triplex lenses, would have had her laughed out of any RAF recruiting station.

Until Archduke Franz Ferdinand's assassination in 1914, the de Bunsens had divided their time between the ambassadorial residence on Metternichgasse and a rented castle in the Tyrol. There was enough privilege to shield the fourth daughter from many of the implications of her disabilities. Then circumstances dragged her back to England and boarding school and games, as they had dragged Volkersz. De Bunsen wondered later if she would have been as fond of flying if she had been better at games and a 'success with men'. As it was, she was 'madly keen' on sports but was always out of breath, and always the worst.

On leaving school she endured several London seasons as a wallflower. She was bookish, and thrilled to take tea with Thomas Hardy and T. E. Lawrence at the summer cottage her parents rented in Dorset. No-one had warned her that life after matric was a harsh marriage market in which her chances would be poor. Flying saved her.

High over Reading in a Cirrus Moth, solo for the first time, she felt born again. Her mother told her whenever she left the house for a flying lesson that she would be burnt alive, but any risk seemed worth taking when drifting towards 'the ghastly fate of the daughter-in-waiting'. Besides, she was seduced by the accoutrements of flying and the brave new Mary de Bunsen they created:

> the delicious leathery smell of a new flying helmet, in which you parade secretly before the looking glass; the firm grip of goggles; a Sidcot suit if you can run to it, and the swashbuckling boots, lined with sheepskin, which give such a wonderful feeling of confidence on frosty mornings.

She did encounter difficulties. On her first attempt to earn a private licence she failed both the practical and medical tests. But the ever-present, ever-helpful Pauline Gower bumped into her at Woodley airfield and gave her the name of a doctor who was 'accustomed to the idea of women pilots' and willing to vouch for her fitness to fly despite her weak right leg and tendency to breathlessness.

De Bunsen's next stroke of luck was to land a public relations job at the ultra-smart Heston aerodrome. Here she could put in hours of cheap practice (and was once given a pearl ring by the Sheikh of Kuwait, who dissolved with mirth at the sight of a kit plane called a Flying Flea being assembled by its French designer; the Sheikh liked to reward those who entertained him, and de Bunsen had arranged the inspection). After that, in the early stages of the war, she worked for a Tiger Moth dealer in Devon as Britain's most improbable test pilot. She had been turned down once by the ATA – 'a bitter moment', she wrote, since those who were accepted that day 'had the dewy, sparkling look of souls reborn'. But eventually, in August 1941, with a note from her oculist in her licence to say that she could see adequately with glasses, she was accepted.

By this time the first two Polish women pilots – Anna Leska and Barbara Wojtulanis – had reached England via Romania and served with the ATA for nearly eight months. Ann Welch, the glider pilot whom Rudolf Hess had failed to impress either as a politician or a skier, had been in for nine. (She described the process of joining up with typical economy: 'The war was just beginning to get serious and I had to be involved; and it had to be in flying. Nothing else could even be contemplated.') They had all been tested either by Gower herself or by one of her trusted lieutenants from the First Eight. The form was simple: climb into a waiting Tiger Moth, start her up, take-off, climb to 2,000 feet, turn one way and then the other, first gently and then in a steep bank, and make a forced landing when the examiner cuts the engine. Instructions came via speaker tube from the rear seat.

A few, like the formidable Lettice Curtis, could affect indifference to the test and to the ATA in general. Most could not. The test was nervewracking regardless of experience, because the stakes were high. It was the gateway to 'the most thrilling work women are doing' – and to the only flying they would be allowed to do for the duration of the war. So an ability to cope with pressure was useful, especially if, as in the case of Diana Barnato, experience was lacking: When she decided to apply to the ATA, she had all of ten hours in her logbook.

In many ways Diana Barnato and Lettice Curtis were polar opposites. One was tall; the other short. One was implacably serious; the other incorrigibly romantic. One was the product of pinched middle-class finances, draughty country houses and institutionalised education; the other, of diamond encrusted opulence and a giddy disregard for rules. Curtis never rivalled Barnato for glamour, and would not have wanted to. Audrey Sale-Barker did, but Diana Barnato eclipsed even her. Until the Americans arrived, no-one could touch First Officer Barnato in the exhausting business of having fun, and even then no-one could fund as much of it as her.

In 1888, Diana's grandfather, Barney Barnato, originally of East London's Mile End Road but latterly of Kimberley, South Africa, found himself standing next to Cecil Rhodes and a bucket full of diamonds. The diamonds were Barnato's. Rhodes wrote him a cheque for them and the mines from which they came for just over £5 million – reputedly the largest cheque in history to that point. Rhodes merged his mines with Barnato's to form De Beers' Consolidated Mines Ltd. For his own part, Barney Barnato wrote a will and, in due course, booked passage on a steamer back to London.

The will provided generously for his wife and three children. But it handed the rest of the fortune to his brother, Solly, who had helped with the management of the Barnato mines. He was with Barney on the promenade deck of the SS *Christiana* on the afternoon that Barney mysteriously went over the side. No-one else was around except a steward, stacking chairs. He later said he heard someone yell 'murder' and turned to see Solly either holding on to Barney's coat or letting go of it; it was not clear which. Barney was dead by the time a lifeboat picked him up. The verdict, in the absence of corroborating witnesses, was suicide. But even Solly's son would later tell Diana that Grandpa Barney had been pushed.

Diana's father, Woolf Barnato, eventually prised most of his rightful inheritance out of Solly through the courts. It was enough. He bought the Bentley Motor Company, an extensive spread in the Surrey Hills, and an exotic new Darracq two-seater sports car for Diana's twenty-first birthday.

Woolf 'Babe' Barnato had kept wicket for Surrey in his youth and won the Le Mans 24-hour race in 1928, 1929 and 1930. He had many friends, among them Ettore Bugatti, founder of the Bugatti marque, with whom he dined in Paris after presenting

Diana with the Darracq outside the Ritz. When she burned out its brand-new clutch en route to the Basilica of Sacré Coeur, Bugatti fixed it.

The year was 1939. War had been declared, and across Europe armies and economies were being urgently reorganised to fight it. If anyone was going to chance a skiing holiday in France at such a time it was the young Miss Barnato. Sure enough, she obtained a pass to enter the country from Count John de Camaran, a friend at the French Embassy, and drove out to Megève and Chamonix with Lorna Harmsworth, daughter of the owner of the *Daily Mail*, for ten days with the Scots Guards.

They paused in Paris on their return for five days with Gogo Schiaparelli, daughter of Elsa, the couturier whom Amy Johnson had favoured with her custom in happier times. Elsa was still very much in business. She did not let the often-photographed Diana continue to Calais without a new wardrobe created for her, and for the moment. It included a heavy tweed coat with a silk lining in red, white and blue.

For Diana, flying was an escape – but hardly from drudgery or want of opportunity. It was an escape from other women. She had been presented to the chaotic court of the future Edward VIII in 1936 and loved being a deb. Unlike so many of her fellow flyers, she thrived at balls. She delighted the hand-picked young men – the 'debs' delights' – and they delighted her. The only fly in this intoxicating ointment was her mother, who chaperoned her to all the main events and deputised a bustling platoon of friends and paid professionals to cover the lesser ones. 'However,' she wrote, 'I was eighteen and didn't like all that molly-coddling anymore.' She knew they taught flying in the middle of her father's favourite motor racing track – at Brooklands – and that most trainers had only two seats, so 'at least nannies, governesses, companions and chaperones wouldn't be able to come along'.

She went solo after six hours, but then lost interest. Or rather, she suffered a fright, the memory of which haunted her for years and probably saved her life several times over. Just before that flight a badly burned man appeared beside her Tiger Moth. She put what happened next into verse:

> He put his claws upon the wing
> Impelling me to turn to him,
> And said, above the engine's din
> 'Don't fly! Don't fly Miss! Look and see
> What aviation's done to me.'
> I scanned his scarred and broken face
> And horror shuddered in my mind
> What flying now could do to me,
> And I would end up same as he.

Rosemary Rees and Diana Barnato both wrote that they would rather die in a crash than survive, horribly disfigured, to endure the rest of a lifetime of staring strangers and conveniently absent friends, and Diana found out soon enough how fickle friends could be.

In the spring of 1941, while out horse riding with her friend Bobby Lowenstein, a bomber pilot and wealthy heir to a Belgian financier, Diana's tired mount crashed through a gate instead of jumping it. The horse was uninjured; not so Diana. She broke her jaw and rearranged her teeth so thoroughly that one of them lodged just beneath her eye. She wrote of the aftermath of the accident, and of a visit from her then boyfriend Claude Strickland, in her memoir, *Spreading My Wings*:

> I was patched up in the London Clinic. The jaws were wired up, and as the risk of blindness receded I was allowed to see my friends. Claude Strickland took one look at me and never came back. Having been my most important love, this was devastating. He moved on to another, more attractive girl, but I didn't blame him.

One late summer afternoon Diana invited me to join her in Surrey for tea and to look at her scrapbooks. Through them marched an extraordinary parade of bravehearts, Spitfire aces returned from battle to the society photographer's studio. They were an absurdly handsome bunch, but Strickland, with curly blond hair and a hint of melancholy in his face, looked even more perfect than the rest.

'Flying Officer Claude Strickland was shot down over Ostend', read a newspaper cutting pasted next to one of his portraits. 'Presumed alive.'

'Wrong,' Diana said.

He never came back, then?

'No.'

I asked how long she had known him: 'Oh, forever. He was a debs' delight when I was a deb. He was a boyfriend . . . but they were all shot down two a penny.'

One friend who did keep visiting was Lowenstein. He and Dick Fairey (son of the founder of Fairey Aviation, soon to lose his legs to gangrene after four days in an open boat off Greenland) had encouraged Diana Barnato to try for the ATA even though she had barely a fiftieth of the experience of the least experienced of the First Eight. Lowenstein and Fairey knew the ATA's chief flying instructor rode in Windsor Great Park each Sunday morning. They had contrived to bump into him there with Diana in tow on a thoroughbred black mare. Startled and socially outshone, the normally unflappable Captain A.R.O. MacMillan, ex-BOAC, agreed to give her a flight test the following Wednesday. There was no legal way of practising in the air, so Diana roared up and down the Egham bypass near her father's home in one of his Bentleys – a silver-grey 1936 four-and-a-half litre. 'I opened all the windows and pretended I was seated in a Tiger [Moth],' she wrote, 'looking out of the side windows at the grass verges so that I could judge what the waving grass looked like when I would be easing off the ground or trying to land again.' In the evenings, Dick and Bobby talked her through every detail of the White Waltham aerodrome and the circuit above it from the orange sofa in an outer hallway of the Barnato mansion.

Captain MacMillan supervised Diana Barnato's test himself. She passed first time.

It was on the day after the test, in the grounds of a house that the Lowensteins maintained in Leicestershire, that Diana had her riding accident. Bobby blamed himself. In the ambulance on the way back to London he told her he loved her and hoped to marry her. For ten days he reported for duty as usual each morning with his bomber squadron, and visited her at the London Clinic after flying. Then, coming into land in a Blenheim, he inadvertently shut down one engine, flipped the aircraft onto its back and was killed.

'Pilot error,' Diana wrote. 'Not to be wondered at. Once more I was devastated. No Claude, plus no Bobby, plus no face.'

Barnato did not report for duty with the ATA for another nine months on account of her smashed-up face, but when she did it was in a leopard-skin coat. Even so, she struck her comrades as curiously unspoilt considering her background. When grounded by bad weather she was a diligent letter writer, undistractable unless she sought distraction. And unlike Audrey Sale-Barker, she was content to order her uniform from Regent Street rather than Savile Row (she still has it; it hangs in her wardrobe in the dry-cleaner's plastic wrap, and comes out at the slightest excuse).

The ATA girls looked sharp. Their gold-trimmed navy uniform turned heads and secured the best rooms in hotels and good tables in restaurants. It was a passport, Veronica Volkersz said; 'it would even get you a seat on the bus'. However much its wearers loathed the 'glamour' word (and even one of those who did had to admit it was 'rather fun walking down the streets in London and having people turn and look at you'), the uniform represented daring and dynamism to the general public.

Most female recruits, like Barnato, were measured up at Austin Reed's, and the fine tailoring on offer there was the one significant concession to feminine vanity made by the ATA on their behalf.

Two pilots thought they could do without it. The results were mixed, and Alison King's unimprovable account of a visit by Margot Gore and Philippa Bennett to the Maidenhead tailor used by most of the ATA's male pilots explains why. No woman, it seems, had set foot in there before, so there was 'a certain amount of consternation' when the serving gentleman discovered that Flight Officers Gore and Bennett were ladies.

Whoever heard of such a thing! But, after much debate behind a screen, he eventually emerged to whisper, almost hysterically, 'that they would see what could be done'.

After some moments he appeared again with two other gentlemen, both rather older than his own fifty-odd years, and these he introduced as Mr Pert and Mr Hix 'who will see to you'. He then hurried away to the far end of the room and pretended to be folding material, but taking all the time quick, alarmed glances at the measurers. Mr Hix had stood himself at a bench with pen and paper, while Mr Pert, having ushered Margot into position, was doing manual things with the tape measure. Length of sleeve, both from shoulder to elbow and elbow to wrist, had gone swimmingly, but his approach to the bust had, they thought, been unusual. He would take a few quick steps, throw the tape measure round the back, catch it in mid-air and, turning his head away as if he couldn't bear to look, wait until the two ends met before giving a fleeting glance to the number of inches it recorded. Then he would cover the five feet or so between himself and the writer, Mr Hix, and whisper his findings in a hairy ear as if they were too awful a secret to bear alone.

Waist and hips again went swimmingly, although the secret numbers were again imparted in a whisper. When it became known that trousers were needed as well as a skirt, there was a hurried consultation, and, after a great deal of eye-rolling and obvious heart-searching, the two gentlemen, as though it were half-time, changed places, and Mr Hix took on the manual duty. Mr Hix did his measurements with ease and dash until it came to the inevitable length from crutch to ankle. This was eventually overcome, but with such delicacy that when poor F/O Gore and F/O Bennett received their long-awaited uniform, the trouser seats hung four inches too low and had to be sent back with carefully chalked instructions and a sharp note.

On 10 May 1941, Lieutenant Colonel J. T. C. Moore-Brabazon, the first man to transport live cargo in an aeroplane (a piglet in a wastepaper basket tied to the wing strut of his French-built Voisin in 1909), paid an official visit to the women's ferry pool at Hatfield. Promoted by Churchill to the critical position of Minister of Aircraft Production because of Lord Beaverbrook's failing health, Brabazon had been in the job all of ten days.

'Brab' must have attached considerable importance to the ATA women's work, or at least to their morale. Or he may simply have enjoyed their company; naturally, he knew most of them socially. He posed with them for a photograph outside one of De Havilland's sturdy brick workshops, hat off, linking arms with Gower on his left and Lois Butler on his right, and they all look unusually jolly. Even Lettice Curtis is smiling.

If the Hatfield tea-party picture taken seventeen months earlier was the first iconic group portrait of the ATA women, this was the second. Its subjects even acquired a nickname – 'Brab's Beauties'. Two of the women are wearing regulation A-line skirts and black silk stockings. These are Audrey Sale-Barker and her saucier namesake, Audrey Macmillan. The rest are in their blue flying slacks. Winnie Crossley, the doctor's daughter, holds a pair of light kid gloves. Lois Butler holds a cigarette in one hand and has thrust the other in her trouser pocket. The picture is imbued with optimism, and, for once, the sun is out.

All anyone wanted to talk about at Hatfield that spring was flying Hurricanes and Spitfires. Gower had proved herself as a player in the aeronautical establishment without alienating its key men. Her women had proved themselves extremely capable pilots. The best of them had moved on from Proctors and Lysanders to Fairey Battles and large, noisy radial-engined Harvards. Hurricanes had to be next. 'Politically,' Lettice Curtis wrote, 'the implications were great, since there were still many men who kidded themselves that only ace pilots could fly fighters.' Practically, therefore, the move had to be incremental, below the radar – a fait accompli.

That bright spring day at Hatfield, Brab lunched with Gower, Butler and Crossley. Lettice Curtis believes that they discussed with him flying a wider range of aircraft (and they surely discussed little else). She also records a theory that Gower effectively clinched the long-awaited promotion to fly operational aircraft by button-holing d'Erlanger at a party a couple of months later. 'I suppose there isn't really any reason why women shouldn't fly Hurricanes,' d'Erlanger is meant to have said, at which point Gower pounced: 'Fine – when can we start?'

Brab may have used the proper channels and written a memo urging the Air Council to require the RAF to allow the use of women in operational planes. If so, it has never been produced. More likely, he simply telephoned d'Erlanger and told him to get on with it. He was one of Churchill's people, after all. He was an aviator's aviator, a pioneer; the man who'd shown that pigs really could fly.

At 9 a.m. on 19 July 1941, the day's assignments went up in chalk as usual on a blackboard outside the Hatfield operations room. In one column were the pilots' names; in the next, the types of aircraft they would be flying. After 'Miss Crossley', written in capitals, was the word 'HURRICANE'. Shortly afterwards, a Captain R. H. Henderson of the ATA's technical department at White Waltham flew over in the department's own Hurricane. Four women flew the plane that day, all from the First Eight. They were Winnie Crossley, Margie Fairweather, Joan Hughes and Rosemary Rees. They were no more experienced than Cunnison, Patterson, Wilberforce or Friedlander; just lucky to find themselves at Hatfield on the appointed day. Crossley went first, with the fate of the women pilots depending on her. The others watched, too anxious and excited to talk, as she climbed in, buckled on her parachute and harness and taxied away. Take-off, circuit and three-point landing were all perfect, and were over in minutes. The Hurricane rumbled back to the spectators. 'It's lovely, darlings,' Winnie smiled as she stepped out onto the wing. 'A beautiful little aeroplane.'

After a brief tour of the cockpit from Captain Henderson, the other three followed. No-one put a foot wrong. One of those watching was Alison King, who was too timid to fly for the ATA but experienced the pilots' entire war vicariously as an operations officer. 'Afterwards there was much laughter and celebration and we eyed each other with furtive, unspoken delight,' she wrote, 'for we knew that that afternoon something momentous had happened.'

To mark that something the women pooled their petrol coupons and drove into London for dinner in St James's at the Ecu de France. Their excitement was at what they had proved, and what they would prove. Because it meant that Spitfires would be next.

10

'The Perfect Lady's Aeroplane'

In January 1942, the Ministry of Information's Crown Film Unit released to cinemas a short documentary called *Ferry Pilot*. The film was about the ATA, and it proved a minor hit. Part of the appeal lay in Captain F. D. Bradbrooke's starring role. He was a senior ATA pilot with a short haircut and a voice indistinguishable from Cary Grant's, and he gave a relaxed and personable depiction of himself as a fatherly jack-of-all-aerial-trades. Part of the appeal lay in the heavy ledgers and clouds of pipesmoke behind which two slightly effete operations officers masterminded a typical day's flying from White Waltham; and part in the unique talent of the chief Spitfire test pilot at Castle Bromwich, Alex Henshaw.

Early in the film, Bradbrooke and an American pilot nick-named Alabam stride into the Castle Bromwich operations room brandishing 'chits': 'Two Spitfires, please,' Bradbrooke says cheerfully, placing his bits of paper on the ops officer's desk. He has jumped a short queue – two young women are already there – but they don't seem to mind. They are easily recognisable as the tiny Joan Hughes, and the willowy, mysterious Audrey Sale-Barker, even though when Bradbrooke addresses Sale-Barker it's as 'Betty'.

'What have you got today, Betty?'

'Trainers,' she mumbles, and leaves the room.

Joan Hughes follows, saying much more brightly: 'Yes, 200 miles an hour's our limit, I'm afraid.'

Outside, a Spitfire hurtles past at shoulder-height. The all-knowing Bradbrooke announces it's Alex Henshaw at the stick: 'Should be worth watching'. Henshaw climbs near-vertically into the sun, twists at the top to give a flash of the Spitfire's elliptical wings, then dives back towards the ground. Alabam can scarcely contain himself; he says he's heard all about Henshaw and sure enough he 'ain't never seen anything quite this'.

Henshaw roars by again, close enough, it seems, to touch. Then he recedes to a faint line against a wash of stratocumulus, and dives again. This time the camera picks out a gentle rise on the ground beyond the aerodrome. Henshaw keeps diving until he disappears behind it. When he re-emerges, much closer and louder, he rolls the Spitfire lazily onto its back, so low that its tail appears to brush the grass.

Hughes and Sale-Barker let their awestruck faces do the talking. Their necks twist sharply as if at Wimbledon. Henshaw's gravity-fed carburettors begin to dry up and his engine sputters, but somehow the Spitfire stays upside down and rock-steady. Alabam promises not to ape the master and he and Bradbrooke head for two Spitfires of their own. The camera lingers on them as they taxi and take off, leaving the ladies firmly on the ground.

Six months before the film was screened in cinemas, Captain Bradbrooke flew into a mountain on the Isle of Arran in a Consolidated Liberator. Newly assigned to BOAC's Atlantic Return Ferry Service, he was killed instantly along with twenty other male ferry pilots, most of them Americans returning home after bringing bombers over from Newfoundland.

Meanwhile, ATA women had been flying Spitfires for five of those six months, even if, as far as the Crown Film Unit was concerned, their speed limit was still a deferential 200 mph. Spitfires were capable of more than double that. They were happy cruising at 300 mph, but were unhappy waiting on the tarmac with their engines idling for more than a few minutes. The American Colonel Jim Goodson, who flew for the RAF from early 1941 onwards, explained somewhat heretically what this could mean for a pilot:

the Spit was a little bitch on the ground. The long nose completely blocking your forward vision meant that you had to constantly weave right and left, and if you took too long before taking off you could lose your brakes entirely through lack of air, or even overheat the engine. The narrow landing gear also made it prone to ground looping on landing.

Spitfires belonged in the air. Up there, their pilots didn't see the aeroplane that had stolen most of the limelight in the Battle of Britain from the manlier Hurricane (responsible for 80 per cent of that battle's kills). They didn't see the plane that Harold Balfour described in 1938 as 'slimly built with a beautifully proportioned body and graceful curves just where they should be'. They saw a big, black, semicircular instrument panel, a dome of sky around it, and a rearview mirror.

The six central instruments – airspeed indicator, artificial horizon, rate of climb indicator, altimeter, turn indicator and gyroscopic compass – were the same as on any operational plane. Everything else was more cramped if you were big or heavyset; more snug if you were small. For women, the whole package was perfect. Without exception, the women aviators of the ATA longed to fly Spitfires because of what they'd seen and heard, but they loved them when they got their hands on them because of how they felt.

First there was the power that kicked them in the back when they released the brakes. It has taken engineers seventy years to work out how to cram as much muscle into a road-going car as was crammed into a 1938 Mark I Spitfire. Later Spitfire marks were vastly more powerful again. The 1,600-horsepower Rolls-Royce Merlin-powered Mark IXs and 2,300-horsepower Griffon-powered F24s spoilt pilots who moved on from them to early jets and found some sluggish by comparison.

After the power, they felt the lift generated by a wing with a slower stalling speed at its tips than close in to the fuselage. This meant that just before it fell out of the sky – in a vertically banked turn, say, or on a misjudged final approach – a Spitfire would shudder. It was a uniquely generous final warning that saved the lives of aces and novices alike.

And finally: the responsiveness that gave meaning to the cliché that you didn't fly a Spitfire at all; you wore it. Or, as Diana Barnato put it: 'You moved, it moved.' This was largely a product of Reginald Mitchell's long experience designing airborne thoroughbreds, and of his intuitive genius. The Spitfire was nose-heavy on the ground and would tip forward if braked harshly, but it was perfectly balanced in flight. It also had an unusual joystick that pivoted forwards and backwards from a fulcrum on the floor but left and right from the neck between the spade-style handle and the stick itself, much higher up. To turn, in other words, you only had to twist your wrist. In skirts or slacks, a pilot's knees never had to be more than 6 inches apart.

The Spitfire is the only fighter plane to have been honoured with a full-length literary biography. Paraphrasing the lustier fighter boys who flew it, its author, Jonathan Glancey, calls the Spitfire 'aerial totty'; a 'mechanical Lady Hamilton'. Certainly, none of the women who flew it thought it masculine. To the contrary, it was every inch the boyish Hawker Hurricane's desirable sister, though the women's feelings for it were more sisterly than carnal, or like those of a teenager with a crush on her pony. But they were no less ardent for that. It was, according to Katie Hirsch, one of the last ATA women to learn to fly it, 'simply bliss'.

'Everyone loved them,' Jadwiga Pilsudska recalled, 'but especially the women.' Some recorded their first Spitfire experiences in quasi-sexual language. 'It seemed the most natural thing in the world to be sitting there in the cockpit,' wrote the South African Jackie Sorour, 'as though my entire life had led to this moment':

> I started up inexpertly and felt the power coursing through the Spitfire's frame. A little awed but stimulated by the urgent throb of the Merlin engine that seemed to tremble with eagerness to be free in its own element, I taxied cautiously to the

down-wind end of the field ... A few seconds later I found myself soaring through the air in a machine that made poetry of flight. Carefully I familiarised myself with the controls as the ground fell away at fantastic speed and felt exhilarated by the eager, sensitive response. Singing with joy and relief I dived and climbed and spiraled round the broken clouds, before turning on to course.

For Helen Richey the Spitfire was 'a fish through water, a sharp knife through butter, a bullet through the sky'. For Veronica Volkersz this was, quite simply, 'the perfect lady's aeroplane'.

The only woman pilot who categorically refused to get carried away by the Spitfire was the very first of the ATA women to fly it. In a letter to her father, Lord Runciman, dated 8 October 1941, Margie Fairweather devoted five paragraphs to thanking him for a gift of money, to news of her and her husband's new life at the Prestwick ferry pool and to her daughter's gratifying enjoyment of her new Oxford boarding school. She then added: 'Knowing your great love of aeroplanes I am sure you will appreciate the great honour [I] have brought to the family by being the first woman to fly in a Spitfire.' She then asked her father to thank her mother for her letters, and signed off.

If the ATA had wanted to keep this latest small step for womankind a secret it could not have chosen a more discreet trailblazer. But any idea that news of the flight would not spread far and fast was ludicrous. By the time Margie Fairweather had written her letter, that news had already reached New York, Pretoria, Santiago and, as we shall see, the scarcely populated estancias of Patagonia.

11

The Originals

Statistically, it was unusual for a woman in wartime Britain to set out to fly fighters and bombers and succeed. One hundred and seventeen British women managed it, or about one in every 200,000. But this ratio represented a positive avalanche compared with the number of women pilots who came from the rest of the world. Of these there were forty-seven (or roughly one in 29 million based on 1941 world population figures). These women were not representative of their gender or their times, except in so far as their times were cataclysmic. They were originals.

Twenty-five came from the United States, too enthralled by the idea of flying combat planes in England to wait and see if they would be allowed to do the same at home. They came from every corner of the country: Maine, Chicago, Kansas City, California, Louisiana and the foothills of the Kettle River range in northern Washington. Others, motivated at least partly by loyalty to Britain and the Empire, came from Canada, Australia, New Zealand, South Africa and – that great 'forgotten colony' – Argentina.

One, Margot Duhalde, came from Chile. Margot had never left the country until she squeezed into a car to drive over the Andes to Mendoza, bound for England and the war, in April 1941. She spoke no English and had no English relatives. What she did have was a commercial pilot's licence – the first ever awarded to a Chilean woman – and a nineteen-year-old's unshaken self-belief.

Duhalde was born in 1921 on a farm near Rio Bueno, 500 miles south of Santiago, the second of twelve children and the oldest of six sisters. She would later write of her difficulty in finding a flying instructor willing to spend time on someone so young who was a woman and 'half-peasant' into the bargain, but in truth the family farm – sitting directly beneath the airmail route from Temuco in the north to Puerto Montt – was prosperous and its owners middle class.

Now in her early eighties, Margot lives in Santiago's diplomatic district. She greeted me at the door of her comfortable apartment in dark red lipstick, aviator sunglasses and a lime green trouser suit. We descended immediately to street level, where the doorman had brought round a shiny silver Peugeot with red seatbelts and racing trim. Weaving past cars that dared to brake in front of her, we drove first to the Air Force Officers' Club for lunch (they knew her here as 'Commandante') and then to the Aeroclub de Santiago at the foot of the Andes. Here Margot found a table on a large, shaded terrace, ordered beer, and talked.

'I dreamed of flying – I wanted to be up there with these dots in the sky,' she said, recalling her childhood memory of the mail planes. Too much dreaming was one of the reasons she was thrown out of school in Rio Bueno and sent as a boarder to the Santiago Lyceo when she was twelve. From there, most days, she would escape to watch the flying at the Aeroclub de Chile.

At sixteen, Duhalde was given a flying lesson for her birthday. With her father's blessing and money, she worked for a year towards her commercial licence and then smuggled herself into El Bosque, the country's top military flying school and a citadel of elitist machismo. As a woman she could never have set foot there officially, so she went as a protégée of Cesar Copeto, the school's maintenance chief. Copeto was something of a national treasure having been, in 1909, the first Chilean to fly. For two years Duhalde came and went as his accessory, learning mechanics and aerodynamics on the Gipsy Moths that he maintained. When the war in Europe came she wanted to be involved, but her only connection to it was her grandfather, who had grown up in the French Basque village of Louhossoa.

Logistically, at least, it was enough. When de Gaulle issued his call to the Free French in June 1940, Margot Duhalde presented herself at the French consulate in Santiago and volunteered. How could she get from there to Europe? 'That was de Gaulle's problem,' she said.

Margot went home to pack and bid a tearful farewell to her mother, whom she tried to reassure with the white lie that she would probably only be sent to Québec or Montreal as a flight instructor. Her father, whose favourite she was, then travelled with her as far as Santiago.

I asked her how much she knew about the war for which she had volunteered. 'Nothing. Just that it had been declared,' she said. 'And the Germans were winning.' She told a little story about a friend and fellow woman pilot of German extraction who warned her just before she left that Britain would be overrun by the time she got there. 'But it's okay,' the friend had said. 'I'll come and rescue you.'

In the end, Margot said, she had made her decision to volunteer for the Allied war effort on instinct – 'an instinct to learn more about France and where I came from, and to find out why my blood wasn't totally Chilean'. She knew what she was doing was unusual, but saw no mystery in it.

In April 1941, 139 Chileans left to join the French, divided into groups according to which force they hoped to join. There were thirteen in the air force group, including one other woman, a nurse. Some went by ship from Valparaiso via Panama. Duhalde, the nurse and two young Basque men were assigned a car to Argentina. They drove north from Santiago, then east up the Valle de Aconcagua beneath South America's highest mountain, to Mendoza. From there they went by train across the Pampas to Buenos Aires, and from there by the *Rangitata*, a Norwegian-registered freighter, to Liverpool.

Duhalde's first impressions of Britain were that it was

'horrible'. Like the Americans who followed her, she was profoundly shocked by the effects of bombing on the fabric of the country, and of rationing on its pinched and pallid people. But there was an additional difficulty for Duhalde. Relations between Churchill and de Gaulle were less than cordial. Despite having ordered the destruction of the French fleet at Oran the previous year, the Prime Minister's strategy towards Marshal Pétain and the collaborators was to keep talking; he could not risk an official state of war with Vichy. And this de Gaulle could not be seen to stomach. He had spent much of 1940 in Libreville, the capital of French Gabon, fuming at perfidious Albion. Churchill was also refusing to take at face value the bona fides of the polyglot volunteer army arriving at British ports under the auspices of the Free French. Who knew where their true allegiances lay? What better cover story for a dedicated Nazi agent than to have come from South America to the defence of France? The result for the thirteen Chileans disembarking from the *Rangitata* in May 1941 was that instead of being welcomed, they were arrested and interned.

'Scotland Yard was waiting for us,' Duhalde remembered. She was taken to London and spent five days in jail there while her story was checked. Only then was she handed over to the Free French, who, unsure what to do with her, put her up in the Morton Hotel on Russell Square.

As she killed time in London, it quickly became clear to Duhalde that in her place de Gaulle's London-based staff had been expecting a man. There was no flying of any sort by women under French command in the war. Margot now believes that her name, in the chaos of setting up a government in exile and communicating with a consulate 8,000 miles away, had become abbreviated and confused with Marcel, or simply reduced to 'M'.

She stayed at the hotel for three miserable months before being sent to Wellingborough in the smog-choked East Midlands to cook and clean for a French woman running a convalescent home for injured pilots. 'I came to work in the war and found myself working as a maid,' she recalled with dismay. In London, she had been scared and lonely. Now she was bored and lonely, and angry with herself for entrusting so much to hope and her imagination.

And then what she describes as 'a miracle' helped her escape Wellingborough. A French military chaplain attached to the Free French in London had noticed her at the hotel in Russell Square, and asked her story. He passed it on to a French pilot, Pierre Orlemans, who happened to have been in Chile three years earlier when Duhalde's success in earning a commercial licence had briefly made the news. Orlemans wrote to her in Wellingborough, telling her about the ATA and offering to arrange an introduction. He spoke little English and no Spanish. Margot spoke neither French nor English. They met in London and continued, largely mute, to Hatfield, Duhalde clutching a letter that Orlemans had written for her and addressed to the only ATA name he knew. That name was Lettice Curtis.

On being presented with Orlemans's letter, the magnificent Lettice, according to Duhalde, read it, said 'not a word' and waved in the direction of Pauline Gower's office. She then disappeared.

Gower received them more warmly and found a French-speaking cadet to translate. Margot was soon airborne again for the first time since leaving Chile four months earlier, this time in a Tiger Moth, which was substantially more powerful than the Gipsy Moths she was used to. A Mrs Ebbage in the front seat issued instructions by means of hand signals.

'I had never seen so many planes in the sky,' Duhalde recalled. 'There was a Dutch elementary flying school in the circuit in some early Mosquitoes and when I made a reasonable landing no-one was more surprised than me.' Accepted in principle by the ATA, she was eventually released from her commitment to the Free French after the intervention of the Chilean ambassador. She reported for duty at Hatfield on 1 September 1941.

Her comrades, Curtis apart, were mildly amused. They nicknamed her 'Chile'. She still spoke virtually no English and knew the layout of England from the air no better than from the ground.

On her first solo cross-country flight, not helped by snow covering most roads and railway lines, she became hopelessly lost among barrage balloons over North London. She eventually decided to force land in a field near Enfield. Duhalde described what happened next with an indulgent grin:

> The field had seemed clean from 2,000 feet, but I was not wearing my spectacles. Close-up, it turned out to be full of wooden posts put there by the local anti-aircraft battalion, but I landed anyway. I had to come down under some power cables but over a low wall which took my wheels off and tipped me forward in the snow.

Onlookers who had watched her descent ran to find her conscious but with blood on her face, no papers, and no command of English. She was arrested. The bemused Enfield police allowed her a telephone call, but when she asked for the ATA she was put through to headquarters at White Waltham rather than the women's pool at Hatfield. They sent a car for her but the driver neither recognised nor understood her and would not vouch for her. 'No-one knew who I was or where Chile was,' she said. 'In the end I just said, "Pauline Gower". And they phoned her and let me go.'

Gower was still acutely sensitive to bad publicity. At this point she seems to have begun to see 'Chile' more as a liability than a brave new pilot heaven-sent from the far end of the world. Duhalde was dispatched to Luton to complete her training. When Luton pointed out that it was hard to teach her anything when she spoke no English, a make-or-break meeting was arranged at White Waltham to decide her fate, to which Duhalde was invited.

'Pauline Gower threw me out,' she said. '"You can't fly; it's not possible," she told me. But I insisted that I could.' In the end, compromise won out. Captain A.R.O. MacMillan, the softhearted chief instructor who had agreed to give Diana Barnato a flight test with only ten hours under her belt, listened to Duhalde's pleas in private and then suggested to Gower that she be allowed to spend three months in the hangars brushing up on Tiger Moth mechanics and, more especially, on her English. Gower agreed. 'But it was MacMillan who gave me that chance,' she said firmly. 'I'd gone into his office and cried like the Magdalena, and no-one tried to stop me after that.'

They all remember the names of the ships that brought them – the *Rangitata*, the *Avila Star*, the *Julius Caesar*, the *Beaver Hill* – and they all kept the tickets of their voyages to England as souvenirs. The *Rangitata* brought Margot Duhalde: a month of zigzagging out of the River Plate and northward round the great bulge of Brazil, two weeks after the scuttling of the *Graf Spee*. The wolf packs had never been further from home, nor more vengeful.

The *Avila Star* had set sail only a few months earlier, in the winter of 1940/41, also from Buenos Aires. It carried only a few passengers bound for England (its captain joked that even the fish were swimming in the opposite direction), but among them were Maureen and Joan Dunlop, sisters travelling without chaperones, which had occasioned a good deal of adverse comment in polite Anglo-Argentine society. They had no idea when or if they would return home, but promised their parents they would write three times a week.

Maureen and Joan had started their journey nearly 1,000 miles south-west of Buenos Aires on a ranch not far from San Carlos de Bariloche, capital of Argentina's Andean Lake District (and ironically a magnet for Nazi fugitives after the war). The ranch was not far, either, from Margot Duhalde's mother and eleven siblings on their Rio Bueno farm in Chile; perhaps a day and a half through the mountains by horse and canoe. But it was an awfully long way from Australia, where Joan and Maureen's father had been born.

Eric Chase Dunlop was 'an amazing man, very tall, terrifically energetic', Maureen recalled, and, like her, he hated being surrounded by people. He had travelled to Patagonia on spec after being wounded three times while serving with the Royal Field

Artillery in the First World War. The vastness and the emptiness suited him and his new English wife, and the Merino sheep he'd imported from his native New South Wales. He worked for the Argentine Southern Land Company. His 'office' was a pair of highland estancias straddling the Maquinchao River and the mountains either side of it. When Maureen said she'd sooner stay there with him than follow her sister to Cheltenham Ladies' College, he entirely understood. So Joan continued her education at boarding school alone, training afterwards to be a nurse. For young Maureen, meanwhile, a governess was hired who in due course was required to leave gaps in her timetables to enable her charge to disappear for flying lessons.

'I always wanted to fly,' she said simply. 'I nearly broke my neck a couple of times jumping off a ledge at the top of the hill behind our house, until I was absolutely forbidden to do it when I was eight or nine years old.'

As a teenager she was shy, but comfortable with horses and with people who flew: people with whom she had a connection that had nothing to do with other people. 'They were a marvellous bunch. They mostly belonged to the Aeroclub Argentino.' They were mostly men, and mostly in oil, cattle or sheep. When she was fifteen, a local Shellmex manager got her into the Aeroclub, which entitled her to cheap tuition. She had her licence two years later.

Maureen now raises Arab horses in Norfolk, but still speaks wistfully of her Patagonian childhood. Once the war came, and soon afterwards an issue of *Flight* magazine with an article about the women of the ATA, there was little discussion about where the Dunlop daughters' duty would take them. 'My father said a war's a war. It's not something you hang about over.'

Six years after gaining her licence in the Argentine, Maureen Dunlop climbed out of a Fairey Barracuda at No. 15 Ferry Pool in her summer flying uniform and became almost famous. She was wearing a white shirt and dark tie with her sleeves rolled up above her elbows. It was hot, and she was relieved to be able to unclip her harness, sling a parachute over her shoulder and shake out her hair. Many of the pilots at the all-women's pool at Hamble had chosen to cut their hair short for reasons of fashion and convenience, but Miss Dunlop had left hers long even though it could be a nuisance to gather up into a flying helmet. As her hair tumbled out, backlit by the afternoon sun, the waiting photographer from the *Picture Post* could hardly believe his luck. Maureen didn't look at him, but she did smile and raise a hand to run through her newly liberated tresses, her long fingers looking as if they had just emerged from a manicure rather than a torpedo bomber's cockpit. As she did so the sun glinted on a gold bracelet on her wrist, contrasting with the functional steel ring on the end of a loose harness strap. It was her cover-girl moment, literally. More than any other single image, the impromptu portrait of Maureen Dunlop that appeared on the front page of the *Picture Post* on 16 September 1944 cemented in the public mind the idea of the ATA as an all-women's outfit, and an intensely enviable one at that.

Maureen became fast friends with 'Chile'. They were posted together to Hamble and there they would talk in the fast, fluid Spanish of the world they'd left behind, a dialect that sounds as if it has been stripped of all consonants by the wind. At Hamble they both found a kindred spirit in a third exotic bird of passage, Jackie Sorour.

Sorour had arrived from Cape Town in 1938 aboard the *Julius Caesar* – 'an overture of sparkling white and expectancy' – making her the only ATA woman of any nationality to leave her native country for England before the war simply to fly. She was also the only ATA woman who confessed freely to wanting to be a celebrity, and was one of the few who had what it took. She had a baby-doll cuteness, an iron will, an ego of solid brass and a deeply conflicted attitude to men that, by her own account, infuriated every one of them who tried to make a pass at her. She took up flying at sixteen as a declaration of independence from two taunting stepbrothers, and of victory over fear – a simple fear of flying that had landed her breakfast in her lap on her first flight as a passenger the year before.

Sorour's need to prove herself brave could easily look like exhibitionism. Soon after her seventeenth birthday, with permission obtained in person from the South African Air Minister, she performed a parachute jump from 5,000 feet over the Swartkop military aerodrome outside Pretoria. She waited a few seconds too long before pulling her ripcord, landed hard, knocked herself out and broke her ankle. The stunt was watched by thousands who had been alerted to it by a radio announcement the night before.

It would be rash to nominate Sorour as the most obsessive woman flyer in the ATA, since obsession was practically a prerequisite for joining. Still, she was a contender. Already an instructor by the age of twenty, she competed fiercely for 'types', which meant jockeying to be the first to fly a new design of aircraft when it came onto the books in the Operations Room at Hamble. After the war she would be the first woman in Britain to fly faster than 600 mph, to captain an airliner and to admit she wanted to break the sound barrier – an admission that immediately disqualified her in the eyes of the RAF, who alone could have made it happen.

In September 1939, she was lodging with a family called Hirons in a farmhouse outside Oxford – digs chosen by her mother for its proximity to the Whitney aerodrome where Jackie was studying for a commercial licence. When the outbreak of war brought her studies to a halt, Sorour wept with envy as the men with whom she had enrolled at flying school went off to join the RAF. Then she turned her feelings of frustration on herself:

> I despised my body, my breasts, all the things that pronounced me woman and left me behind as solitary and desolate as a discarded mistress . . . I looked malignantly at my breasts, symbols of weakness rooted firmly on my chest, and remembered Mr Hirons' cut-throat razor in the bathroom.

No ATA woman was ever quite so confessional – not even Jackie Cochran, the most outspoken woman pilot of them all.

12

Team Cochran

To understand why a group of young American women crossed the Atlantic to fly Spitfires for the ATA, it helps to know about the last flight of Betty Taylor Wood. Betty was a WASP – a Women's Air Force Service Pilot – posted to the US Army's Camp Davis in the swamps of North Carolina for a 'special assignment' towing targets for trainee anti-aircraft gunners. Originally from California, she was a recent graduate of the WASP training programme set up at Avenger Field near Sweetwater, Texas. The WASPs were the outcome of a titanic struggle between the Pentagon and Jackie Cochran, the aviatrix and cosmetics mogul who had returned from London and the ATA the previous year. Betty was not as well known as Cochran, even at Camp Davis. She was considered shy. She had been married a month.

One clear September afternoon in 1943 she went up for a routine training flight in a Douglas Dauntless A-24, a workhorse of the dangerous but necessary target-towing business. On her final approach she overshot and told the control tower she was going round again. She opened the A-24's throttle but its engine failed to respond. The plane landed hard and too far down the runway. It bounced and turned over, crushing Betty in her cockpit.

Cochran was immediately alerted in Washington. She flew down the following morning. Meanwhile, another WASP who had had problems with exactly the same A-24 walked over to the Camp Davis maintenance hangar and asked for its records. On an earlier flight this pilot had experienced a delay of several seconds between opening the throttle and feeling an increase in power; when the power came she had had to stamp on the right rudder to stop the plane rolling onto its back as result of the sudden surge of anticlockwise torque on the fuselage. She had duly noted 'sticky throttle' on the plane's service record, but when she looked at it again she saw no mention of repairs. It appeared that Betty had died through simple negligence on the part of the mechanics.

She was buried the following afternoon. Before the funeral, Cochran held a private meeting with the hangar staff and left Camp Davis without telling anyone what she had discovered, fearing it would trigger an insurrection. Everyone at the Camp Davis meeting agreed that the A-24 had not exploded. In fact, its fuel tanks had not even ruptured – but in them had been found traces of enough sugar 'to stop an engine in no time at all'.

It is possible, of course, that the sugar story was concocted by maintenance staff anxious to avoid disciplinary action. But Cochran was convinced the aircraft had been sabotaged, and for no better reason than that it was being flown by a woman. She knew at first hand how women pilots were regarded on both sides of the Atlantic, and on the American side sabotage seemed all too plausible. Indeed, the US Army Air Corps in the middle years of the war was tainted by an institutionalised and potentially murderous misogyny that did not exist in the ATA and was subordinated in the RAF – if it existed there – to the overwhelmingly urgent demands of war.

It was the air war in Britain that gave Cochran the opportunity to show what American women were made of before she was allowed to demonstrate it at home. But even after that, at the time of Betty Taylor Wood's death, she was under no illusion that any of her work would eradicate a deep conviction among American military flyers that they were a brotherhood, and sisters be damned. She knew that some of the men who resented the WASPs most bitterly were those who had to work with them in the US Army Air Corps and felt belittled by the experience. There had been other similar incidents of sabotage: loose throttle quadrants that had started coming away in WASPs' hands at Sweetwater; severed rudder cables that nearly killed a woman pilot of a B-13.

And there had been Cochran's own experience in the cockpit of a Lockheed Hudson in Newfoundland two years earlier.

Rich and successful beyond her wildest dreams, Jackie Cochran was, by 1941, accustomed to being taken seriously. Yet when the war came she felt something was missing. She had yet to find a role that used her undoubted talents or adequately reflected her accomplishments as champion air racer, entrepreneur, industrialist's wife and all-purpose rags to riches inspiration. For all her clout, the war had so far proved a frustratingly male and European affair.

Then she was invited to the White House. The occasion was the presentation of a medal to the designers of a high-altitude oxygen mask. Afterwards, at lunch, the conversation turned to the urgent need for pilots for transatlantic ferrying. Someone – probably the US Army Air Corps' General 'Hap' Arnold – suggested that Jackie fly a bomber to Britain to boost recruitment. It is not too uncharitable to suggest that visions of headlines swam before her eyes. Immediately she cabled Lord Beaverbrook in London. She and her husband had known him socially before the war, dining occasionally at his London home with Churchill and Viscount Castlerosse (who went on to write the screenplay for *They Flew Alone* in memory of Amy Johnson, and who, Cochran wrote in her memoir, 'usually had his 300-lb body encased in an evening suit of coloured velvet with velvet shoes to match').

Beaverbrook, then Minister of Aircraft Production, gave his approval. He asked the British Embassy in Washington to issue the necessary clearances and help this formidable friend of aviation find a bomber. There were none handy; none, at any rate, with an empty captain's seat and a co-pilot willing to be flown across the Atlantic by a woman with fancy friends but no experience on two or more engines. In the end Floyd Odlum had to rent a Lockheed Lodestar for his wife to practise in over Long Island.

She proceeded to Boston, where a friend at Northeast Airlines put her through the tests used to select pilots for their Boston to Iceland route. Finally she headed to Montreal, where Atlantic Ferry Command tried everything to ground her.

'You think you're pretty hot, don't you?', a Captain Cipher said before Cochran's first official flight test in a four-engined plane. This was an understatement, and she did not deny it. Unable to fail her at first, Cipher wore her out with emergency stops while taxiing, and then recommended vetoing the transatlantic flight on the grounds that Cochran's right arm had become sore from heaving on the handbrake. She claimed she had been made to perform no fewer than sixty emergency stops and swore she would make Captain Cipher and his Ferry Command cronies sorry they had ever heard her name.

The truth was they were already sorry. More than that, the other Atlantic ferry pilots based in Montreal were incensed that a woman would volunteer to do for free something that earned them danger money and a certain amount of swagger. They called a meeting and threatened to strike. They called the *Boston Herald* in the hope of embarrassing her; the Germans would shoot her down to make an example of her, they said. They even called the US State Department to try to prevent her being allowed into a war zone – but they had no real idea who they were dealing with.

'In a contest of power and friends, I knew I could win,' Cochran boasted. Sure enough, her visa arrived on time at the US Consulate in Montreal and the Atfero boys appeared to give in. One of them was cleared to act as her co-pilot on the condition that he take the controls for take-off and landing. Cochran wasn't pleased, but she knew when to compromise.

As it turned out, compromise wasn't enough. On the morning of her planned departure from Montreal, her Hudson's antifreeze tank was drained and its oxygen supply was hooked up the wrong way round. In case she thought to check it while still on the ground, which she did, a socket wrench designed exclusively for turning on the oxygen once airborne went missing from the cockpit. Cochran checked that too, and bought another one. At Gander, her first refuelling stop, the wrench disappeared again. She bought a third. The cockpit window was broken when her back was turned. She fixed it with duct tape.

'I wanted to scream, as only I knew how,' she said. But instead she flew for twelve hours at 135 mph, peering through the Perspex into the short northern night, with the inky Atlantic below her and the Aurora Borealis above and to her left, to the west coast of Scotland. It was a stunt, a first, a point scored for women and an act of homage to Lindbergh and her lost friend Amelia Earhart all at the same time.

After landing at Prestwick, Cochran travelled down to London to call on Lord Beaverbrook and thank him for his help (she also bartered two Florida oranges for a framed cartoon of the great man as the Pied Piper of Hamelin). At his suggestion she then visited Pauline Gower at White Waltham to find out how she had finagled women into military aircraft. She then returned to New York in the bomb-bay of a B-24 Liberator, arriving so frazzled that she instructed the maid at the Cochran-Odlum residence on East End Avenue that she was not to be woken before noon, even for the White House.

Roosevelt phoned at nine the next morning. Pearl Harbor was still half a year in the future, and the President, summering at his Hyde Park estate in upstate New York, was preoccupied with finding ways to help Britain while remaining neutral. He asked Cochran to join him, his wife and Princess Martha of Norway for lunch. With help from police outriders she covered the seventy miles up the east bank of the Hudson just in time. After the meal she was debriefed privately by the President for two hours. He wanted an American's unvarnished view of the country whose Prime Minister was so eloquently – and desperately – seeking his assistance. Oddly, one of the things she remembered explaining to him with great confidence was that England could not afford to plough up all her pastureland for wheat and potatoes. (Her brother-in-law was 'one of the great agriculturists in England ... and had just

Joan Hughes, the youngest woman in the ATA, never married in case it meant putting a husband before flying.

Jackie Sorour, who wrote that flying a Spitfire for the first time 'seemed the most natural thing in the world...as though my entire life had led to this moment'.

Freydis Leaf, who flew every class of aircraft except four-engined bombers with the ATA.

For Mary de Bunsen, seen here in a Mosquito, flying was an escape from 'the ghastly fate of the daughter-in-waiting'. She was lame from polio, with poor eye-sight and a hole in her heart.

The elite women pilots cleared to fly on four-engines liked to remind sceptical men that the aircraft were designed to carry them, not vice versa. Here Joan Hughes is dwarfed by a Short Stirling.

Maureen Dunlop, from Argentina, preferred the company of animals to people and shot to fame as *Picture Post*'s cover girl in September 1944.

Ann Wood, airborne at sunset. She also flew under the Severn Railway Bridge, twice.

Above Ann Wood (seated) with her fellow flying pupils in Maine before Pearl Harbor. She craved the company of 'honest to goodness' American men when in London.

Left Waiting to be cleared for take-off in a Spitfire.

The ATA's Ansons flew ten million miles with no loss of life through mechanical failure; their boxy cabins accommodated card games, impromptu concerts and, on one occasion, a goat.

Ann Blackwell in a Typhoon.

The 'greatest woman pilot in history' is how Jackie Cochran wanted to be remembered. The British tried to put her in her place, and failed.

(*left to right*) Helen Harrison, Ann Wood and Suzanne Ford, the 'flying socialite', in Montreal for flight tests before sailing to Liverpool.

Pauline Gower fought hard for women to be allowed to fly in trousers. In this photocall at White Waltham to mark the arrival of the first American pilots in 1942, only Audrey Sale-Barker (*2nd from right*) wears a skirt. The others are (*left to right*) Virginia Farr, Louise Schuurman, Helen Richey, Gower, Zita Irwin, Pamela Gollan, Diane Williams and Jackie Cochran.

Jackie Cochran was an orphan and millionairess from Florida by way of Manhattan. Pauline Gower was the daughter of a Tory MP. Flying was all they had in common.

King George VI and Queen Elizabeth (later the Queen Mother) visited White Waltham in 1941.

Eleanor Roosevelt visited White Waltham in a downpour in October 1942. After this parade the pilots gorged themselves on American food in a nearby hangar.

made these things plain to me in terms of overall economy'.)

Cochran took the opportunity to bend Roosevelt's ear on the subject of women pilots. Fired up by the sight of Pauline Gower's heroines in blue and gold, she proposed an American equivalent: bigger, better and answering to Jackie. The President and First Lady endorsed the plan. But his generals emphatically did not and it was not enough of a priority for Roosevelt to force the issue. Cochran's consolation prize was that she would be to be allowed to start recruiting women pilots for the Brits.

Cochran never flew a Spitfire during the war, but without her none of her protégées would have flown one either. To this extent, she and Gower were equivalents. They were both busybodies and enablers, tireless opportunists and fervent believers in women. On this level of generality, they were so alike that their coming together at White Waltham, and then at the cinema on Leicester Square, might look like fate. But they were not alike. As people, they could hardly have been more different.

The opening line of Cochran's story, wherever she told it, was: 'I am a refugee from Sawdust Road.' By that she meant the back roads along Route 231 that ate into the logging country of northern Florida, sprouting camps that paid able-bodied men a dollar a day to turn pine trees into planks. She also meant the wrong side of the tracks anywhere. It was certainly a long way from Gower's Tunbridge Wells. She was an orphan. Eventually she hired a private detective to trace her natural parents, but she handed his report unread to her husband, who never read it either. So neither of them knew where or to whom she was born, or when.

This singular life started sometime between 1906 and 1910. She would tell rapt audiences that she wore flour sacks and no shoes as a child, running wild by day and sleeping on the floor of the couple who adopted her. She referred to herself as 'a real harum-scarum ragamuffin'. Nastier types called her 'white trash', but her whole existence was geared to confounding them. She had no formal schooling. Instead, she started twelve-hour shifts at a Pensacola sawmill aged eight – or thereabouts – graduating to a hair salon in Montgomery, Alabama, where she chose a new name more or less at random from the phone book and became much requested for her Nestlé perms.

Though obsessed with beauty, Cochran was not regarded as beautiful (Dorothy Furey said she had 'a face like a dog'). She did have beautiful skin, which one friend described as like 'the loveliest whipped cream'. She also had an unshakeable faith in the power of cosmetics and used them almost as heavily as she promoted them.

When she tired of Montgomery she took her perming skills to Philadelphia, and added to them, learning the Marcel wave technique. Eventually she reached Manhattan, hairdressing capital of the world, where Charles of the Ritz blew his chance of hiring her by insisting that she cut off most of her own hair. But Antoine of Sax Fifth Avenue accepted her terms.

During the winter hairdressing seasons Cochran would travel with Antoine to Miami, where he had a salon on the beach. And it was in Miami, as 'the much-needed extra woman' at a dinner party hosted by Stanton Griffis, a former US ambassador to Spain, that she met Floyd Odlum. He was a pale, freckled, sandy-haired son of a Methodist preacher who had studied hard for his law degree and anticipated the Crash. That enabled him to buy up near worthless trust funds, whose holdings, once American capitalism had dusted itself down, turned out to be anything but worthless. He acquired major stakes in RKO pictures, Hilton Hotels and Consolidated Aircraft, and as the war progressed he invested heavily in uranium. He acquired a nickname in lower Manhattan, 'Fifty Percent', which was the margin he liked to insist upon before reselling a business. That evening in Miami he was tired of small talk, and when he heard that one of the women present actually worked for a living he asked Griffis to be seated next to her. Jackie Cochran had no idea who he was, but she liked his style.

The story they were to agree on states that that very night she saw in him her destiny, and he said that if she really wanted to start her own cosmetics business she would have to learn to fly in order to keep track of it as it expanded. They reconvened for dinner in New York on the day Cochran had chosen as her birthday. Floyd was charmed and fascinated. They married four years later. Before that she followed his advice and took up flying. She went solo on her third day of lessons and headed for Canada on her first flight beyond the confines of Long Island's Roosevelt Field.

'They became a most unusual duet,' a mutual friend said later. 'He was enthralled with her accomplishments and wanted to keep her going.' Not that this was hard – he owned several large aircraft factories.

Once married, Jackie and Floyd combined the two ranches they had each bought separately in Southern California's blistering Coachella Valley, and held court there to anyone who could withstand the heat and Jackie's hyperactivity. They siphoned water from the Colorado River to create a defiant twentieth-century Eden, heady with citrus and exotic blooms. One regular visitor was Amelia Earhart, who relaxed beside the Cochran-Odlum swimming pool before her final flight in 1937. Another was Howard Hughes, whom Odlum remembered as permanently short of cash.

In the tight and sometimes fetid circles that adjudicate on the competing claims of twentieth-century aviators, there is an enduring fashion for rubbishing Jackie Cochran. She was gauche, it is said. She was brash. She fetishised beauty and elegance but lacked either. She browbeat her critics, overwhelmed her admirers, appalled the British, invented large chunks of her autobiography, sponged off her sugar daddy and could only ever see the big picture if she was in the middle of it.

Some of this is true, but it misses the point that the core of the Cochran legend – that of a penniless orphan with the name chosen from a phone book, who married a millionaire, took a bomber and a group of women pilots to wartime Britain, founded the WASP and after the war broke the sound barrier – is undisputed and remarkable by anyone's standards. It is also easy to forget that Cochran would have been unlikely to achieve anything without the sort of self-belief from which timider souls tend to recoil. She was, apart from anything else, a thrill-seeker. 'To live without risk would have been tantamount to death,' she said, and this helps explain her manic enthusiasm for air racing.

When Cochran followed Amy Johnson into the clouds above Mildenhall in 1934, she was hoping to win the inaugural air race from England to Australia. But she was in a death trap called a Gee Bee, made by the Granville Brothers of Springfield, Massachusetts. Not only did the Gee Bee stall at the slightest excuse, the secondary fuel tank switch on Cochran's aircraft had been connected upside down. She and her co-pilot were about to bale out over the snowbound Carpathians when she realised 'off' meant 'on'.

After her marriage, instead of settling down she spent her summers screaming across the American heartland in sleek silver prototypes in pursuit of the Bendix Trophy for the fastest flight from Long Beach to Cleveland. She eventually won it in 1938 against an otherwise all-male field. When the world went off to war, it was no surprise that she wanted to join in. When her own best contacts in Washington had declined her offers, and when Air Marshal Arthur T. Harris of the RAF said that actually he could use some of her pilots, it was no surprise that she practically mugged him.

In the summer of 1941, Harris was based in Washington as head of the RAF delegation. Soon after Cochran's luncheon with Roosevelt on her return from England in June, Harris, too, was summoned to see the President, this time at the White House. Roosevelt asked what the RAF and British aviation in general needed most urgently, and Harris mentioned ferry pilots. 'My request was forlorn,' he wrote.

I knew that the bottom of the barrel had already been scraped. The President said that he would instruct General 'Hap'

Arnold, and the latter rang me up next day to say that he could not raise a single spare pilot but that he was sending 'the only person who could help' round immediately. He added somewhat cryptically, 'and don't laugh'. Within a few minutes into my office erupted a blonde bombshell.

She introduced herself as Jackie Cochran and offered 'maybe six' women pilots at once – 'but I could soon make it 60, and later maybe 600'.

Cochran was trying to be helpful to Britain, but most of all she was out to confound the sceptics at home: 'I went to England to prove to General Arnold and others in Washington, DC, that American women pilots were just as capable as English women pilots,' she said. 'Twenty-five young American women and I did it to prove a large point to the folks back home.'

The announcement that Miss Cochran (she was Mrs Odlum only in private life) would be recruiting women for the ATA was made at a dinner she hosted at the St Regis Hotel in New York on 23 January 1942. The details had been ironed out at the White House the week before with Eleanor Roosevelt, ever the friend of women flyers, and a Captain Norman Edgar of the ATA. Cochran received him at her apartment before the dinner for cocktails and for photographs – which were released to the press that day and showed him looking variously condescending and bemused. In one of them either Cochran or the photographer persuaded Captain Edgar to join her at the globe in her trophy room and stare down at it, lit from below, as if planning to take over the world. Edgar earned his supper at the St Regis, however, thrilling his female audience with the news that some of the aircraft the Americans would be flying would have guns loaded and ready to fire; and predicting that if 'Jerry' sprang a surprise attack on any of them, they'd shoot back 'just as fast as a man'.

Cochran was desperate to retain sole charge of the project. Her husband's friend and publicist, Harry Bruno, who was also a neighbour of theirs in California, released a statement the same day outlining the recruitment plan and asking that applications for service in 'the Cochran unit' be sent to her newly established headquarters in Rockefeller Plaza. In fact, 125 women whom she considered prime candidates on the strength of flying records lodged with the Civil Aeronautics Administration in Washington had already received telegrams before the next day's papers hit the streets. But Cochran would soon find that she had no monopoly on initiative.

Five months earlier, the spectacular Dorothy Furey had been killing time and hoping for stray joyride passengers at the airport outside New Orleans where she had learnt to fly. She was surprised to see two uniformed British officers walk in out of the sun. They had been observing US war games on the beaches of the Gulf of Mexico, but Furey was more interested in the rumour they passed on that a British air organisation might soon be flight-testing women in Montreal. Furey instantly ingratiated herself with these unlikely messengers. 'I said, "Well, what are your plans?" And they said, "We have to go to Washington, and we have to be there about a week, and then we're going over to Montreal." So I said, "How about if I pick you up in Washington?"'

The two men accepted this remarkable offer. That gave Furey about four days to quit her job, pack up her New Orleans life and head north for the nation's capital in a nearly-new Studebaker she had picked up for interest-only payments of just $25 a month, and of which she was immensely proud. She kept her rendezvous with her new British friends and drove them to Montreal. There she became, by several months, the first American woman to be cleared to ferry British warplanes, and the only one to do so before Pearl Harbor.

In a sense this was only fair. Though a regular truant from high school, Furey had always been ahead of the game: she read *Mein Kampf* at seventeen, and when Hitler invaded the Rhineland the following year she wrote an editorial in the *Louisiana Women's*

Weekly forecasting war. But her speed off the mark infuriated Cochran.

'She [Cochran] was livid with the way I went to Montreal without her stamp of approval,' Furey recalled shortly before her death sixty-five years later. Then she told a story about how Jackie Cochran had faked an application form from Furey in her anxiety to show history that every last one of her twenty-five pilots was really 'hers':

> It had all my statistics, the number of hours I had, everything ... She never filed it. She was afraid to do that, but one of the girls who worked with her told me about it. [Cochran] wanted to make out that she had sent me the job, and many, many years later when we were both living in the same luxury apartment building in New York City I thought maybe I'd ask her and her husband up for a drink. She said no, she didn't feel well.

Furey never liked Cochran. She felt she owed her nothing and she disowned her as soon as she arrived in Britain. But others owed Cochran the defining years of their lives, and never forgot it.

Ann Wood was one. Cochran's telegram found her at home in Waldeboro, Maine, where she was living with her widowed mother while teaching cadets to fly in Piper Cub seaplanes as part of a government pilot training scheme. She had wanted to go to war as a reporter – and had written to all the names she admired in the *New York Times* to find out how to go about it. They had not been particularly helpful, and flying seemed a perfectly suitable alternative. Ann telephoned New York immediately and was summoned to the Cochran-Odlum apartment at River House. A Northeast Airlines Dakota from Portland and a taxi from La Guardia put her outside Cochran's front door feeling, unusually for Wood, 'a little timid'.

Inside, like Captain Edgar before her, she was invited to admire the trophy room. It had a giant inlaid marble compass on the floor and a glass screen shielding a wall of memorabilia that included a cigarette case encrusted with rubies and emeralds (a gift from Floyd). The emeralds formed Jackie's winning route across America in the Bendix Trophy race; the rubies were her refuelling stops.

The whole place was humming. Odlum and Cochran each had separate staffs and tended to work from home. Wood struck Cochran as sufficiently presentable – each of her girls would have to serve as ambassadors as well as pilots – but insufficiently experienced in the air. Cochran said she'd be in touch. But it would only take a few candidates to fail the flight test in Montreal for Wood's name to get to the top of Cochran's list. When in May it did, she bade farewell to her mother and left for Canada: 'My mother was very pleased that I'd managed to get going, that I was accepted and that I was going to do a useful job,' Wood later reflected; 'she was very keen about the war. She believed in it. She hated Hitler.'

Roberta Sandoz's telegram had to be redirected in order to reach her. It was sent to the address she gave as home – Evans, a place twenty miles from the Canadian border in north-eastern Washington state. Evans was the last town on the Columbia River before the river slowed and broadened to fill its own valley along 120 miles of its length, held back by the Grand Coulee Dam. On reaching Evans, the telegram had to go upriver to a giant plant run by the Spokane-Portland Cement Company, just south of the border, where Roberta Sandoz's Swiss stepfather was chief engineer. His status meant that she was not raised in Cochran-style destitution, but she still rode to school on a horse and the camp was still a hard day's drive on unmetalled roads to the nearest sidewalk, in Spokane.

'We lived at a great excavation place where limestone was dug out of the mountain and shipped to Spokane, where it was crushed up,' she told me. 'It wasn't a town. There were three houses – a bunkhouse for the men who worked there, a cookhouse to feed them, our house and that was it.' That was the isolation from which Roberta's first real escape came, aged ten, in a barnstormer's aeroplane above a little town called Marcus that has since been drowned by the Grand Coulee Dam. Before then she had paid annual visits to Spokane with her family to buy new shoes, but this was different: 'It changes your perspective of the world, once you see it from the air. This was the sensation that interested me: a wonderful feeling of expansion.'

Sandoz left the camp to go to college – having dashed her mother's hopes of making 'a little Lady' out of her – and set her heart on seeing the world. Her first job was as a San Francisco social worker, near Chinatown on Telegraph Hill. 'Life began for me in San Francisco,' she said. She led gymnastics classes for immigrant children, and broke up their fights, and in her spare time made a nuisance of herself among the window dressers of the Gump department store on Post Street, pestering them with questions about flower preserving and English country life. She also took an evening class in aeronautics and was rewarded for her diligence by being recommended for the cut-price Civilian Pilot Training Programme.

Talking in her room in a bustling high-rise retirement community in Oregon, Sandoz sounded a little dreamy. She had ventured to suggest on the telephone that she still had all her marbles, and she had a bucketful: a steel-trap mind that might have been inclined to rage against the dying of the light but for a rather humbling wisdom. Recalling her pilot training she laughed and rubbed her hands involuntarily. 'Oh!' she said, as if about to sing:

> It was so exciting learning to fly. I get goosebumps just re-membering. I had one forced landing while I was learning. My own darn fault. Ran out of gasoline and landed in a cow pasture. And the operator, the man who owned the airplane, was so delighted that I hadn't wrecked it that he gave me five free hours. Do you know how much that represented? That was better than a diamond bracelet. Five hours. It was an overwhelming gift to me. I quit my social worker job and I worked for that operator, took letters, swept the office, gassed the aeroplanes, anything.

That gift took her to Belmont, a grass airfield halfway to San Jose. When she completed her training she went looking for any paid employment that would keep her in the air. She found a job in Corcoran in the Great Central Valley, where a farmer took her on to crop-dust and scare off pests in an old Porterfield Tandem that she had had to buy herself. It was in Corcoran – best known today for its exceptionally brutal penitentiary – that the Cochran telegram caught up with her.

'Those were the days when you received a telegram, you sat down before you opened it,' Sandoz recalled. 'Telegrams were a couple of lines, usually bad news. Well, in Cochran style this was a page and a half. The stuff that really thrilled was the word "secret" in there: "Do not contact the press." This was undercover stuff.'

In fact Sandoz was one step ahead of Cochran. She had already made enquiries as to how she might use her flying skills in the war effort. As a child she had spent summers in British Columbia and grown fond of what she thought of as British orderliness and accents: 'I suddenly began wanting to go and help them win their war. I made myself ridiculous writing to the Royal Air Force and the Royal Canadian Air Force and the British Air Ministry, and got no useful response until someone in Canada said get in touch with Jacqueline Cochran.'

She replied at once to the telegram and the madly mobile Cochran flew to the nearest respectable airport in Fresno, California, to meet her. Ann Wood, no stranger to East Coast glitz, had found herself swept along by Cochran's can-do, must-do dynamism; but Roberta Sandoz was less worldly and more inclined to doubt herself. Knowing something of Cochran's reputation, she had made an effort with her clothes and hair and even plastered on a layer of unfamiliar make-up. The result: 'I think I impressed her as the wrong type of person – a floozy'. Cochran misread the bundle of nerves and curiosity in front of her and lectured her sternly on the cold and hunger that came with the work she had in mind. She promised nothing, and

Roberta Sandoz went back to inspecting crops in her Porterfield Tandem.

Luckily for her, Harry Smith, the check pilot whom Pop d'Erlanger had assigned to test the women Cochran was sending up to Montreal, was finding a lot of would-be recruits too bumptious for his taste. They had the hours – or they would never have made it onto Cochran's list – but he just wasn't passing them. Like the women climbing in and out of his big radial-engined Harvard AT6 trainer at Montreal's Dorval airport, Harry Smith was American. But this did not mean any special favours. On the contrary, he made no secret of his view that a woman's place was in the kitchen. If you were smart, you understood that arguing with him was likely to be construed as evidence of inability to fly. 'He was not a monster,' Bobby recalled. 'He just wasn't going to be pushed around by a lot of pushy women.'

Cochran had promised Sandoz nothing, but neither had she forgotten her. The invitation to meet Harry Smith came through in the spring of 1942, and with it a one-way train ticket for the Santa Fe Chief to New York, from where onward transport would be arranged to Montreal. By this time America had entered the war and Sandoz had become engaged to a navy cadet bound for the Pacific. She drove home with what possessions she could fit into his car, and told her parents she would write often and be careful. Then she drove back to California to catch her train.

Dorothy Furey cooled her heels in Montreal for the whole autumn of 1941. She had beaten all of Cochran's girls out there, but then had to wait for them before embarking for England. There were two consolations: an ex-boyfriend now based at Dorval with the Atlantic Ferry Command had managed to find her a smart apartment in the city, and the grateful British taxpayer was paying for it. Furey spent most of her time in the library, reading up on her new employers. 'When I got to England I knew more British history than the Brits did,' she said proudly in her sunroom in Virginia, looking west towards the Shenandoah Mountains. 'I could tell you every King and Prime Minister from Alfred and the cakes right on up to the present time.' Little did she know then that one British Prime Minister not yet on the list would fall in love with her and in the process risk a career that took the world back to the brink of war at Suez. Meanwhile, she read history books and watched the leaves turn gold along the St Lawrence River, and waited.

In early January, Jackie Cochran set off from New York for England on a BOAC flying boat, travelling via Baltimore, Bermuda and Lisbon. She was determined to be in London before her charges and to meet them in style. Her trip was not a pleasant one, however. She had recently developed a suppurating leg ulcer which needed constant dressing and dousing with sulphur powder.

By February 1942, Cochran's girls had started arriving in Montreal in numbers. Depending on their staggered departure dates for England, which started in the spring, they stayed at the Mount Royal Hotel for weeks or even months. And they partied hard on expenses. There were tales of all-night benders with the Atlantic ferry boys, and of shower curtains filled with water and dropped bomb-like down the hotel stairwell. Not everyone took part. Ann Wood found the whole scene unedifying and went back to Maine to wait for her crossing, while Roberta Sandoz and her new friend Emily Chapin, a fellow recruit from Rye, New York, sensibly took Harry Smith out for a quiet drink and urged him to talk about himself. (He passed them both.)

In fairness to the young lady hooligans at the Mount Royal, they may have wanted to distract themselves from the fact that, unlike Cochran, they would be travelling to England by ship when there was no surer way of tempting fate. Dorothy Furey had been told that the transatlantic convoy before hers had lost six of its ten ships. She would also have known that eleven male pilots had drowned the previous year en route to the ATA when their ship, the SS *Nerissa*, was sunk 200 miles from the English coast. Furey was told not to expect other ships to pick up survivors if her ship, the *Beaver Hill*, was hit, since that was what the U-boats would be waiting for. The ATA recruits were divided into four groups of five and one (the first) of four, so that they could not all be lost to one torpedo as on the *Nerissa*. In Furey's group were Louise Schuurman, a Dutch national also from New Orleans whose father was an honorary consul there; Winnie Pierce, from upstate New York; and Virginia Farr, from West Orange, New Jersey.

The *Beaver Hill* spent the final days of January mustering with the rest of its convoy in bitter cold in the relative safety of the river downstream of Quebec, waiting until Canadian submarine spotters judged it the least bad moment to make a dash through the blockade of the Gulf of St Lawrence. Furey was fatalistic. 'I had no fear,' she said: the ship had carried coal and been converted to a troop carrier,

> so we were all well below the waterline. I figured that if we were going to be hit we weren't going to get out, especially considering we were five girls and the rest were men, and they weren't going to stand back and say 'you go first'. So I just didn't think about it. Besides, I kind of felt nothing was really going to kill me anyway just then.

Ann Wood, likewise, gave little thought to the likelihood of drowning, even though three ships were lost in the Gulf of St Lawrence the week before her departure. She had been briefed on the shipboard routine – lifejackets at all times; no stopping if other ships in the convoy were torpedoed, even to pick up survivors. But she preferred to focus on the far horizon, and the business of pitching in as part of the war effort when she got there.

It was a fine day when at last the *Indochinois*, with twenty-three passengers and a 'cherubic-looking Frenchman' for a captain, was cleared to head towards Quebec. It was delayed again at Trois-Rivières as the previous week's wrecks were hauled out of the shipping lanes downstream. Ann cabled her mother to let her know her ship was still afloat. After watching a group of Flying

Fortresses pass overhead, heading back towards Montreal, she wrote in her diary: 'Perhaps some day it will be my chance to have a crack at one of those crates.'

The *Indochinois* passed the Heights of Abraham in a line of six ships late on 16 May 1942. It was another beautiful evening, and Ann had one final farewell to remember. She had a younger sister attending a convent in Quebec not far from the Château Frontenac, the city's most opulent hotel. The hotel rose like a citadel from the Heights on the north bank of the St Lawrence. Next to it was a lawn with a clear but distant view of anything passing along the great river below. 'My sister was anxious to get to the Frontenac to wave to me as I went by,' Ann said. 'I'm not sure she ever did, but we like to pretend we saw each other. I certainly was there, hoping she was there.'

The crossing to England took nine days. The food was good, plentiful (four meals a day) and French. The atmosphere was convivial, to put it mildly. Five days out, somewhere south of Iceland, a lady passenger celebrated her birthday with a cocktail party that Wood, a dedicated Catholic, considered 'revoltingly wild'. Her cabin mate 'went completely animalistic and was messing about with the captain', Ann wrote in her diary. 'It makes me wonder whether my unawareness is due to a so-called protected life – or am I to find out that twenty-five people out of every hundred are utter fools?'

In the middle of the cocktail party the ship received an order to change course because of submarine activity, though the captain took three hours to find the code book to work out which way he was supposed to turn. Otherwise, the U-boats left the *Indochinois* alone. Indeed, they spared all the ships carrying Cochran's girls.

By the end of the voyage Dorothy Furey had become engaged to one of her fellow passengers – chiefly, she claimed, to keep the others at bay. 'He wasn't handsome,' she said of Lieutenant Richard Bragg, a Canadian and the first of her four husbands, 'but he was sweet and charming and well-educated and of all the men who would queue up to see who would take me to dinner, Rick did it the most times. And I got to liking him.' They were married a month later.

On the *Mosdale* Roberta Sandoz – already engaged – romanced no-one, and neither was she romanced. But she did spend a night playing poker with Emily Chapin under a lifeboat, fearful that they might have to use it as their ship lurched and zigzagged across the ocean without explanation. She found out later that the point of the manoeuvres had been to avoid a convoy, not a U-boat; the Norwegians preferred to sail alone. The *Mosdale* was also carrying Mary Nicholson, of Greensboro, North Carolina, formerly Jackie Cochran's most trusted personal secretary and now her final ATA recruit. The ship was last of the five that brought Cochran's pilots from America. It arrived off Liverpool at dawn on 10 August, to be guided into port through thick fog along an avenue of upended wrecks. A breakfast of oily yellow kippers awaited the young women at the Adelphi Hotel.

After more than a year of planning and an exceptionally good few months for the bar at the Mount Royal Hotel in Montreal, Team Cochran had landed.

13

Over Here

Several months after disembarking at Liverpool – possibly on 27 March 1943, but she was coy about it in her letters home out of respect for the censors – Ann Wood took off from Castle Bromwich in a Spitfire. By this time she had been posted to No. 6 Ferry Pool at Ratcliffe Hall in Leicestershire, a friendly, popular place owned by Sir Lindsay Everard, a brewing magnate and Conservative MP.

No. 6 Pool had been set up expressly to clear the great Castle Bromwich factory of its Spitfires before they could be bombed. Sir Lindsay was passionately air-minded. He had relinquished the use of his private aerodrome together with many of its out-buildings to the ATA for the duration of the war, and Ann was billeted above his eight-car garage in digs originally intended for visiting cricketers. She made good friends at Ratcliffe, and among them was Johnnie Jordan, the wealthy and strong-willed grandson of the Bedfordshire manufacturer of breakfast cereals.

Wood and Jordan would remain friends until their deaths within weeks of each other sixty-three years later, but even after that other ATA veterans were at pains to stress that Johnnie's flying style did not reflect that of his comrades. Most ATA types took their mission of delivering planes intact extremely seriously. Jordan was different. Though skilled as a pilot, he was utterly undisciplined. Having chafed at his grandfather's draconian way of running the family business, he had left the firm. He was later court-martialled by the RAF for 'borrowing' a Swordfish biplane in order to escape from his bomber squadron's base, to which he had been confined for hedge-hopping.

The ATA gave him much greater freedom 'to express himself in the air' – and to lead other pilots astray. He loved the feel of his weight on his shoulder straps and blood rushing to his head so much that he once spent ten minutes inverted in a Spitfire before force-landing it at Edgefield when its engine failed. At Castle Bromwich it was said that Alex Henshaw, the test pilot, liked to hold his aircraft down until it gained enough speed to pull up into a half loop that left him upside down but above the barrage balloons and heading in the opposite direction. Henshaw denied the story, but the more exuberant Ratcliffe pilots liked to emulate what they had heard about him and Jordan surely would not have missed the opportunity. (Wood was not averse to the occasional loop, either. 'I always believed that aerobatics was a good way to familiarise yourself with your aircraft,' she told me, and she once lost all power while upside-down in a Miles Magister. Like Jordan at Edgefield, she told no-one about the inversion and was commended for not losing the plane.)

Jordan was with Ann at Castle Bromwich that spring day in 1943, in another Spitfire; so too was a third pilot whom Wood remembered as Don Spain, although his real name was probably Leslie Swain. They took off in quick succession into a corridor of barrage balloons that dead-ended a mile or two beyond the runway.

Initially Wood followed normal ATA procedure, executing a smart 180-degree turn before climbing out of reach of the balloons. All three Spitfires then turned south towards Bristol, heading, as far as Wood knew, for the ATA's No. 2 Ferry Pool at Whitchurch. 'We didn't have any radio so we couldn't communicate with one another, but before we took off we organised that we would fly in line,' Wood recalled.

I was to be tail-end Charlie and Johnnie was number one and Don was number two, and of course when we get down near to Bristol and we see the Severn Johnnie goes right down on top of the river and you know very well what he's about to do, and of course it happened to be low tide and there was lots of space. When I tried it [again] on my own a while later it happened to be high tide, and that just shows what kind of head I didn't use.

The Severn Railway Bridge, with its twenty-one arched spans of girders, each a little over seventy feet wide and supported by stone pillars and giant lengths of iron pipe, was a deeply functional piece of engineering. After two barges collided with it and exploded in 1960 it was torn down, but until then its plodding, unambitious structure made it seem closer to the water than it really was. The sight of three Spitfires diving as if to strafe it, then choosing their span and skimming under it at 300 mph, would have been thrilling enough, especially if seen from above by the good people on the 9.15 from Cardiff to Paddington. But most would have found it hard to believe that the third aircraft was being flown by a rangy New England society gal and graduate of D'Youville College who was also a qualified flying instructor. And their disbelief would have turned to alarm had they seen Ann's second, solo run. Between low and high tide the water level under the bridge rose by more than 30 feet – the second-largest differential in the world after Canada's Bay of Fundy. And here was the same young woman, strapped legally and officially into one of His Majesty's deadliest warplanes, barrelling down once more towards the surface of the River Severn so that she could pull off on her own the stunt that she had hitherto performed only as tail-end Charlie to two ungovernable fly boys who'd thought it funny to lead her into it without telling her; and finding, too late, in a moment of quiet terror, that she had 30 foot less clearance than the first time around. Truly she would have a line to shoot if she ever made it back to Ratcliffe alive.

In later years, when Jordan told his part of the story, he would say it transpired further south under the Clifton Suspension

Bridge. He probably did fly under this bridge, and possibly more than once: it was clearly visible from the Whitchurch aerodrome, leaping the Avon Gorge as impudently as ever between Brunel's stubby white towers. It was a magnet for daredevils throughout the war and after, until Flight Lieutenant John Crossley of the RAF's 501 Squadron made the last confirmed fly-through one February morning in 1957, hurtling under the span at 450 mph in a Vampire jet and slamming into Leigh Woods on the south side of the gorge when he failed to get his nose up in time. The aircraft burned for two hours; afterwards only a smouldering clearing in the steeply sloping trees remained. But the Avon gorge is so deep that the level of the tide would have made little difference to Ann Wood's clearance on her second run. And in any case, when shown a photograph of the Clifton bridge in her retirement she said confidently, 'that's not my bridge'.

It was only after her death that I learned from Chris Witts, author of *Disasters on the Severn*, that RAF Spitfire pilots made such a habit of buzzing the railway bridge that a policeman had to be stationed on the front lawn of the Severn Hotel on the Lydney side to take down their call signs. Whichever bridge was 'hers', when asked why she went under it a second time, Ann replied that it was because the first had been 'grand fun'.

Ann Wood had her disagreements with the English, with their ways of eating and relating to each other and to Americans, and with their approach to fighting wars. 'I honestly believe,' she wrote in her diary in September 1942, 'that if there is an inconvenient or difficult way of doing something, the English will think of it.' But on the whole she kept such views to herself and adapted easily to life on the edge of war.

Dorothy Bragg (née Furey) found the whole process harder. She was so incensed at having to sit through a talk on her arrival in London on how she would be expected to behave that she nearly turned straight round and sailed for home. And when she and the other American women from the *Beaver Hill* finally reached the nerve centre of the ATA at White Waltham, they had to run a gauntlet of chilly curiosity from the men there.

Besides the three one-armed First World War veterans and 'Doc' Barbour, the medic who liked people to strip for their physicals, there was First Officer Stefan Karpeles Schenker, an exiled Austrian businessman who had been interned on the Isle of Man at the start of the war until his bona fides could be established; First Officer Gwynn Johns, a world champion parachutist; Flight Captain Jim Mollison, the moody and reckless former husband of Amy Johnson; and Chief Supply Officer Captain F. Ellam, who had written in all seriousness to the Ministry of Aircraft Production seeking funds for two elephants being sold off by a circus in Horley. (The idea was to use them to pull aircraft stuck in mud. A budget was agreed and plans were made to enrol the circus mahout as a uniformed member of the ATA, but the purchase was cancelled at the last minute because of fears that the elephants might panic during an air raid.)

The place was 'an utter madhouse', Wood decided later. In fact it was a model of flexible management and improvisational genius, even if it sometimes felt like a boarding school for grown men. Before wondering about elephants – but after being bombed with no warning or defences in the first summer of the war – the ferry pool commanders had authorised the construction of a 'tank'. It consisted of a truck chassis, armour-plating of welded scrap iron and the gun turret from a decommissioned Avro Anson.

White Waltham was a hive of functional and usually amiable eccentrics, but they could be intimidating. Their preconception of American womanhood had been formed almost entirely by Hollywood and it was 'all blonde and glamour, all singy and dancy', according to Ops Officer Alison King. When the time came to see whether the real thing measured up, the men did little to disguise their curiosity.

Virginia Farr from New Jersey said she would never forget her arrival at the airfield: 'the walk past the windows filled with silent male faces, all dropping as they saw the travel-stained girls – you could feel their thoughts,' she said; 'why, one's fat, one's definitely strapping – no glamour, no glamour anywhere'. In a half-hearted show of solidarity, King noted that 'actually, they were all good-looking girls, each in her own way, but when you expect Hollywood and you get instead ordinary flesh and blood. Well!'.

If ever the new arrivals needed a mother hen, it was now, and Jackie Cochran had assigned herself the role. She had rented a Chelsea apartment in which to entertain high-ranking members of General Eisenhower's staff, but also to show her recruits that she cared about their welfare. She summoned each of them to dinner on their first two days' leave – six weeks into their contracts – even if by that time they had settled in and wanted nothing more to do with her. For Dorothy Bragg it would have been comic had it not also been embarrassing: Cochran, after all, had faked a job application on her behalf. But Ann Wood was always loyal to Jackie and was repaid with frequent invitations which were worth accepting if only because they meant unrationed food and honest-to-goodness American company.

'Bobby' Sandoz, likewise, was appreciative. Her crossing on the *Mosdale* had been nervewracking; her first English billet, with a hard-pressed couple in Luton, depressing. And then she received the news that her fiancé, her college sweetheart of three years, had been listed as missing in action in the Pacific. When Cochran opened the door to her at her Chelsea apartment, Sandoz dissolved in tears: 'Jackie said something like "What the hell is the matter with you",' Sandoz recalled, 'and I lost it. I just lost it.'

Cochran took her in and cooked her southern fried chicken and told her everything would be all right, and in the end it was. Sandoz was 'scared to death most of the time' by the sheer power of the aircraft she had to fly, but she was skilled enough to tame them. Sometimes the gaucheries of her fellow Americans left her feeling mortified, but she was no killjoy. After her fiancé's 'missing in action' turned out to mean 'killed' she mourned him in the breaks between flying, then let a British officer whom she had met in a pub in Mayfair pursue her all the way to a respectable London altar.

It was Cochran herself who never found her feet in England. She always maintained that she left on her own terms to lead her own all-American legion of uniformed airwomen. But even her staunchest supporters admit the fuller story of her time in London is one of a self-taught bull in a china shop of over-educated mandarins. According to Sandoz, she was let down by her 'lack of background'. She was also let down by Brits who took thin-lipped delight in humiliating her.

Cochran was always on edge in London. Ann Wood realised this on her very first visit to White Waltham. She was overdue there herself: the ATA had failed to send anyone to Liverpool to meet the *Indochinois*, which Wood had taken as a signal that she was free to plan her own itinerary through the great blacked-out capital of free Europe about which she had read so much. Her fellow recruits, at Helen Harrison's suggestion, checked into the Savoy. Wood opted for the Grosvenor House, and then went sight-seeing. She took in Big Ben and a bombsite or two before making her own way to the aerodrome, where she found 'La Cochran trés gaie in uniform', but agitated. Cochran was, firstly, 'greatly distressed that we were not met at Liverpool,' Wood wrote in her diary; 'then embarrassed on my behalf because I wasn't with the other gals and she thought I was in London sobering up. But as I have quickly gathered she is conversationally and mentally in a dither all of the time.'

Cochran had been in even more of a dither with the first group's arrival, over the vexed question of Dr Barbour's nude physicals. None of the British women had objected to stripping for him. But Cochran did, so vehemently that Barbour was forced to back down. She won that fight, but lost any hope of earning the respect of the ATA rank and file by failing to ferry any aircraft herself. She awarded herself the rank of flight captain and the right to wear the ATA uniform, but never submitted herself to a flight test even with the indulgent Captain MacMillan. Dorothy Bragg believed this was because she couldn't navigate from a map and was afraid of failing or flying into a stray hill. Wood insisted that 'Jackie never intended to fly in the ATA. Her mission, strictly, was to convince the American generals that women could be used.' But if so, she went about that mission in a way few could fathom. She would disappear to London for days at a time, then reappear at White Waltham unannounced to offer her unsolicited Pensacola dime's worth of advice on how to run an organisation that thought it had been running itself rather well for three particularly stressful years. Wood concluded:

> I think it was too bad that she wasn't able to face up to it with Pauline [Gower] and say, 'Look, this is why I'm here, this is what I'm not going to do. You may not like it, but there it is.' Instead of which she remained silent on what she was up to to the extent that she was suspect. The ATA didn't understand her. They didn't like her. Why did she come? Why did she live so extravagantly? Why did she wear a mink coat?

She was a long way from the Coachella Valley and may have been feeling the cold; but she was also anxious to impress people at the Air Ministry, whom she visited as often as twice a week in a borrowed Daimler with a full American colonel 'to make sure she behaved herself a little bit', and with Ann Wood sitting next to her in the back seat.

'She always had a tiny dictionary in her pocketbook,' Ann remembered, 'and when she came out would throw it at me and say, "Annie, you went to college, look these words up for me." And I recognised that she couldn't look them up herself because she didn't know the alphabet properly.' They would practise five or six words at a time in the back of the Daimler; words the Air Ministry people had been using that she hadn't understood. 'And if you were with her any time subsequent to that she'd be chucking those words out all the time. She was a very fast learner.'

In July 1942, after six months in London during which US bomber squadrons based in Britain had suffered appalling losses in their daylight raids on Germany, General Arnold of the US Army Air Corps let Cochran know that he thought he might be able to use her women pilots after all. She threw a final, bittersweet dinner party for her charges, then packed her mink coat, returned the Daimler and flew at once to Washington. Thirteen years later 'Bomber' Harris warned in his introduction to Cochran's autobiography that British readers would resent what it revealed about the behaviour of their own authorities, 'who used her services and those of the American women pilots whom she brought over, and omitted to send her even so much as a thank you when she left'. The truth was that at the time, few were sad to see her go.

14

Flygirls in London

This . . . is London. This is Trafalgar Square. The noise that
you hear at the moment is the sound of the air-raid siren. A
searchlight just burst into action, off in the distance, an
immense single beam sweeping the sky above me now.
People are walking along very quietly. We're just at the
entrance of an air-raid shelter here, and I must move the
cable over just a bit, so people can walk in.

Edward R. Murrow, chief reporter for the American Columbia
Broadcasting System, was speaking live to both coasts at
11.30 p.m., London time, on 24 August 1940 in the middle of
the Battle of Britain. During the Phoney War, Murrow had tired
of British inaction and wondered aloud if it was not a mask for
ineptitude or worse. But as the raids began and Londoners started
to show their mettle under attack, Murrow swung behind them.
By New Year's Eve, 1940, in the middle of the Blitz, he was needling his listeners to come and help: 'You will have no dawn raids,
as we shall probably have if the weather is right. You may walk
this night in the light. Your families are not scattered by the winds
of war. You may drive your high-powered car as far as time and
money will permit . . .'.

For some of the Spitfire women, the Blitz had been their first
brush with mortal danger, and the fact that they had survived it
toughened them. Kay Hirsch, who would join the ATA in 1944,

spent the early part of the war working at Allders department store in Croydon, directly under the path of the Junkers squadrons droning up the A23 towards Westminster Bridge. 'One Blockbuster bomb fell at the end of the High Street, down South Croydon end,' she recalled.

> They tried to defuse it. They couldn't, and it went off, and that thing blew out every glass window for a mile ... Most Croydon homes don't have basements, so we reinforced the ceiling in the dining room. We bricked up the window because flying glass was the worst thing, and that's where we slept, in our clothes, every night for three or four months.

Veronica Volkersz and Diana Barnato drove ambulances with the Red Cross. Mary de Bunsen desperately wanted to drive a fire engine. She had to make do with the running boards as an Auxiliary Fire Service Volunteer, but she still found her baptism by bombs exhilarating. Called to a Palmolive perfume factory in Twickenham after a direct hit, she distributed hot chocolate, wearing dungarees and a tin hat, as 'all the perfumes of Arabia wafted up into the smoky air'.

De Bunsen was enthralled by the extraordinariness of war. This brainy onlooker at a dozen coming-out balls, who embraced flying as an escape from the dreadful expectation of a good marriage, embraced the just war as fervently as any soldier. In most of her writing she is whimsical, as if she knew whimsy was what would be expected of an overgrown schoolgirl and did not want to disappoint. But on the role of conflict in history and her life, she switches without warning to righteousness: 'I believe that fighting is a law of nature without which we rot, and I know that, under tyranny, worse things happen than death.'

And pity the softies who didn't understand. 'After the panicky people and most of the rich ones had run away,' she wrote, London life became 'tolerable and then positively inspiring'. It was a city 'purged of parasites and cleared for action', hushed and tense between the sirens and the start of the anti-aircraft guns, 'not with fear and self-pity . . . but with the awareness of danger and the imminence of death, without which none of us are truly alive'.

Parasites! De Bunsen was so thrilled to be shot of them that she invited her mother to visit from the country and see what Battle Station London felt like. Lady de Bunsen happened to choose the night of the worst raid of the war and loved every minute of it. They lunched voraciously at Claridge's the next day to celebrate being alive.

One imagines Ed Murrow would have found the de Bunsens good copy had he encountered them on a Mayfair rooftop admiring the air-bursts and inhaling deeply of the cordite. And one imagines Ann Wood listening to Murrow in Waldeboro, Maine, and picturing herself in his adopted hero city. 'I wanted to be a part of that, however I could be,' she said. It would be a good fit in her mind. She was not unduly modest, and she had a hunch even before the Cochran telegram arrived that a twenty-four-year-old college graduate and flying instructor, unintimidated by men, women or rank, could make herself useful in the defence of freedom. And it was a good fit in reality. Perhaps more than any of the other woman pilots, Wood squeezed wartime London for all the education and excitement it could offer. In the process, she came to see Murrow's assessment of the place as so much propaganda.

For most of 31 May 1942, it rained. In London this at least washed the smog out of the air. Up the A1 at the new ATA training pool in Luton, established after the De Havilland factory at Hatfield had switched from building Moths to Mosquitoes, the weather meant flying was washed out. And for the latest recruits – Americans – that meant ground school; navigation and mechanics with a Captain Sloper, even though it was a Sunday. Afterwards, most of them trudged or bicycled back to their billets. Thanks to double summertime the night was young, even if the weather was sodden. The RAF had sent more than a thousand bombers to Cologne the night before and reprisal raids were expected over London. Undaunted, Wood took the 7.15 p.m. to St Pancras under a balloon barrage that ringed the city at cloud height. She shared a compartment with a snooty and facetious Englishman (a fellow pilot), had a quiet supper at the Grosvenor House Hotel with friends (the reprisals hit Canterbury, not London), and spent the night at the Red Cross Club on Charles Street. She wrote in her diary before bed: 'Somehow these jaunts to London fill me with utter glee.'

It is not hard to see why. Wood had the heightened awareness of the newcomer and the heightened status of the well-connected American. Never mind that Austin Reed's hadn't yet finished her uniform. That would turn heads and turn them again in due course, as civilians mistook her for Free French and then clocked the gold 'USA' flash on her shoulder and realised she was altogether more exotic. She was already informally connected, through Jackie Cochran and an early upbringing in polite Philadelphia society, to the American military and civilian elite now pouring into West London with a budget for expensive leases and an assignment to 'meet Hitler and beat him on his own ground'. She was also a natural networker. After being greeted by General Eisenhower at the US Embassy's Fourth of July party on Grosvenor Square, she found herself 'infatuated' with Crown Prince Olaf of Norway. So she buttonholed him in the garden before the General could extricate himself from the receiving line and do the same thing.

Wood was a frequent visitor to the Red Cross Club, as much for heady talk about affairs of state as for the milkshakes and Coca-Cola on offer there. The club was run by a Mrs Biddle, wife of the former US ambassador to Poland, with whom Wood became firm friends. She also greatly impressed Mr Biddle, whose new role was as Roosevelt's liaison with the Polish government in exile. Biddle later used Wood to set up a meeting with the radiant Jadwiga Pilsudska, who he hoped might open back-channels to the Warsaw underground. It is not clear whether the meeting changed the course of history, but it is clear that Wood was tickled to be involved. 'Little does Biddle know, that's right up my alley,' she wrote in her diary, firmly underlining it.

Through Cochran, Wood met and befriended Colonel Peter Beasley, Cochran's minder in her dealings with Whitehall. And it was while dining with Beasley and his wife in Mayfair in September 1943 that Wood found herself sitting a few feet from Clark Gable and a girlfriend (whom she didn't recognise). 'Poor guy,' she wrote. 'So stared at that he couldn't take his eyes off his lassie without confronting a hundred other pairs of eyes.' Gable was still mourning the loss of his wife, the actress Carole Lombard, whose plane had crashed into a mountain near Las Vegas the previous year. In London, he was desperately trying to blend in while on a hybrid mission to make a movie about the brave air gunners of the 8th Air Force, while at the same time being one himself.

Unlike most of her fellow diners, Wood was nonchalant about Hollywood royalty; though less so about the real thing. She was fascinated by King Peter of Yugoslavia, with whom she had been invited to dine by a mutual friend: he was 'nervous and excitable' and she was gratified that His Majesty was so ardently pro-American. 'It was a big night for me and I loved every minute,' she wrote afterwards; 'have terrific desire to meet all kinds of people, and love it when you can find what makes them tick.'

For people anxious to meet people, London was, of course, the only place to be. Blacked-out, dirty and haunted by balloons, it was teeming with half the world's exiles. Wood went 'up to town' whenever she had leave.

Pilsudska and Barbara Wojtulanis – two thirds of the ATA's female Polish contingent – opted to live in rented rooms near Paddington and commute to White Waltham to be closer to their exiled compatriots since they were the only source of news from home. 'If it happened that somebody came from Poland and you were there in London and met them, they would give you the personal information,' Pilsudska said. 'If you were not in London, you just didn't get it.'

It was at Polish dinner parties, cobbled together from ration books and carefully hoarded vodka, that Pilsudska and Anna Leska met the brave young officers who became their husbands. Pilsudska's served in the Polish navy on one of three ships to escape from Gdynia before the port's capture. Leska's was an air force navigator who was shot down over Germany and spent two years in Stalag Luft III.

In London, even Margot Duhalde could find a familiar accent – the Chilean ambassador's. 'His name was Manuel Vianchi, and he regarded me as his daughter,' Duhalde recalled with a smile. Days off without her boyfriend, Squadron Leader Gordon Scotter, meant trains to Waterloo and hot baths and long evenings unwinding at the official residence, where His Excellency made an apartment available for Margot's exclusive use. Ambassador Vianchi often hosted all-night fiestas at which guests would be expected to join him on the dancefloor for the conga.

Bombs or no bombs, London was a standing invitation to live for now and forget tomorrow. There were two largely irreconcilable views on whether the Spitfire women should do so. 'People who were sensible would cut out parties and do nothing but try to keep themselves in good shape for flying,' said Rosemary Rees, who had had her fun on the pre-war European party circuit and at Hamble would play the role of prefect (she was second-in-command to Margot Gore). But not everyone was sensible.

Most of the Americans were inclined to work hard and play hard, and to think that the Brits did less of both. Ann Wood stayed up late, but her preference for milk and cookies with Mrs Biddle was exceptional. Winnie Pierce and Suzanne Ford, both New Yorkers, would gravitate to bars at the Dorchester or the Savoy when on leave, and to the Lansdowne at Hyde Park Corner for the music. Even the demure and 'unsophisticated' Bobby Sandoz liked the Lansdowne, because she loved to dance – and so did her fellow ATA flyer, Opal Pearl Anderson – a rough-tongued Chicago lady on a sabbatical from motherhood; she had left a three-year-old son behind in the care of relatives. Sandoz well remembered the time when Opal brought the Lansdowne to a shuddering halt just by walking in and saying hello: 'She saw me – now it was a big area – and she yelled, "Hi Bobby, y'old sonofabitch, how are ya?" and it got silent on the whole place; you know, "Who's this?", because that was very offensive to some people, but that was Opal all over. She had a little boy and she swore a great deal.'

As much as anyone in uniform, the women of the ATA felt the recklessness of youth and deracination, and the knowledge that death could come at any time. Cockpit hangovers were par for the course, not least because drinking was by no means confined to days off. Suzanne Ford (known as a 'flying socialite' before she even left New York) was posted to Prestwick at her own request to be with fellow Americans from the Atlantic Ferry Command. There she offered refrigeration services as well as convivial company, loading beer into suitable aircraft and cooling it unmercifully by spiralling up to 10,000 feet over the Firth of Clyde. She also rode to hounds and, as Ann Wood gathered from talking to her, 'if you hunted you drank pretty well'.

No-one partied quite as well as Helen Harrison, however, and her alcohol consumption vexed and then simply baffled the more serious-minded Wood. The two of them shared a room at the Red Cross Club a few days before their first English Christmas, but kept different hours. 'Was awakened by 8 a.m. to patter of HH just coming in,' Wood wrote. 'Amazing what she can take night after night. Should think she would feel dreadful, but apparently it is worth it to her. She is in spite of all the best-natured soul and when happy far too generous.'

For her own part, Wood sought out men who wouldn't bore her. One worked for the US Army's Signal Corps, carrying sensitive messages between Eisenhower's headquarters on Grosvenor Square and Churchill's on Horseguards Parade. Another flew bombers until he had to bale out of one over Kiel. A third was Jackson Kelly, Pan Am executive and old family acquaintance from Philadelphia. Ann married him in the end, but when she first bumped into him in London he was seeing Cathy Harriman, daughter of Averell Harriman, the American railway magnate and

Roosevelt confidante. Later in the war Harriman was posted to Moscow as US ambassador and took his daughter with him, at which point Kelly started thinking less about girlfriends and more about prospective wives. 'And I guess that's how I came into the picture,' Ann said.

In the meantime there had been a fourth man, not romanced, but pumped for insights in the normal Wood way. He was John Daly, Ed Murrow's colleague and rival at CBS. Ann liked him initially for his name, which she assumed meant he was Irish and Catholic. He turned out to be South African-born and lapsed as far as religion was concerned. She admired his candour and his 'sound, logical mind'. Like Ann, he had arrived in London with his mind full of Murrow soundbites about a city and people on the edge of the abyss, living a half-scavenger, half-troglodyte existence without soap, warmth, money or much sleep or food. But it was a template he found difficult to reconcile with the London he came to know best: a schizoid town that had seen real hardship, but where men still deferred reflexively to officers, and Embassy parties were livelier than ever, and the 400 Club never stopped serving steak and champagne to those who could afford it.

Daly walked into the Red Cross Club one Sunday evening in the summer of 1943 after the day's live broadcast to New York. Wood collared him for a 'nice, meaty chat' and soaked up his broodings about 'social climbing' journalists willing to report the news as fed to them, and the gulf between that and what he saw as reality. She wrote in her diary:

> Perhaps Murrow's plan was to paint a picture so pathetic that American sympathy would be aroused – regardless [of the fact that] it is far from the truth . . . [the] prevalent American idea of this being a beleaguered isle is ridiculous. Daly remarked that [a] happy day would be when having made sufficient money to ensure his family's safety he could be independent and speak the truth.

*　　*　　*

In 1942 the US War Department produced a pamphlet for GIs heading to Europe entitled 'Instructions for American Servicemen in Britain'. It was a brilliant piece of propaganda, aimed not at the enemy but at bridging an Anglo-American cultural chasm that could have wrecked the most important alliance of the war. It was respectful but not deferential towards the Brits. It was informal but informed – or at least it appeared to be – and it quickly became famous. *The Times* even recommended it to British readers for 'the spotlight directness of this revelation of plain common horse sense understanding of evident truths'.

'Don't be misled by the British tendency to be soft-spoken and polite,' the Instructions advised. 'The English language didn't spread across the oceans, and over the mountains and jungles and swamps of the world because these people were panty-waists.'

As it happened, no one was accusing them of being panty-waists, or namby-pambies, as the Brits themselves might have said. But nor did they seem to some of the American newcomers as tough, soft-spoken or polite as advertised. Ann Wood's sense of shock at the grime and dirt of England three years into the war was more or less as forecast in the Instructions. But her disappointment with Britain's puny-looking men, with their greasy macs and Kaiserish moustaches, went further. She was often aware of the British straining to eavesdrop on her conversations with fellow recruits, especially when the talk turned to pay. They were habitually rude about and to those whom they considered their social inferiors. Wood was especially angered by RAF officers' prevailing attitude to WAAFs, noting on one occasion that at least American officers treated their female colleagues as humans rather than animals. And she was appalled at the way some members of the officer class were happy to observe one set of rules for themselves and another for everybody else:

> Wednesday, July 22 – 1942 – Poor day – Rain.
> Am more confused than usual – was thoroughly shocked when Air Vice Marshal [an unnamed officer with whom she

was billeted] told me he was changing billet, for this one is
too close to the aerodrome and he can't get any petrol, but
being further away (out of walking distance) he will be given
a ration. And that is how we are fighting a war – am sure
that men who sail in tankers would be pleased with his
comments . . .

Wood's diary was no more than her version of the truth,
but it is shot through with compelling directness and plausible
indignation. She sympathised with her hosts when she was at the
Luton training pool, the hard-pressed Stockhams. But she also
chided them: 'It does seem that the likes of them sacrifice and
sacrifice and never ask why, while the so-called social bracket type
do little or nothing . . . perhaps with more thought [their] sacrifices
would be less and these made more fruitful.' That day's entry
concluded with an assessment of the White Waltham catering
operation: 'The canteen is something to marvel at – it is an utter
and complete mess and is so bad that you really don't want to eat
at all.'

Wood twigged immediately that the 'so-called social bracket
type' regarded themselves as a breed apart. Their sense of
entitlement and disdain for others bothered her whenever she
encountered it. So did British inertia. 'Mustn't rush them,' she
reminded herself after visiting London's oldest church to find that
it had not been cleaned in the year and a half since being bombed.
Like a true American revolutionary, she recoiled at a health system
that seemed to assign private rooms to cut-glass accents and ward
beds to Cockney ones, and she saw in the bombsites round
St Paul's the tragedy of lives lost, but also 'the folly and greed
of the men with money – who contrived to draw rent out of
condemned slum areas that weren't fit for animals'.

But nothing irritated her more than the idea that setbacks in
the war, and in particular in North Africa before El Alamein, were
somehow America's fault.

Thursday, June 25 [1942]   Beautiful Day
Did a final circuit in Hart trainer with my pal Rockford, and
that being OK was checked out. Then on to Maggie [Miles
Magister] test with Captain Woods which consisted of turning
on magnetic headings and then estimating to Broxbourne
and Henlow, then a forced landing . . .

Stockhams had guests and man played piano beautifully
and all was well until War Conversation came up – always
there is tension – America blamed for anything and everything – I gather it is insinuated that had we supplied Africa
better it might have held – they forget it held previously
with much less, but the average citizen rarely questions their
government and so must look about for the fault.

Two weeks later the news from Libya was little better. All the
same, the dinner conversation at the Stockhams turned to England's 'glorious stand' there. Wood kept her thoughts to herself
but scribbled them down later:

Had I been English it wouldn't have seemed glorious . . . for
the life of me can't help but think there is tremendous and
rank incompetence in many places, and the slow old methods
of everyday life make one wonder: if they do the same in
battle it is little wonder that the outcomes are so adverse.

Like most of her fellow recruits, Wood went into the war and
emerged from it an Anglophile. They all made English friends,
though perhaps fewer than some of them expected to. In the
interim, they and their hosts were treated to the same feast of
contrasts that the American war machine provided with the British
home front. To the Brits, the GIs may have seemed overpaid,
oversexed and over here but to the Cochran girls they were won-
derfully familiar. 'Real men,' Ann reckoned. Smart, clean, honest-
to-goodness Americans. She was immensely proud to be one;
proud of Mrs Biddle's gleaming oasis on Charles Street; proud of
the free donuts at a US base that she visited with a (for once)
appreciative English 'lassie' at Bovington; proud of the gigantic

magnets that only the Americans could supply to lift several tonnes of old nails out of a top-dressing of new soil applied to the White Waltham runway in 1943; proud of the Jeep that screeched to a halt beside her Spitfire when she jazzed over to another US base at Aldermaston; and proud of FDR, who John Daly assured her was every bit as splendid and farseeing as she hoped he was.

'DON'T BE A SHOW-OFF,' the servicemen's instructions warned GIs. 'The British dislike bragging.' Wood was smart enough to know this. But others bragged, or so Bobby Sandoz thought. 'The British couldn't help but be offended,' she said, and she couldn't help but be ashamed. 'I liked England. I liked the British and I liked the dependable, organised life, and my heart bled at the things I saw happening around me . . . Someone would say, "Oh, you're an American," and I would say "yes, can you forgive me for that?" And it would bring us to a level communication.'

One of many embarrassments Sandoz's ATA compatriots caused her was their penchant for motorbikes. Winnie Pierce bought one and quite quickly put herself in hospital because of it. Wood thought long and hard, and then bought one too. Sandoz considered motorbikes to be bragging on wheels; few Brits could afford them, and petrol was strictly rationed even if you were unscrupulous enough to siphon the odd gallon of 100 octane out of your Spit. But to the others, motorbikes meant freedom from clanking, freezing trains and ever-stopping buses, and excitement when the Brits or their weather threatened to ration that too.

To Jackie Cochran, bragging was no more than public relations. She expected it in others and practised it herself, and it never occurred to her that the 'Instructions for Servicemen' might apply to her as well. She bragged about her first trip over in a bomber. She bragged about winning the Bendix race, to those who had heard of it and those who had not. And she bragged about the bigger, brassier women's flying operation she was going to set up in the States as soon as she had proved the worth of women flyers.

On her return to Washington in the summer of 1942 she

started recruiting again almost at once – 'clean cut, stable young women' with at least 200 hours in their log books, this time for what became the WASP. In her account of this, she is practically begged to take on the new role by General Arnold after dinner with him and Lord Beaverbrook in London earlier that summer; she reluctantly assents. Another version has her browbeating Arnold into promising her the command of any American women's flying outfit, then storming back to the US on hearing that Nancy Harkness Love (an altogether more reserved and elegant aviatrix, with award-winning legs) has beaten her to it. The upshot was the same: Cochran and the ATA parted company, too baffled by each other to go on pretending they could work together.

Cochran's departure from London would have left Ann Wood in the role of Queen Bee or at least sorority president to the American women, had she wanted it. She was the only natural leader among them. In the event they were not much interested in being led, and Wood preferred to think of herself as a lone wolf. But it did fall to her to restore morale and soothe flared tempers when pilot Helen Richey was effectively sacked by Pauline Gower in January 1943 for damaging one too many planes. Wood did this by floating the idea that Richey was actually taking the flak for Cochran, who had driven the ATA slowly nuts but had been impossible to remove because of her connections. Richey spent three weeks at Claridge's on full pay, then flew home and joined the WASPs. (She was well-known in the States, having been hired by Central Airlines as the country's first female airline pilot in 1934. But she seems to have been inconsolable when her wartime flying ended and nothing as exciting came along to fill the void. One Saturday in January, 1947, she gave a small party in her rented New York flat at which, guests said, she seemed depressed. She died the following evening from an overdose of pills.)

Wood had lost one of her two London bolt-holes – the Cochran pied-à-terre in Chelsea. But there was compensation: she was posted to the mixed ferry pool at Ratcliffe, where she stayed for most of the war, shovelling Spitfires away from the great Vickers factory at Castle Bromwich before the Luftwaffe could destroy them. It was at Ratcliffe that she learned to love the Brits, perhaps because a different sort tended to gravitate there – mainly male, more worldly and less snooty than those she had encountered at Luton and White Waltham, and diluted by large numbers of Americans and other foreigners. She would shock some of them by standing up after dinner in the oak-panelled dining room in Ratcliffe Hall to help clear the dishes. But the fact that she and other pilots were dining there at all spoke volumes about the unusually grown-up ambiance of the place: it was a flying club mobilised for war, rather than a boarding school with aeroplanes for hockey sticks.

It was at Ratcliffe that she first met Johnny Jordan and Don Spain, her partners in the illicit 300 mph bridge-buzzing and general treetop hell-for-leather japery. ('Sat. March 27 – 1943 – Luscious day – not very busy. Spit to Sherburn, went up with Jordan – had fun shooting up things en route – got Proctor back to Rat. – then got a Spit Castle Bromwich to Hucknall. The latter was deserted, so I practised circuits and bumps until the Anson came . . .') Ann also approved heartily of the rich, suave and handsome Frankie Francis, assigned to Ratcliffe from White Waltham in 1943. She considered him a 'nifty' commanding officer and established by gentle probing that his wealth derived from being half American; he was related to the Marshall Field family of Chicago. And she clicked naturally with Sir Lindsay Everard, MP, the gregarious Lord of the Manor, who, in return for lending the ATA his private aerodrome, had been allowed to keep his domestic servants. That, and the clever use of ration books and his own market garden, enabled him to host lavish dinners to which a broad range of politicians as well as pilots would be invited.

One of these gatherings got out of hand, with fatal consequences. After D-Day, with the end in sight, Don Spain got into a drunken brawl with the ferry pool's second-in-command and choked to death on his vomit while waiting in hospital to have his face patched up. That cast a pall over Ratcliffe that never quite blew on for Ann, but it did not affect her friendship with her host.

On days when fog over the Midlands kept Ratcliffe's pilots grounded, and parliamentary recesses gave Sir Lindsay nothing to do in London, Ann would help him prune his rose bushes, or take tea with him in the pantry. Later in the war he beckoned her conspiratorially, jangling an ancient set of keys, and led her down into a many-alcoved cellar, each alcove stacked high with wine, each bottle listed according to provenance and vintage. Sir Lindsay chose a bottle of champagne and they drained it together before resurfacing. 'It was fun,' she wrote to her mother, 'a bit of the old world which is easy to take and a bit that I think I'll incorporate into my life come peace.'

It was 'fun'. It may also have been a mildly racy English gentleman's way of saying thank you for coming all this way when no one forced you to, and risking your neck for us. If so, he was not the only one to show some gratitude to Ann as an American. On 13 April 1945, the day after President Roosevelt's death, Wood had a delivery to make from Castle Bromwich. As she stepped out of the taxi Anson that had brought her from Ratcliffe and went looking for her Spitfire, the entire staff of the factory aerodrome downed tools, pens, telephones and cups of tea, and came out to offer their condolences. Ann was distressed by the news from Washington and had little faith in Roosevelt's successor. On landing in East Anglia, she took out a pen and wrote to her mother that 'the thought of Truman taking [Roosevelt's] place makes it utterly tragic, for somehow regardless of what went wrong or what I might have disapproved of in his way of doing things, I always felt and hoped that he had the final answer up his sleeve'.

But for once, spring meant sunshine. Ann had rolled up her trousers and sprawled on the grass, waiting for another taxi plane to pick her up. As she wrote, pressing on her parachute, perhaps, or an overnight bag slim enough to fit in the four-inch gap to the left of a Spitfire pilot's seat and behind the throttle, the momentous death was analysed and put aside. Within a page it had been dealt with, and a twenty-seven-year-old daughter, fulfilled, appreciated and warmed by an unusually generous English sun, felt bound to tell her mother, 'this is really a most heavenly day'.

15

Hamble

After Rudolf Hess visited Ann Welch at the Rossfeld ski hut above Berchtesgaden, he made a more famous trip, to Scotland. His purpose was the same – to gauge Britain's appetite for war and argue for an armistice. This time he flew in secret and apparently without the Führer's knowledge or permission up the North Sea to visit a man he had once seen across a crowded room, but never spoken to – the Duke of Hamilton. Douglas Douglas-Hamilton was at once ogre and Adonis: huge, fierce, handsome and immensely strong. He was also fair. Hess must have thought of him as a Teuton under the skin. He was the first man to fly over Everest, then went to the Berlin Olympics as a former boxing champion and guest of the hosts. His brothers included David, hero of the Battle of Malta, and Geordie, the man Audrey Sale-Barker would marry. He sent Hess packing, and at last the Nazis got the message.

They could equally have got the message by visiting the East End of London, of course – or Hamble, in Hampshire. In peace Hamble was timeless and bucolic. In war it was suddenly busy, brave and bristling with defences. It was also enlivened by the antics of its visitors.

Mary de Bunsen was a Hamble stalwart. Until she became embarrassed at having damaged one too many Spitfires and asked to be reassigned to the 'salt mines' of Kirkbride, she enhanced the place with a crackpot recreational style that appeared to be inherited. Her first act on arriving was to rent a collapsible canoe with blue canvas decks from her landlady, because she loved water and Hamble was hemmed in by it on three sides. Her weak heart never deterred her. One dark, sleeting November afternoon in 1943 she put her seventy-three-year-old mother in the canoe and paddled her towards Southampton as far as the port's submarine barrage, surfing across the open water on the wakes of steamships and horrifying the rest of the ferry pool as they watched from the Yacht Club, trying to work out whether they were witnessing matricide or suicide. 'Though apparently mad it was, of course, the perfect antidote to the tension of flying,' de Bunsen wrote, and one can only believe her. The de Bunsens, after all, had watched the worst night of the Blitz from a Mayfair rooftop and loved every minute of it.

Hamble's position on a neck between the Solent and the Hamble River, and its aerodrome, made it the obvious jumping-off point for the 8,000 Spitfires built at the Vickers Supermarine works in Southampton during the war. The business of flying them to camouflaged country airfields like the nearby Chattis Hill and High Post on the edge of Salisbury Plain, where they were test-flown and armed, could be monotonous, but it was never straight-forward: for long periods Southampton was constantly under attack, and when the sirens sounded barrage balloons had pre-cedence over aircraft movements – even of brand-new Spitfires lined up like ducks on the grass at Hamble. When the balloons went up, they left only a narrow corridor for friendly incoming aircraft, and the corridor's alignment changed from day to day. Unlike test pilot Alex Henshaw at Castle Bromwich, the women ATA pilots were not trained in aerobatics. For most of them, a perky half loop to get out of balloon danger was not an option. But there were compensations. Day in, day out, they were flying the perfect lady's aeroplane, and it seems that an enlightened Pop d'Erlanger chose Hamble for his first all-women's pool precisely so that they would be flying the aircraft that suited them best.

D'Erlanger had been forced to begin moving his women pilots away from Hatfield by mid-1941, when the De Havilland plant there began re-tooling to build twin-engined Mosquitoes – which none of the women was yet cleared to fly – instead of Moths. In due course a second all-women's pool was established at Cosford, near Wolverhampton, and women were posted on an ad-hoc basis to Ratcliffe, Kirkbride, Prestwick, White Waltham and elsewhere. But full integration was never an option. Sir Francis Shelmerdine, Director of Civil Aviation, had written to his director of finance in September 1939: 'It will be necessary for obvious reasons to keep the women's section separate from the men's section of the ATA, and to have a woman in administrative charge of it.' Sir Francis did not trouble to set out what those 'obvious reasons' were, and in truth the idea that most of her pilots should be lumped together geographically by gender was one that Pauline Gower never resisted. This was partly because those posted to Hamble were almost always pleased to be there.

For all the stinking refineries and sawtooth factory roofs spreading towards it from Southampton, Hamble was still, in 1941, an Anglo-Saxon seaside gem. When Margot Gore, the new commanding officer of No. 15 Ferry Pool, and Alison King, its operations officer, first set out from the airfield to explore it, they felt drawn into a timewarp. 'A quiet hard drizzle had set in with a cold, eating wind,' King remembered. 'Suddenly we turned from a wide windy road round the corner and down the sloping lane into something that had been in a world of its own since the fourteenth century.' The High Street led past ancient trellised porches on one side and Hookers the baker and Spakes the grocer on the other, and dead-ended in the water. The signs of half a dozen hostelries beckoned from the gloom, catering in peacetime to armchair sea dogs and now, in wartime, to nightly refugees from the air raids. It had its pubs, of course – the Ye Olde White Hart, the Victory, the King & Queen and, facing the water next to the yacht club, the Bugle, famous for lobster. 'We stood in the rain to get our first full view of the river,' Ops Officer King wrote, 'and listened to the greedy, querulous sound of the gulls as they whirred, and to the ripple and lapping of the grey-green leaden water, opaque as the earth and empty now of its small bright boats. The far bank of the river hung still with blue mist, mysterious and silent,'

It was idyllic – and still in danger of being overrun by Germans. This was the official line, at any rate. The Battle of Britain might have been won, but if as a consequence Hitler had called off his invasion plans the news had yet to filter down to the mouth of the Hamble River. Here, in a large, sealed envelope marked 'Invasion Orders', were detailed instructions to Commanding Officer Gore on how to save her planes and pilots and regroup for the fightback when the sky filled with parachutes and the Solent with swastikas. The envelope was not to be opened until an attack was imminent. However, Gore knew the broad outlines of its contents already, having diligently organised a field trip to her ferry pool's first inland mustering point. It was forty miles away: a former racetrack north-west of Salisbury. When she and Alison King arrived there one washed-out winter's afternoon in their official Humber, they were shown a potting shed containing four large tents, four crates of tinned food and a hatchet. After being served a cup of tea, they signed for the shed keys and drove glumly back to Hamble. 'There we were then,' King wrote afterwards. 'Ready for invasion.' The next day Gore ordered every-one in her command to pack an invasion bag containing pyjamas, jersey, chocolate, toothbrush, mug, knife and a plate if desired, to be ready at a moment's notice at all times.

Boarding school was never quite like this. But in other respects, once the invasion threat receded and the Americans began arriving in the summer of 1942, boarding school is what Hamble came to resemble. It was cliquey, hierarchical and run to a strict timetable, but with rules that existed largely to be broken: being a civilian organisation, the ATA's only serious sanction for bad behaviour was dismissal, and this was seldom used because pilots were needed and pilot training was expensive.

Hamble was smaller than its mainly male headquarters in White Waltham, but no less eccentric. It was home to one woman

(Jackie Sorour) who insisted that she knew how to fly before she knew even the most basic facts of life; and to another (Barbara Wojtulanis), who knew how to fly before she could ride a bicycle. Sorour liked to perform headstands in the mess before taking to the air because she felt her blood was more urgently needed in her head than her feet. Others used the curling linoleum floor for more conventional exercises; they had figures to maintain, and flying taxed the mind more than the behind. Idle hours were passed with bridge games, letter-writing, *The Times* and the music from *The Strawberry Blonde* on the gramophone. Visiting males, if not too intimidated by the women, or so intimidated that they could think of nothing to say to them, would sometimes attempt a tour of the mess without touching its floor, using only window sills, chair backs and the chocolate-coloured dado rail. Visitors were also expected to sign the curtains.

Most of the women were billeted in bijou cottages along the river or on the edge of the green expanse from which they flew (and which remains undeveloped even now; a tussocky meadow reached via 'Spitfire Way'). Lucky with their lodgings, many also remembered Hamble as a place of easy camaraderie. It was, but not for everyone. Most of the Americans gravitated in the evenings to the newsagent's wife's house on the outskirts of the village where at least two of them were always billeted. They mixed a little with the English, but much more with each other. Dorothy Bragg was an exception. She bridled at being asked to share a room with one of her compatriots and checked into South-ampton's Polygon Hotel. And Margot Duhalde, released from her crash course in the English language with the White Waltham mechanics, became sucked into a feud with Anna Leska that could have killed them both.

It is not clear how the argument started. Duhalde herself cannot remember. She suggested that her connection to the Free French may have been resented by Leska, whose brief stay in France on a long journey from Poland had not been an entirely happy one. 'In the end we just didn't like each other,' Duhalde said. 'We fought over everything, in the ground and in the air. We would barge in front of each other when taxiing to take off or cut each other off when we were coming into land. It was crazy, and I suppose it was dangerous.' Her boyfriend at the time, a Squadron Leader Gordon Scotter, certainly thought so. He flew into Hamble frequently, 'and he saw us fighting in the air', Duhalde remembered ruefully. Deciding betrayal would be the better part of valour, he had a quiet chat with Margot Gore. 'Leska and I had to go and see her, and she said, "One of you will have to go, and that person is you Margot unless you say sorry." So I said sorry in front of her, but outside I told Leska that after the war I'd knock her teeth out.'

Duhalde patched things up with Scotter, but never with 'La Polacka'. As she explained: 'The only time we exchanged more than courtesies after that was at a reunion in the presence of the Duke of Kent. We said hello to him, then started quarrelling again.'

Such discord does not feature in the placid photographs that survive of Spitfire women at leisure in their Hamble mess. And nor does sex. In fact, sex scarcely rears its unprofessional head in all the women pilots' writings and reminiscences, whether intended for public or private consumption. But did human yearning and biology put itself on ice while humanity took care of Hitler? Not if countless thousands of war brides and babies are any indication, and not in Hamble.

'We were called the lesbians' pool, of course,' said Rosemary Rees, presumably referring to RAF and other male banter. She didn't know of any real lesbians there, and there may have been none. On the other hand, some of the surviving pilots suggest quite casually, in the old-fashioned way, that there may have been one or two among them who were 'not the marrying sort'. There were certainly a good many who never married for whatever reason. Then there was Joy Ferguson, a pioneering transsexual who after the war announced that she had become a man and changed her name to Jonathan. (As a civil servant at the Ministry of Supply, this automatically entitled her to a pay rise.) And there was the woman who eventually became Dorothy Furey Bragg Beatty Hewitt.

By the time Dorothy Bragg arrived at Hamble, in the autumn of 1942, it was clear to her fellow pilots that she *was* the marrying sort. Lieutenant Richard Bragg, her successful suitor from the *Beaver Hill*, had been killed in action shortly after their wedding in March. She insisted later that she had never been in love with him, but she was clearly in the mood for it now. In the presence of men she had an eerie absence of inhibition by the standards of most of the rest of the ferry pool. She had shunned Hamble's cosy après-fly existence by choosing to live in Southampton, and she understood better than anyone that if all was fair in love and war, then to be in both at once must be very fair indeed:

> I lived in the hotel there in Southampton, and I used to go down and sit in the bar in the evenings. The boys there were in the Navy. I would sit down and have a drink with them, and one night I saw this older man, just staring and staring at me.
>
> A couple of days later our commandant, Margot Gore, got an invitation from Lord Beatty, who said that he'd been at sea a long time and his men were tired and he was going to give them a ball, and he was inviting all the ladies to come. And he would arrange transport for us. So naturally I went. I didn't have any idea who he was or what he was, and he danced with me all night . . .

'Oh!,' Dorothy sighed as she remembered Beatty – and the 'oh' seemed to float out of her and up towards the ceiling of her sunroom like a dandelion. 'He was *very* romantic.'

Dancing all night with whomsoever he desired turned out to be this gentleman's prerogative, for he was, by a long way, the most senior man in the room. He was Commander Lord Beatty, beetle-browed son of the more famous admiral who had fought the Kaiser's fleet at Jutland in 1916. He, too, was already married – to another American Dorothy, as it happened – but unhappily.

Beatty family legend had it that this other Dorothy had left twin boys in the States and told a friend: 'I sold all my jewels and I'm going to England to catch me a Lord.' She caught one, but having done so failed to provide an heir, and Beatty wanted one.

The younger Dorothy, in her *Gone With The Wind* red dress and black choker brought over in the *Beaver Hill*, learned soon enough that in David Beatty's set even a happy marriage was no bar to serial adultery. 'Marriage meant nothing,' she found out. 'People just slept around.' But that night Beatty had reason to feel more than usually reckless. His men were tired and in need of entertainment because he had just led them on the worst British naval disaster of the war. With Stalin demanding a second European front to slow the German momentum towards Stalingrad, Churchill had reluctantly approved a hasty, half-baked plan to attack German forces in Dieppe. Beatty had been given command of a flotilla of transport and patrol boats, with orders to support the mainly Canadian troops going ashore. Over the course of the operation, on 19 August 1942, 555 sailors lost their lives. It could have been worse. German defences in this part of the Channel were all but impregnable, which was why Eisenhower left them well to port on D-Day. Beatty had simply drawn a short straw in an absurdly grand game of geopolitics.

He murmured the gist of the story into Dorothy Bragg's enraptured ear that evening in the Polygon ballroom, unaware until she pressed him for more detail that this closeness to the real war thrilled her quite as much as his uniform or eyebrows, or his strangulated accent. 'He swept me off my feet,' she said.

Sixty-three years later Bobby Sandoz begged to differ. 'I think the shoe was on the other foot,' she told me with considerable feeling. 'And that was only the beginning. Damn, I wish it hadn't happened, for the impression of Americans in England. We came to do a job, we wanted to fit in. We didn't want to make trouble.'

But was it really seen as trouble to allow a senior British naval officer to dance with you, I asked?

It was by me. Oh, she was just gorgeous-looking. We all had to have our hair off of our collar in uniform, and we got used to wearing it up. But I remember going to the ladies' room with Dorothy that night and helping her let her hair down and widen the neck of the dress. She knew that I didn't approve of her, but I helped her anyway. I felt unsophisticated, whereas she was glamorous and worldly.

I must have been a kind of pain in the ass, I guess. A lot of the gals were into having a good time, but I was so devastated by seeing young men, younger than I, lost every damned day . . . I didn't have time for flirtation quite yet.

Only one of the English pilots could match Dorothy Bragg's impact at a ball. This was Diana Barnato, a latecomer to the all-women's pool at Hamble, who as far as she was aware had been sent there from White Waltham to keep her out of trouble.

Before joining the ATA, Barnato had grown used to a dual existence in London. By day she was, like Veronica Volkersz, a volunteer angel – an ambulance driver with the Red Cross. By night she was a party animal with a very full dance card. It was hardly sustainable, but then not much was about the war. It required a full ration of coffee and cigarettes, but it enabled her to squeeze the marrow out of a life that she knew could end at any moment. It was exhilarating, and what had proved exhilarating as an ambulance driver she was reluctant to abandon as a ferry pilot.

She never did abandon it, though the authorities at ATA headquarters did their best to make her. One senior official whom she will still not name – or forgive – thought he saw a chance to clip Barnato's wings in the spring of 1942.

While based at White Waltham she lived in a house her father had given her on the Chelsea Embankment, within easy striking distance (by train or by Bentley) of her favourite clubs and restaurants. She was especially well known at the 400 Club on Leicester Square because her father was also a regular there. As a pre-war motor-racing hero to many of the fighter boys who showed up at the 400 after a hard day's work over France or the Home Counties, Woolf Barnato helped set the tone. The dance floor was tiny, but it tended to be full because of the irresistible Fat Tim and his band. 'And the maitre d' was called Rossi,' Diana remembered:

> Tim and Rossi. It was all very skilfully done, with plenty of pillars so if you didn't want to see someone you could always go round a corner. I'd come in, all tarted up in a long dress mostly, and Rossi would take me aside and say, 'Your father is here, Miss Barnato,' as if I shouldn't know. He'd be there with one of his girlfriends, and of course I'd go over and give him an enormous hug.

There had been no flying for two weeks because of fog, but then the murk evaporated and Barnato was assigned a Spitfire delivery to Somerset. It was her one job for the day. To anyone with an ounce of wanderlust a chit for a Spit with a clear sky and a full tank of fuel constituted grave temptation. Even at the regulation ATA cruising speed of 250 mph, almost nowhere in England was more than an hour away.

Barnato gave herself a joyride down the Cornish coast and had lunch with a friend at RAF St Eval. She was spotted signing in there and was reported to her commanding officer. He demoted her for misuse of fuel, lectured her on the terrible risks run by tanker crews to get the precious 100 octane past the U-boats, and took the opportunity to move her to Hamble. She was led to believe it was, apart from anything, for her own good. 'I flew all day and was out all night. I suppose they thought if I didn't let up I'd break my neck.'

Instead of letting up, though, she befriended two obliging London cabbies whom she remembers as Bert and Ozzie. They joined what began to look like a broad-based conspiracy to save both her life and her lifestyle, as did Max Aitken, Billy Clyde and Tony Bartley. Aitken was Lord Beaverbrook's bronzed and charismatic son, and a skiing companion of the Barnatos from before the war. Clyde had fought with him in 601 Squadron in the Battle of Britain. Bartley had originally introduced Barnato to her first love, Humphrey Gilbert (who had been killed taking off in his Spitfire, nine months earlier). All were still serving fighter pilots, and all of them joined Diana at the 400 Club on the evening of 19 January 1943. There they learnt for the first time that ATA ferry pilots were expected to fly with no wireless or instrument training. They were appalled: did this mean that Diana couldn't fly blind? It did.

'Max got out his fountain pen, and, to my horror, drew an instrument panel on the pink linen tablecloth,' Diana said. 'He gave me a lesson there and then on what to do on instruments, and I needed it the next day or I wouldn't be here.'

Diana left the club at about 2.30 a.m. and went home to Chelsea to change. Bert – or Ozzie, they were brothers and she never knew which it would be – was waiting as usual. She shed her gown, pulled on her uniform and over it a large, furry Afghan coat that smelt rotten when wet but kept out the cold. Then she slipped out again into the night to curl up in the back of the cab. Ozzie – or Bert – drove across the river to Waterloo and Diana caught the 3.40 a.m. milk train to Eastleigh. That gave her a little over an hour's sleep. She had left a secondhand Vauxhall her father had given her at Eastleigh station, and there would be another hour or two in bed in her little-used digs at Hamble before the 9 a.m. rush to the aerodrome.

The morning of 20 January started clear, and Diana was given a Mark IX Spitfire to deliver to Cosford. It should have been an easy half-hour hop in the RAF's ultimate flying machine, with a top speed and rate of climb that left the Mark V wallowing in its slipstream and was, at last, more than a match for the Messerschmitt 109.

Barnato was high over the Cotswolds, enjoying the view, when a slight fall in the temperature outside filled the sky with an instant, impenetrable blanket of condensation. It had not been forecast because it was not a front, but it looked like one and presented exactly the same risk of sudden death for a pilot unsure how to use her instruments.

The night before, with the help of the pink tablecloth, Max Aitken had stressed two things: a pilot almost never flies head-first into cloud because of the instinct to look for a way around it, so first, he said, straighten up. And secondly, remember the last spot height on the map, add a safe margin, then turn through 180 degrees and descend as gradually as possible. Oh, he'd said, 'and think'.

Barnato thought, feverishly. She also remembered a final piece of advice from Aitken: if there was still no visibility at her safe break-off height she was to climb fast and bale out. This presented a problem. She was in her regulation skirt rather than slacks. Under it she was wearing large knickers made from parachute silk and wartime stockings that ended just above the knee. She wasn't bashful, but she did have a reputation to consider. She put the Spitfire into a shallow dive from 6,000 feet. At 800 feet, 50 feet above what she hoped against hope might be the Little Rissington aerodrome in Gloucestershire, she was still in thick cloud.

'But we didn't bale out, we came on down,' she said, remembering the plane as half of a two-person team. She broke out of the cloud in driving rain at 200 mph and 600 feet, which in that part of the Cotswolds turned out to be treetop height. A glimpse of a parked aircraft on a waterlogged grassy airfield flashed by under her port wing and she threw the Spitfire into an immediate tight turn to get back to it. Another turn, and she was down, falling out of the sky into a series of enormous puddles. Through luck or instinct, she managed to keep her nose up despite the natural tendency of the huge engine inside it to tip the plane forward into the mud. She opened the canopy and felt her knees buckle as she climbed out of the cockpit. A startled RAF officer was already striding over with a cape. To disguise her jellied legs Barnato knelt on the wing, pretending to scrabble in the cockpit for stray maps.

'I say, miss,' the gallant officer remarked as he reached up with the cape, 'you must be good on instruments.'

He led her back to a Nissen hut at RAF Windrush from which she telephoned ATA headquarters. The commanding officer there was relieved to hear from her. The instant cloud, caused by an unusually high dew point, had covered the whole of England. An entire training pool had had to force land and two pilots had been killed.

16

Heroines

'No glamour', the British women pilots would insist to reporters. No glamour, the men of No. 1 Ferry Pool ruefully agreed when they saw the first Americans. No glamour, Jackie Cochran must have thought so often in White Waltham that she wanted to scream.

Even in 2006, surviving ATA veterans in several countries warned me darkly against romanticising what they'd done in the war. But in the end it is impossible to oblige. There is a limit to how long one can soberly agree that there was nothing particularly special about criss-crossing Britain in Spitfires and Hurricanes as a young woman in the early 1940s. In the end one has little choice but to grant the women pilots their compulsive understatement, and then, respectfully, break their golden rule and see them as others did; as Flying Officer Henryk Jagowy of the Polish Air Force did, for instance.

Jagowy was posted to RAF Millom in remotest Cumberland in 1943. As he recalled at a Polish Air Force Association reunion after the war, glamour dropped in unannounced one lunchtime as his officers' mess was filling up with hungry men:

The skies over the airfield were clear when out of the blue appeared an aircraft that started to perform lively aerobatics. Seeing this reprehensible flying, the Station Commander rushed out of the officers' mess, jumped into his car and drove to the watch office, stopping on his way to pick up a guardsman to arrest the pilot when the plane landed. This sort of flying was strictly forbidden at all operational stations.

By the time the Station Commander arrived at the watch office, the plane had landed and taxied up and the pilot had climbed out. To the amazement of the commander, the pilot was a woman. For a while he stood bewildered, then he sent the guardsman away and asked the pilot into his car and invited her to lunch at the officers' mess. Still dazed at this new experience, and out of character, he bought everybody a round of drinks. To add to his amazement, the woman pilot was a young Polish girl – Jadwiga Pilsudska – the daughter of the Marshal of Poland.

I showed Jadwiga a transcript of this account at her home in Warsaw, and she shook her head gravely. 'Not true,' she said. 'Not true at all.' It was nonsense. As the station commander in this fictional episode appeared to understand full well, at least in principle, this type of flying was strictly forbidden. There had been no aerobatics.

At first I was unable to hide my disappointment. Then I realised she was not denying everything, only the aerobatics. Did she have any recollection of the lunch? She smiled, but only a little. She admitted that such hospitality was not unheard of.

In fact, by pure chance it seems to be corroborated in this case by a written account left to the Imperial War Museum by an impressionable Edgar Featherstone of the RAF Volunteer Reserve, posted to RAF Millom between 1941 and 1943. 'I was on duty crew when I saw my first (and only) World War II female pilot,' Featherstone wrote,

> and she was at the controls of a Spitfire. I didn't know the gender of the pilot as I marshalled the aircraft into the allotted space near the control tower, placed the chocks in front of and behind the wheels and then made to climb on the wing to see if I could be of any help with the straps etc. From my

ground-level viewpoint I saw the helmet come off, and head give a shake, and the blonde hair come streaming out in the breeze. I was very impressed with everything that happened after that, including the 'swarm' of young officers, who seemed to come from every corner to see this ATA phenomenon. Where had they been hiding? I was right out of the scene, of course, but I would dearly have liked to have been very much a part of it.

Glamour, it turned out, was in the eye and imagination of the beholder. Pilsudska would have known this even if she preferred not to admit it. Why else the constant presence of photographers during her weekend gliding trips outside Warsaw before the war? Maureen Dunlop learned the same lesson the easy way, stepping out of a Barracuda onto the cover of *Picture Post* and then, mercifully for someone so shy, never being bothered by the press again. Diana Barnato revelled in all the glamour she could generate, but in the end the self-effacers set the tone. Some might have carried powder compacts with their parachutes, but glamour in the form of 'blonde hair streaming out in the breeze' was the exception, not the rule.

Consider the apparently workaday 50-mile ferry flight by Ann Welch on 3 February 1942, from Chattis Hill to Colerne in north Wiltshire in a Spitfire. Chattis was a heavily camouflaged grass aerodrome outside Stockbridge with a gentle hillside for a runway. Spitfires built at the original Supermarine works and its satellites in Southampton were assembled and test-flown there before being distributed to wherever they were needed. It had been snowing for three days by the time Welch climbed into her cockpit. Two of those she had spent in a freezing hut in her Sidcot suit, sipping tea from a Thermos flask, or just sitting, saying little. Visibility had been close to zero and the forecast gloomy. To have taken off without instrument training or the use of wireless would have been suicidal.

Ordinarily, Welch's commanding officer would have been able

to 'wash out' and send her home at noon each day as long as the foul weather continued, but this Spitfire was a PW1 – a 'Priority 1 Wait'. She had orders to stay by it from dawn to dusk and take off at the first hint of an improvement in the weather. The only clue to the reason for the urgency was the aircraft's unusual colour scheme. It was pale blue on its underside and khaki from above. This was also a time when angry questions were being asked in the House of Commons about Germany's increasing strength in North Africa and the Allies' apparent inability to do anything about it.

That month, 1,300 miles to the south, in perfect weather, the island fortress of Malta was being bombed back to the Middle Ages. For an island so critical to British control of the Mediterranean its aerial defences were pitiful. The RAF had started the Battle of Malta with four aircraft, all biplanes – Gloster Gladiators borrowed from the navy. When one was shot down, the others were named Faith, Hope and Charity. By March 1942 Malta was defended by twenty serviceable fighters, of which no more than six were likely to be flyable on any given day. Each day that month, Field Marshal Kesselring, based less than 200 miles away in Sicily, sent over 150 bombers with orders to destroy the Grand Harbour at Valletta, all three of the island's air force bases, and anything that moved. The pounding was having its desired effect. German convoys were getting through to North Africa again.

Worse still, there was every chance that Malta would be lost. Six weeks before Welch got her PW1 Spitfire, Lord Cranborne, the Secretary of State for the Colonies, had written to Churchill warning that if the island were not resupplied within two months it would only be a matter of time before it fell. Since then a supply convoy had set out for the island, but only two ships had reached it and they were bombed in the harbour. At Churchill's pleading Roosevelt had loaned Britain an aircraft carrier, the USS *Wasp*, for one trip only, to deliver Spitfires to Malta. The war could not be won as long as Germany was undefeated in North Africa. Victory there was hard to imagine without the island. Malta was desperate for food, fuel, ammunition and, above all, Spitfires. The *Wasp* was waiting in the Clyde to take them there, but none had arrived. Welch was sitting in one of them, waiting for a break in the weather.

She knew what was at stake; the parliamentary questions had been reported on the BBC. But she could not even see the trees at the top of the hill that served as a runway, and snow was still falling. There was nothing she could do and nothing much worth saying. Lettice Curtis, not often given to sympathy, was sympathetic. Everyone who took off that day 'frightened themselves in a way that is known only to those who, of their own free will, pit their lives against the clearness of their thinking', she wrote. 'And there can be few things more frightening than finding oneself committed to chasing through the sky . . . pressed down by a vast greyness, knowing that if reference with the ground is lost even for an instant one's chances of a safe return to Earth are not worth the proverbial row of beans.'

Welch had a plan. If the trees at the top of the hill appeared she would take off and follow a memorised sequence of roads and railways that would get her to Colerne as long as she stuck to it rigidly. The route included a double loop in the Savernake Forest branch railway line as it went through the hills on the north side of the Vale of Pewsey. She would follow every yard of each loop, circling as if lost in order not to get lost. And she would fly as low as necessary to keep the tracks visible beneath her.

A slight improvement in the weather was forecast for mid-morning, and soon after 11 a.m. the trees did appear. Visibility extended briefly to 700 yards under a sagging, sodden blanket of dark cloud. A snowplough cleared a strip up the middle of the slope and Welch warmed up her engine. She took off with the cloudbase at 300 feet and headed north by north-west, flying lower than she ever had before, peering intently down to her left, then her right, then her left again as she banked to follow each curve of her route.

The plan worked. 'I flew as slowly as possible, flaps down,' she recalled. 'It was not possible to fly with the wheels down on a Spit for extra drag as the undercarriage leg obscured the oil cooler. The weather did not improve, but neither did it worsen, and I picked my way along the roads and railway tracks at 140 mph, flying the last mile along a lane uphill to the aerodrome.'

On arrival she was pulled from the cockpit by engineers waiting to fit out the aircraft with a full complement of instruments and weapons before it continued to Renfrew. No other Spitfire made it to Colerne that day; the only other one that had been able to follow Welch into the air from Chattis Hill before the fog closed in again had turned straight round and even then had fallen out of the murk and back onto the cleared strip more by luck than skill. Ops Officer Alison King, waiting for news at Hamble, feared Welch was dead until she heard her voice on the telephone, and even then was not convinced she wasn't talking to a ghost. Her voice was 'bleached and expressionless . . . it was as though she was drained of feeling and didn't want to talk about it'. What she actually said was: 'It was very bad indeed; worse than I've ever known.'

It wasn't combat, but Welch had run a series of risks that combat pilots rarely ran. It wasn't glamorous in the peer-reviewed sense, since no-one was watching her terrifying slow-dance over the Savernake Forest to ascribe any glamour to it (though the engineers waiting for her at Colerne may have recognised something special in an uphill final approach). But it was exceptionally brave, and, unusually for an individual ferry flight, it had its own toehold in history.

The USS *Wasp* finally sailed from Port Glasgow carrying forty-seven Spitfires on 13 April 1942. It passed through the Strait of Gibraltar six days later with an escort of three cruisers and eight destroyers. Starting at 5:45 a.m. on the 20th, all forty-seven planes took off with nearly 700 miles still to go to Malta. (Half of them were led by Lord David Douglas-Hamilton, a 6 foot 4 former Oxford University boxing champion, and a tighter fit in a Spitfire than Audrey Sale-Barker, who married his brother after the war.)

The Spitfires landed without incident and their pilots went to get some lunch. Immediately, Kesselring attacked: 300 German bombers hit the new Spitfires where they were lined up on the ground. The following morning six were still serviceable. It was a terrible, avoidable disaster, watched by many of the pilots themselves as they stood outside in their tin hats. But the RAF did learn from it. An SOS went back to London for 'Spitfires and more Spitfires'. Roosevelt allowed the *Wasp* to make a second trip. The ATA flew forty-seven more Spitfires up to Renfrew, and this time they were back in the air above Malta within ten minutes of arriving. Kesselring had lost his chance to conquer Malta, and the tide in Africa soon turned.

There was also a less grand footnote to Ann Welch's heroic hop from Chattis Hill to Colerne. Once she had landed, the operations room at Hamble had to work out how to get her back. Ordinarily a taxi aircraft would be sent to pick her up. That did not seem possible given the weather, but a junior pilot volunteered. She was Third Officer Bridget Hill, not long out of Wycombe Abbey Girls' School, 'wise and mature beyond her years', according to a friend, and very promising in the cockpit. She astonished Welch by puttering out of the murk at Colerne in a Puss Moth twenty minutes after Welch had got there in a Spitfire. She had the advantage of a much lower stalling speed and a better view of the ground, but it was still an achievement not to have crashed, and Welch rewarded her by letting her fly the return leg, too.

Hill flew back to Hamble at treetop height along two sides of a large triangle via Oxford. When Welch asked why, her chauffeur replied calmly that her parents lived in Oxford, so she knew the way. Less than a month later, Hill was dead. Another taxi plane in which she was a passenger crashed into a house near White Waltham after being roughly handled by its male pilot. He, Hill and another ATA pilot, Betty Sayer, died. Three more ATA pilots were killed on the same day, two of them while trying to find a way round the rugged lobe of western Scotland between Prestwick and Kirkbride in zero visibility. It was the ATA's blackest day. It was also a jolt for many newer recruits; confirmation that they were in the war, not watching it. A moment's lapse in concentration, as Ann Wood wrote to herself, and you were apt to be a goner. Or maimed or burned beyond recognition, which many considered worse.

It did not help morale that Bridget Hill and Betty Sayer spun into the ground so close to White Waltham. Three months later it happened again in plain view of many on the ground. Flying Officer Castle recorded the aftermath in his diary on 6 June: 'Joan Marshall was killed today. She was solo in a Master, doing a circuit . . . she made her final turn into wind, went into a normal power approach and then turned off to the right in a steepening turn which finished in a spin.'

Marshall crashed within five minutes' walk of Castle's billet. That evening he and three other pilots went along to see the wreck. 'It is between the houses in a garden. And is a dreadful sight. The whole tail unit has broken off and the rest is just small pieces. Why it did not burn is a mystery. It is a great shock to everyone . . . I wonder how many more of us have been marked out for the same fate.'

Over the course of the war, the 'wastage rate' of female pilots was fewer than one in ten, twice as economical as the men, who lost nearly one in three of those enrolled by February 1940 (a rate comparable to that of Fighter Command). But it was still death on a significant, non-civilian scale, close to what the Romans called decimation; and it took some getting used to.

The women of the ATA were living the days of their lives. They were often embarrassed by the intensity of the thrill of flying such 'lovely, powerful, fast, exciting war aeroplanes'. Ordinarily, the experience might have forged a special bond between them and with many it did – but this mainly came after the war, once they had had time to reflect. Until then their comrades – their partners in flying, bridge, filmgoing, cocktailing and line-shooting – were people who might on any given day let their mind wander for a moment from the railway line below; or hit an unforecast fogbank and then a steeple; or pull a dud chit from their operations officer and climb into a dud Spit with gummed-up spark plugs; or they might just lose a propeller – watch it detach in front of their eyes and disappear in a useless spiral ahead of them – and panic, and perish in a matter of seconds.

For many the best defence against falling apart was not to get too close to one's comrades. Margaret Frost, convivial by nature (and my grandparents' neighbour for many years) knew this intuitively. When asked who her closest friends were during the war she didn't have to think long. 'I don't know that you made close friends,' she said.

Alison King at Hamble tried to help by rubbing out the names of the dead in the left-hand column of the giant blackboard on which she wrote out each day's programme. Each name below would quickly move up a line. But she and the pilots she dispatched still had to acquire that 'strange philosophy of life where friends went out on their appointed tasks and did not return'.

Unlike combat pilots, the ferry pilots flew without radios, instrument training or weapons in aircraft that were nonetheless legitimate targets for any Luftwaffe pilot who saw them, and they flew in any weather except the certifiably foul. They flew continuously, not just when grand strategy demanded it. They were sometimes mistaken for enemy aircraft by bored ack-ack units. They were frequently required to fly badly damaged planes to maintenance units for repair or to be broken up, and they took special pride in being able to fly a new type of aircraft with no notice or familiarisation apart from twenty minutes alone in the cockpit with their ring-bound A6 bible – the official 'Ferry Pilot's Notes'. With no surplus syllables and hardly a verb anywhere, these cards gave take-off, flying and landing settings for every knob, flap and fuelcock in every aircraft flown by the Allies into or out of Britain in the war. They fitted neatly into the breast pockets of the ATA uniform. It was 'all THERE', as Ann Welch once put it with the delight of a pirate clutching a treasure map. Even pilots trained from scratch later in the war used them to fly dozens of different types before it was over, and sometimes three or four in a day.

For passengers foolish enough to ask what was going on, being flown by a pilot who had to bury her nose in a ring binder before take-off and again before landing because she had never sat in this sort of cockpit before could be a disquieting experience. Nothing similar was ever asked of combat pilots. It was a sustained aerial stunt that one seasoned British Airways instructor long after the war called, simply, 'mind-boggling'.

In all, the ATA delivered 308,567 aircraft, including 57,286 Spitfires, 29,401 Hurricanes, 9,805 Lancasters and 7,039 Barracudas of the type that took Betty Keith-Jopp to the dark floor of the Firth of Forth. In mid-1942, when British aircraft production reached its peak, the ATA was moving more planes each day than British Airways did on a typical day in 2006. Its taxi Ansons alone covered ten million miles with no fatal mechanical failure. But this was not achieved casually. The pilots – the best of them, at any rate – lived in a continual state of stress. Keeping themselves and their aircraft in one piece was a nervewracking business.

When asked, aged ninety, if she would like to have flown in combat, Lettice Curtis rolled her eyes and groped for words. She would clearly have liked nothing better than for her interviewer to leave. When she had composed herself, she said: 'This is the sort of imagination I am very much against. There was no question of it, and it was not a question you asked. It just never came up.'

I left it at that. But a few months later I asked Sir Peter Mursell, director of training at White Waltham for the last three years of the war, if he thought any of the women whose progress he was responsible for monitoring would have made good combat pilots. 'I'm sure Lettice would have,' he said without hesitation.

Apart from a week's rest at Cliveden hospital after a crash that almost killed her, Curtis flew continuously from July 1940 to

September 1945; thirteen days on, two off, for sixty-two consecutive months. In that time she ferried nearly 1,500 aircraft including 331 four-engined bombers. She was never given command of a ferry pool because she never got on with Pauline Gower, but she was still the alpha female of the ATA. If Margie Fairweather was the Cold Front, Curtis was the Ice Queen, the Iron Maiden, the *prima inter pares*. More particularly, she was the embodiment of the ATA's most important sociological discovery – that any man who clung to the view that aircraft were for men only was liable to be made a fool of.

It was not that Curtis didn't suffer fools gladly; she didn't suffer them – or anyone who had not somehow proved that they deserved her respect – at all. She would simply ignore them, or cut them off with a conversational carving knife. Naomi Allen, the flamboyant ex-parachutist and glider pilot, once recorded in her diary telling Curtis that she would be seeing Jim Mollison, Amy Johnson's estranged husband. 'Oh,' Curtis replied. 'Give him my hate will you?'

To this day some of Curtis's defenders explain away her spectacular *froideur* as proof of crippling shyness. But Peter Mursell, who knew her well, said she wasn't a bit shy as long as she was 'on firm ground', and firm ground was Lettice Curtis's speciality, even in the air.

Her father was a country lawyer, too hard of hearing to engage in more than perfunctory conversation. He sent her away to boarding school when she was six. At seven, after scandalising her nurse on a weekend at home by telling her she was expected at her new school to share a bath and bedroom with a boy called Monty, Curtis was moved to an all girls' establishment on the north side of Dartmoor. It was run by three spinsters, victims of the man-drought left by the First World War, who gave her a solid grounding in all subjects along lines set out by the Parents' National Educational Union. The school had a library, where Lettice found herself indifferent to Dickens but entranced by the adventure novels of Rider Haggard. Aged thirteen she was moved again, to

Benenden public school, in Kent, which taught her 'the importance of exams and passing them', and the loneliness of wanting,
above all, to win.

'Benenden was to some extent a bittersweet experience,' she
wrote in her autobiography, 'as until I became House and School
Captain, when I thoroughly enjoyed being a leader, I never completely fitted in . . .'. She was, she said, extremely competitive. 'To
me, second place at anything was a failure.' She went to Oxford
University in 1933, longing 'to be told the right way to do
everything'.

Academically, Oxford disappointed Curtis, and vice versa,
since her college, St Hilda's, had no mathematics tutor of its own.
So she concentrated on sport, which naturally entailed sweeping
all before her. She was a triple blue in fencing, tennis and lacrosse.

She joined the ATA reluctantly, so she said, having scared
herself in bad weather over the Pennines while doing aerial survey
work for the army before the war. She also claimed to find her
fellow women pilots pleasant and intelligent, but hamstrung by
'a fundamental lack of enterprise – a willingness to cling perhaps
a little too rigidly to rules and customs good or bad'.

This was her explanation for applying to be posted from all-
female Hamble to the all-male headquarters at White Waltham. It
appears no coincidence, however, that the commanding officer
there was the darkhaired, blue-eyed Frankie Francis, leader of men
and enchanter of women. Curtis would have known of Francis
from ferry flights in and out of White Waltham, and from gossip,
and the most poignant strand of the Curtis legend holds that she
had something deeper than a crush on him; that she lobbied for
White Waltham postings to be near him, and that she even allowed
herself to think of a life with him. In her history of the ATA her
formal narrative tone is dropped for two subjects: Spitfires and
Francis. 'All the girls fell for Frankie and I was no exception,' she
wrote. 'I thought he was wonderful.' There is a sense at this point
of the incorrigible, binary-minded competitor aching to elaborate
on something unfamiliar and mushy, and to an extent she does.

She writes about her marathon backgammon sessions with Francis, and her admiration for his methodical and scientific approach to winning them.

Whatever motivated her to aim for White Waltham, she was there one sodden October morning in 1942 when Eleanor Roosevelt came calling, and that visit propelled her into history.

17

Girl Flies Halifax

There were any number of stories that the papers could have told about the First Lady's visit to White Waltham. Apart from anything, the Germans bombed the place while she was there.

Mrs Roosevelt, in greatcoat and fox fur, had just finished a short speech of thanks and encouragement in front of a Lockheed Hudson draped with the Stars and Stripes. Her invited audience, including most of Jackie Cochran's recruits, then repaired to the mess to eat bountiful American food and to bombard her with questions about when women would be flying back home. 'We proceeded to gorge ourselves,' Ann Wood wrote that night, 'when suddenly the siren went and we were all told to make for the shelter. It was rather a weird awakening, and my first into-the-shelter raid. I couldn't help but marvel at the German timing.'

No-one was hurt, so the raid's newsworthiness was deemed marginal. The reporters covering the visit were similarly uninterested in the Cochran angle. Where was she? Why had she gone home so soon? Would it not have been appropriate for her to return with Mrs Roosevelt since without her there would have been no American women pilots for her to visit? But Cochran was three months' gone, and long forgotten.

A piquant human interest story also went unsampled – that of Mary Zerbel, petite, attractive and beside herself with worry as the others delighted in the attention of the 'soft and kindly' Mrs Roosevelt and her 'very cute' companion, Mrs Clementine

Churchill. Zerbel had learned to fly in Southern California and lived in Hollywood until her boyfriend, Wesley Ford, was posted to England soon after Pearl Harbor. She leapt at the chance Cochran offered, not so much to fly as to follow Wes. They were married in Sir Lindsay Everard's private chapel at Ratcliffe Hall. Now Wes was missing, and had been for two weeks; shot down over Germany. Ann Wood did not foresee a happy ending: 'Mary is being terribly plucky,' she wrote, 'but it must be quite an effort as [I] don't believe she was ever too thrilled with her work, nor the people, and it was only the nearness to Wes that made the job passable at all.'

It was Mrs Roosevelt's encounter with Lettice Curtis that made the headlines the following day. For the First Lady's walkabout before her speech, Curtis was positioned under the giant wing of a Handley Page Halifax, which provided shelter from the rain and a conversation point. Curtis was at this stage the only woman in the world to have taken the controls of a four-engined bomber, having earned the privilege with relentless work and a blemishless record. She would gloss over the achievement afterwards, saying she had merely been 'lucky enough to be in the right place at the right time'. But her promotion to four engines opened the way for her and a select few other women to a class of planes that included Short Stirlings, American Liberators and Fortresses, and the mighty Avro Lancaster. When she met Mrs Churchill, Curtis had yet to go solo in the lumbering monster that shielded them both from the rain, but that didn't bother the gentlemen of the press. 'Girl Flies Halifax', they announced the next day, which meant there was no turning back now even if the girl had wanted to.

The ATA's assault on the last bastion of male air supremacy began, typically, with no fanfare and the quiet help of some supportive men. Commander Frankie Francis put Curtis up for what was known as 'Class V conversion' because he thought she was ready for it. Chief Instructor Captain Macmillan agreed. The only possible objection anyone else might have had was that she was a woman, but the d'Erlanger-Gower doctrine that gender was no bar to anything had been established thirteen months earlier by Winnie ('It's lovely, darlings') Crossley in her first Hurricane. There were, of course, still men who believed that 30 tonnes of aeroplane needed at least 200 lbs of man to fly. But any of them inclined to grumble to *Aeroplane* magazine would have thought better of it when they learned that the insurgent 130 lbs of woman belonged to the triple blue with the frozen sense of humour and angular jaw who played backgammon marathons with Frankie Francis. And in any case, the grumblers were wrong, as Rosemary Rees explained briskly to one of them after joining the women's Class V elite in 1943: 'I remember having quite an argument with a Wing Commander about an [Avro] York I was collecting,' she wrote. 'He said it was so heavy compared with my five foot three and seven stone weight. I pointed out that I was not proposing to attempt to carry it after all, but on the contrary to make it carry me.' Taxiing a four-engined bomber in a strong wind could take a bit of elbow grease, Rees admitted, but 'the controls of a big aircraft were not at all heavy in the air'.

Before the Roosevelt visit, Lettice Curtis had done several dual circuits in a Halifax with a mild-mannered Polish instructor called Klemens Dlugaszewski, also known as Double Whisky. He had founded LOT, the Polish national airline, in 1929, and escaped to England ten years later. He was much loved: a model of probity, patriotism and pride in his pupils; and it was up to him when Curtis would go solo. She did so before the 'Girl Flies Halifax' headline became fish-and-chip paper.

On 27 October 1943, Dlugaszewski clambered down from a Mark II Halifax that he had flown for her to an airstrip with a convenient east-west runway, and left Curtis to get on with it. She flew a perfect circuit and remembered long afterwards the sight of Dlugaszewski standing at the edge of the runway and saluting as she taxied it back towards him. Someone, at least, had witnessed this little piece of progress. But if Dlugaszewski was proud of her, she would not confess to any pride in herself. Granted, it might have helped that she was tall and strong, even if physical strength was no particular requirement to fly big planes. Granted, it might have helped that she had got herself posted to the otherwise all-male White Waltham pool. But you weren't proud, she said. You had a job to do.

That evening the instructors held a party at White Waltham to which Curtis was invited. I made the mistake of asking if it had been in her honour, and quickly understood that a more preposterous question had not been asked in the whole history of aviation. Too much celebration would, in fact, have been premature. Gender politics intervened just before Curtis was cleared to ferry heavy bombers: she was required to make ten perfect landings, rather than the usual seven, and Freddie Laker (the future airline tycoon) accused her of bouncing on one of them. He was her flight engineer and may have been alarmed at being flown by a woman; Dlugaszewski happened to be watching the landing from outside, and vouched for the fact that it was 'perfect'.

Curtis finally completed her Class V conversion at RAF Pocklington in Yorkshire in February 1943. She was lonely there, and self-conscious about having to request landing permission by radio in line with RAF procedure. She wrote simply: 'I went solo on my second flight.' But it was not that perfunctory from where her new instructor, Captain Henderson, was sitting. He wrote an account of it in 1946:

> The Halifax had barely taken off when the Control Room was invaded by no less a person that the Group Captain commanding the Station, accompanied by an Army Staff General. Everyone snapped to attention, momentarily overpowered by the weight of red tabs and 'scrambled eggs' [gold braids].
>
> 'Oh hello, Henderson! No work this morning?' asked the Station-master in a fatherly manner.
>
> 'Just watching a first solo, Sir,' I replied.
>
> The Control Officer could contain himself no longer.
>
> 'It's a woman pilot, Sir.'

'It's a WHAT?' gasped the S.M., and, turning to the General: 'Come on Fred, we must watch this.' He led the way hastily out on to the balcony. Arriving there he discovered that the runway in use was the one adjacent to the Control Tower and passing it within about thirty yards. He thereupon returned to the Control Tower as hastily as he had left it.

'Which way will the Halifax swing when it lands?' He sounded urgent.

'Away from the Control Tower, Sir, with this cross-wind,' replied the Control Officer.

The S.M. was relieved, and returned to the balcony with 'Fred'.

I said nothing. Suddenly the loudspeaker began to buzz and Lettice's voice came through: 'May I come in to land? Over.' The Control Officer nodded: 'You may land' returned the Operator. 'Over.' I watched confidently; the others excitedly.

The great undercarriage appeared and slowly extended itself. The Halifax slowed perceptibly, made its final turn toward the aerodrome and descended steadily towards the runway. It crossed the hedge, checked its descent and held off just above the ground. Then the wheels kissed the surface gently and the 30-ton aircraft rolled steadily down the runway in the smooth manner which seldom characterizes a first solo, and came to a dignified halt.

'It didn't swing!' said the S.M. in a musing tone. 'It didn't even bounce! And my lads have always kidded me how difficult Halifaxes are. Why damn it, they must be easy if a little girl can fly them like that!'

I said that Lettice wasn't so little. He snorted. I told him that Lettice had 2,000 hours and a lot of variegated types in her log book.

'Has she, by Gad!'

He thought for a moment, then: 'Come on, Fred, let's drink a half-can before lunch.' And departed.

There was now no logical bar to women flying any type of aircraft – only an illogical ban on their presence on flying boats. The reason, apparently, was the risk of untoward intimacy among mixed-sex flight crews should they find themselves left with no alternative to sleeping on board. But the ban affected few of the ATA women; only eleven of them were ever cleared to fly Class V planes, the prerequisite for anyone hoping to move on to flying boats. The remaining 153 women pilots found the awesome power of fighters and fighter-bombers challenge enough.

18

Mayfair 120

From the 'Standing Orders for Delivery Pilots', given to each of them on signature of contract and posted at all ferry pools in case of emergency:

> If you have a forced landing, ring up 'Mayfair 120' extension 4, and give your particulars to the Transit Officer (Central Dispatch Pool) LONDON ...

> In the case of a forced landing or crash you are responsible for unloading guns.
> Tel. 'Mayfair 120' each day no later than 10 a.m. if still unable to proceed.

> If you have a crash, send a written and signed report immediately to O.C. Central Dispatch Pool. THIS IS MOST IMPORTANT.

Occasionally, after a crash, unloading one's guns and telephoning Mayfair 120 (a central search, rescue and salvage number for the RAF as well as the ATA) was not immediately practicable. This was certainly the case when another Diana ran into difficulties after taking off from Langley, near Slough, in a Hawker Tempest in 1943. First Officer Diana Ramsay (known as 'Wamsay' because she couldn't say her 'r's) was a dainty young woman with an upturned nose and light brown hair held back with a blue velvet ribbon. She joined the ATA the same month as Diana Barnato, who was at White Waltham as she flew overhead in serious trouble.

With a monstrous 2,500-horsepower Centaurus engine, Wamsay's Tempest was one of the fastest piston-powered aircraft of the war. It could cruise at 350 mph and sustain 450 mph for brief periods at maximum boost, making it perfect for chasing flying bombs. But it proved a handful when anything went wrong.

Soon after take-off, bound for Henlow to the north of London, 'Wamsay' felt an unsolicited surge of power and saw her airspeed indicator climb smartly to 400 mph. At that speed she would be at Henlow in less than three minutes, but with no hope of surviving a landing. She tried to throttle back and cut her boost setting, but found to her alarm that both were stuck at maximum. At this point, she told the Accidents Committee, she altered course, turning west for White Waltham, because she knew the aerodrome and surrounding area better. (She also knew that as a training school White Waltham had a practised crash wagon and its own blood cart.)

Unable to lower the undercarriage at 400 mph, she hurtled over Wembley and tried to climb to lose speed. It didn't work; she simply gained height and knew she would accelerate again when the time came to lose it. Not wanting to bale out over such a built-up area, she made a low pass over White Waltham at full power and full speed, shattering the mid-morning calm in the operations room; then she cut her engine. She was still travelling at close to 400 mph in an aircraft designed to land at not more than 100 mph. The crash wagon was already racing across the grass as she turned and began a last-ditch final approach. Diana Barnato and others emerged from the administration block to see her 'trying to lose speed in a series of humps, like a Dover sole or flatfish along the bottom of the sea'. The Tempest whistled clear across the aerodrome, pulled up to avoid a church spire and disappeared. Arthur 'Doc' Whitehurst – who had taken over as Commanding Officer at White Waltham when Frankie Francis was reassigned to Ratcliffe in December 1942 – ran for his car and invited Diana Barnato to go with him.

Dreading what they might find they drove to the edge of the aerodrome, then walked quickly across two fields in the direction the Tempest had been flying when last seen. The first sign of the crash was a series of cuts in the soft turf from the propeller. A section of wing and a heavy branch lay on the ground between two oak trees at the edge of a third field in which a small herd of cows had been grazing. Beyond this, something large and powerful had heaved itself over a ditch, smashed into a wood and kept going. Barnato and Whitehurst picked their way through the tunnel of torn branches it had left behind and came to a circle of flattened trees which looked, Diana wrote, 'as if a couple of dinosaurs had had a fight in there'. On the far side the Tempest's fuselage, shorn of wings and tail, was wedged up against a final bulwark of larger trees. Sitting astride its engine, minus her flying helmet but with hardly a bruise, was 'Wamsay'. She had begun to walk back towards the aerodrome, she said apologetically, but thought better of it since she was afraid of cows. In any case, she had left a velvet ribbon somewhere in the trees.

Even on delivery flights, the 'lovely warplanes' that Rosemary Rees and the rest of the ATA women delighted in flying travelled about 200 mph faster than the unlovely box kites that passed for warplanes in the First World War. An inevitable result was a much lower survival rate from 'prangs'. But a more curious result – or it may have been a series of extraordinary flukes – was that many of those who somehow survived potentially fatal accidents did so virtually uninjured.

In January 1943 Helen Richey hit a hangar at full power seconds after taking off from Llandow in a twin-engine Vickers Wellington. She lost three feet of wing, spun involuntary back onto the airfield and walked off smoking a cigarette. (Shortly afterwards she was expelled from the ATA for damaging too many aircraft and returned home to the States.) Three months later Jean Bird crashed in flames in a Hudson bomber when it stalled on take-off from Gosport in Hampshire. Margot Gore flew there immediately from Hamble in a Fairchild taxi plane, assuming Bird was dead. She was actually in the mess having a cup of tea. Hazel Raines, from Macon, Georgia, who sailed with Ann Wood on the *Indochinois*, spun out of the cloud and into a barn in a Spitfire and escaped with a blow to the head. In April 1944, Lettice Curtis suffered a fuel failure in a Typhoon on approach to Langley. She didn't make it, landing wheels-up in a field short of the runway having somersaulted when the aircraft's giant ventral cooling scoop dug into the grass. She wriggled out of the upside-down cockpit with gashes to her head and leg and insisted that the ambulance driver take her to the Royal Canadian Hospital at Cliveden (rather than Slough hospital). There she bumped into Lady Astor, who found a doctor to stitch her up. All these pilots had to telephone Mayfair 120 in due course, but at least Pauline Gower did not have to telephone their mothers.

19

Over The Top

The surest way to avoid an accident was, of course, to refuse to fly. In certain circumstances ATA pilots were within their rights to do this. In fact, in principle, they were encouraged to stay on the ground if they had any doubts about the wisdom of taking off. 'We pay you to be safe, not brave,' said a reminder notice above the entrance to the Hamble Ops Room. And, from the 'Standing Orders' again:

i) Bad weather flying is strictly prohibited . . .

ii) Competition between pilots is strictly prohibited. The idea that if A gets through and B does not, this is a reflection on B, is quite erroneous.

iii) No flight shall be commenced unless at the place of departure the cloud base is at least 800 feet, and the horizontal visibility at least 2,000 yards.

Furthermore, each pilot was her own captain. Completion of training entitled her to a Flight Authorisation Card which went everywhere with her along with her cherished Ferry Pilot's Notes. It was her passport to the skies. It was also what she showed to any uppity RAF or WAAF operative who presumed to question her judgement or tell her what to do.

Few pilots ever had to put their cards to the test, but the incomparable Mary de Bunsen did. She once made an unscheduled landing at Stratford-upon-Avon in a Hurricane and stayed there for eight straight days. A plume of smoke was billowing in a dark stripe down the middle of the country from the smokestacks of Wolverhampton directly over the Shakespeare Memorial Theatre, and de Bunsen refused to move as long as it did. To the east and west the skies were clear. Aircraft were flitting constructively back and forth. ATA pilots were stacking up hours in their logbooks. The weather people had said nothing about Stratford disappearing into a meteorological black hole. Operations at Hatfield, where de Bunsen was based, were incredulous. The RAF officers at her adopted aerodrome thought she was 'a frightful sissy'. One of them, after a few drinks, lurched up to her in the RAF mess where she was whiling away time and said: 'Why the hell don't you take off?' The answer was that de Bunsen loved flying even more than Bach's chromatic 'Fantasia and Fugue', and dreaded being sacked: she had 'bent' more than her share of Hurricanes already, and even though each accident report had exonerated her she knew that any report would count against her if she bent another. Even if it meant bunking for eight nights with secretly envious, earthbound WAAFs, she was taking her ATA minima – her 800 feet and her 2,000 yards – very seriously indeed.

There was a hitch. Pilots could be legitimately sacked for breaking weather minima, but they could also be illegitimately sacked (which amounted to the same thing) for not delivering enough aircraft. While de Bunsen was camping out at Stratford, Lois Butler, ATA pilot and wife of the chairman of De Havilland's, flew in in a De Havilland Rapide and gently told de Bunsen that underproductive pilots were being quietly let go. Men only so far, but . . .

De Bunsen understood. She told Butler she thought Rapides were easier to fly than Hurricanes in this sort of muck. Butler agreed, and took off into it. De Bunsen stayed put, and eventually the wind shifted to the west.

In such a fix, the solution for less admirably stubborn souls was to break the ATA's most basic rule and 'go over the top': climb through the overcast – the concrete, as Bobby Sandoz thought of

it – and worry about landing later. The moment a pilot took this decision she unburdened her employer of responsibility for her welfare, because it was expressly forbidden. Yet everyone knew that if every pilot obeyed this rule all the time only a fraction of the planes required to defeat Hitler would be delivered. Therefore the employer routinely turned a blind eye to such rule-breaking, and the pilot routinely took it upon herself to accept responsibility for her own life.

It was a nervy business. Amy Johnson got dragged into it and died. As Diana Barnato put it: 'She broke the rules and got caught out.' But of course Barnato broke them, too. A few months after tumbling out of the sky into the puddles at RAF Windrush, in another Spitfire, she ran into bad weather midway between East-leigh and Cosford over the Severn Valley and had to risk passing out from hypoxia to get over it. Lucky to find a hole in the clouds exactly where she needed one, she stood the Spitfire on its nose and dived from 12,000 feet to 400 feet, levelling out immediately above Cosford. Even allowing for an element of line-shoot, it was a close-run thing.

Veronica Volkersz insisted that the ATA's supposedly strict minima were broken time and time again simply to get the work done. Even the unbending Lettice Curtis admitted breaking them – though not actually going over the top. She described the despair, disembodiment and 'sickening frustration' of being ambushed by cloud over hilly country west of Cosford, near Wolverhampton, in a Lysander:

> 'Please God,' I prayed, 'get me out of this and I promise never to let myself get caught out like this again.' In situations like this one becomes schizophrenic, half of the brain searching for an excuse to opt out of the whole situation, whilst the other, driven by an instinct for survival, continues to battle for a way out.

The risks posed to ferry pilots by the British weather were invariably life-threatening. The ATA could have mitigated them

substantially by training its pilots to fly on instruments, but chose not to. No convincing reason for this decision was ever given. Barnato suggested, not entirely facetiously, that it was to prevent pilots joyriding beyond the British Isles (and in the end, in her case, it failed even to do that). Eric Viles, a former ATA cadet on heavy twins and four-engined bombers who subsequently became a public relations officer for Concorde, said there was simply no time for blind-flying training. Others have argued that refusing to give it helped to enforce the rule against flying in bad weather. This was clearly true, but it also helped kill those who were forced to break those rules. In any case it was a circular argument: if pilots had been taught how to fly in bad weather there would have been no need to forbid it and there would have been many fewer delivery bottlenecks, especially in winter.

The more enterprising pilots understood that they were risking their necks more than was necessary, and did something about it. When Diana Barnato landed at RAF Windrush, the officer who walked her to the Nissen hut under a cape explained that the aerodrome was a blind-flying school, and he was the instructor on its Link trainer simulator. She sat down with him immediately for an hour's tuition. Freydis Leaf told me she 'realised very early on that although they said not to do instrument flying you had to learn to do it so that when you got into cloud, you could just turn round and get out of it'. Whenever she found herself stuck out at an RAF station she would go in search of its simulator. 'And you know the officer in charge was generally delighted to give me an hour's training.' One well-known senior woman pilot was shocked, after the war, to learn of such brazen initiative.

There is a loyal consensus among most ATA veterans that their training was second to none. It was certainly remarkable as far as it went. Never before (to adapt Churchill) had such an eclectic crew of civilians flown so many different types of aircraft in such trying circumstances with so few mishaps, all things considered. The Times' aeronautical correspondent likened the achievement to 'taking a bunch of suburban motorists and, after a month or two's

Helen Richey, a well-known air racer in the US before the war, left the ATA in 1943 and committed suicide four years later.

After early resistance to the idea of women flying its aircraft, the RAF came to appreciate the heroic labours of the ATA – even if Margot Duhalde (second from left) and Ann Wood (right) were less than deferential to its officers.

(*Left to right*) Bobby Sandoz, Opal Anderson, Jadwiga Pilsudska and Mary Zerbel-Ford, who came from California to be close to her fiancé.

'A tough bunch of babies' – Diana Barnato Walker's description of her Hamble comrades. She is second from right, second row from the back. To her right are Margot Duhalde and Jackie Sorour, who hitchhiked by plane to South Africa and back to see her ailing mother.

Stewart Keith-Jopp, uncle of his namesake, Betty, lost an arm and an eye in the First World War but ferried aircraft throughout the Second.

Betty Keith-Jopp, survivor of one of the most miraculous escapes of the war, in a Harvard in 1945.

Audrey Sale-Barker lowers the ATA flag for the last time at White Waltham in November 1945.

'There was no-one to compare with me,' said Dorothy Hewitt. Here the acknowledged siren of the American pilots is pictured with her second husband, Lord Beatty.

Ann Wood on Remembrance Sunday in London in the late 1990s. She said in 1946: 'I will always deem it the greatest privilege of my life to have served the British Government in its hour of need.'

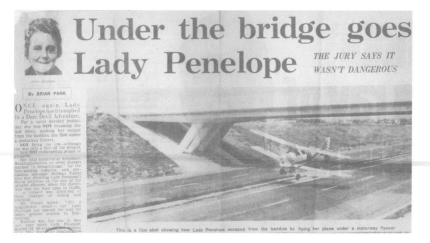

Under the bridge goes Lady Penelope

THE JURY SAYS IT WASN'T DANGEROUS

By BRIAN PARK

ONCE again, Lady Penelope has triumphed in a Dare Devil Adventure.

For a court decided yesterday she was NOT breaking the law when, making her escape from the baddies, she flew under a motorway flyover.

NOT flying too low—although she was only a foot off the ground.

And NOT endangering people or property.

Her total acquittal at Aylesbury, Buckinghamshire, on seven charges marked "a breakthrough" for the film-making industry, said production manager Norman Foster, who was directing Lady Penelope's flying activities on the day of the alleged offences, when the motorway was not then open to traffic.

Mr. Foster added: "It's a magnificent result — our Lady Penelope has opened the way for much greater realism in film-making."

Realism was the aim in May last year when Lady Penelope soared by 48-year-old spinster Joan Hughes...

This is a film shot showing how Lady Penelope escaped from the baddies by flying her plane under a motorway flyover

Joan Hughes was prosecuted for dangerous flying after standing in for Lady Penelope in a Tiger Moth for this stunt for the film *Thunderbirds 6* in 1968. She was acquitted.

Margot Duhalde sailed from Buenos Aires in 1941, hoping to fly for the Free French. She was still flying light aircraft from near her home in Santiago aged eighty-three.

In 1963, Diana Barnato Walker became the fastest woman in the world and the first British woman through the sound barrier. She was diagnosed with cancer the same week.

practice, turning them loose at Brooklands to discover that they can equal the professionals at their game'. He was right. But the failure to teach pilots how to save their own lives simply by using the information on the instrument panels in front of them was egregious and pointless. At the Aeroclub de Santiago, far from the English reunions and obituary desks where the loyal consensus was forged, Margot Duhalde called this failure 'criminal'.

One of its victims was a friend of Duhalde's called Honor Salmon. She was the granddaughter of the inventor of shorthand, Sir Isaac Pitman, and had not been married long when she flew into a hill near her parents' home on the Wiltshire Downs. It happened on 19 April 1943. A cold front had been forecast to arrive from the west in the late afternoon but it was over the Cotswolds by mid-morning, a wall of cloud and rain moving steadily across the country like a giant automatic car wash.

Salmon was supposed to be delivering an Airspeed Oxford to Colerne, the same type of aircraft that carried Amy Johnson on her last flight from Squires Gate two years earlier. On the same route and the same day, Veronica Volkersz was assigned a rare Mark XII Spitfire – the very latest thoroughbred from the Supermarine stable, with a snarling 2,035-horsepowered Griffon engine that could pull it along at 435 mph. Volkersz flew cautiously and turned back as soon as she ran into the front. Salmon was less experienced and possibly felt less vulnerable in the slower, roomier plane. Next to the rollercoaster Spitfire her Oxford was a bus, and famously dependable. Flying directly into the oncoming front rather than with it or along it, she would have known it couldn't last forever. Moreover, she may have thought she could wriggle through under the worst of the weather since she knew those particular hills so well. She hit one of them near Devizes and was killed instantly. She had been a team player, not a prima donna, and was never more noticed than when Margot Gore called everyone together on the Tannoy to tell them she was dead.

Six pilots from Hamble attended the funeral, Volkersz among them. Honor's mother asked them to share out the possessions left in her locker between her fellow pilots. 'After the ceremony we went back to the Pitmans' house, where refreshments had been prepared,' Veronica wrote. 'Trying desperately to smile, Honor's mother told us: "I do want this to be a jolly funeral, for I know Honor would like it that way." The gallantry of those words haunted me for many days.'

But it could only be for days. Quiet, kindly Honor Isabel Pomeroy Salmon had her name rubbed off the board at Hamble as the still-living had to get on with the war, still untrained on instruments.

Prince Chirasakti of Siam was another casualty of the British weather and the unspoken agreement that pilots would keep flying, edging into it, until they started getting killed. So were First Officers Ronald Porter and Alexander Scott. They took off from Kirkbride on 15 March 1942 in priority Spitfires for Prestwick under cloud at 200 feet and slammed into the first mountains they came to on the north side of the Solway Firth. Such was the fate of perhaps half the 170 ATA pilots of both sexes who were killed while flying during the war.

A few others died because of pilot error: their own or that of a taxi pilot. Others were victims of catastrophic mechanical failure resulting from combat damage, hasty or botched repairs or the sort of freak malfunction that the law of averages ensured was never more than a few engine beats from sending even the most careful pilot into a sickening, terminal spin.

Irene Arkless, 'the flying schoolgirl of Carlisle', was a proud pre-war pupil of the Border Counties Flying Club. She applied to join the ATA after her fiancé, Flight Lieutenant Thomas Lockyer of Chorley, Lancashire, had been shot down over Germany on a bombing raid. On being accepted, Arkless told her local paper she planned to fly over there and 'bring him home'. But she stalled and crashed in flames near Cambridge three days into 1943. She was hauled alive from the wreckage of her aircraft with severe shock, a badly broken femur and a fractured skull. She died later from her injuries.

Dora Lang died in a Mosquito in March 1944, with Janet Harrington, one of the ATA's four female flight engineers. The aircraft reared up, flipped onto its back and hit the ground seconds before what should have been a routine landing at Lasham in Hampshire. She may have lost one of the two engines and, with only twenty feet between her and the runway, failed to control the other. She may simply have stalled. The accident report was inconclusive, not least because the explosion on impact destroyed much of the evidence.

In the strange case of Mary Nicholson the accident report stated exactly what happened:

> A failure of lubrication to the reduction gear [between the engine and the propeller shaft] caused extreme overheating. Part of a pinion wheel race became loose and cut through the reduction gear to break away. On gliding down, the aircraft struck some farm buildings, caught fire and was destroyed.

In lay language, she lost her propeller; it was recovered several miles away. The accident happened around 5 p.m. on 22 May 1943 near the village of Littleworth in rolling Staffordshire farmland, about fifteen miles south of Stoke-on-Trent.

The report was posted on a noticeboard at Hamble a few days later. It was the first detailed information Bobby Sandoz gleaned on the death of her friend and fellow veteran of the good ship *Mosdale*. But the few cold lines about pinion wheels and reduction gear failed to satisfy her. When her next leave came due, Sandoz went to Littleworth to find out more.

20

Eyes Wide Shut?

Mary Nicholson was the only American woman to be killed while flying in Britain in the war. She died a long way from her family home in Greensboro, North Carolina, and there was little consolation for her parents when the telegram arrived there two days later, beyond the cliché that she died doing what she loved best. But she would never have been creeping up the Severn Valley in a Miles Magister on a cloudy late spring afternoon had she not practically begged Jackie Cochran to be among her twenty-five recruits. And she would never have had to beg had she not already been Cochran's most trusted secretary.

Nicholson was as awestruck as Cochran herself by the possibilities of flying. 'It's not for the thrill that's in it that I love it,' she declared of aviation in a speech to a women's group not long before she left for Montreal. 'I believe that it has a great future, and I believe that girls and women will take a great part of its development.'

She did love the thrill of it as well. The daughter of a Greensboro banker, Mary left her home state in 1925 with a degree in music and followed her new husband to Portsmouth, Ohio. For three years she worked there as a secretary, and chafed at the ordinariness of married life. In 1927 she flew for the first time. It was a joyride with an itinerant barnstormer. The following year she asked her husband for a divorce, and within a week of signing away her marriage she reached a deal with Portsmouth's Raven

Rock Flying School: if she performed three parachute jumps at the Carter County Fair to publicise the school, they would teach her to fly. She jumped, with no training to speak of (parachuting being less widely practised in those days than murder), from the lower wing of a three-seater biplane that would climb to 1,200 feet over the fairground and circle until she was ready. The chute went up in its own hand-held bag. The role of the second passenger was to unpack it and hold onto it until she jumped.

If Nicholson knew fear, she controlled it well. She kept her part of the bargain and did all three jumps. The Raven Rock Flying School duly coached her for her private licence, and on returning to Greensboro to help her family after the great Crash of 1929 she qualified as an instructor.

As secretary of the local flying club, and a strong, beautiful divorcee, Mary Nicholson was often to be found there borrowing other people's aeroplanes. She caught the eye of a famous aviator and altitude record-breaker named Frank Hawkes. It was he who recommended her to Cochran, who was frequently in need of secretaries because few of those she hired could stand her pace. Nicholson became her constant companion, taking furious dictation but also flying coast-to-coast with her and moving into the fabulous penthouse on the East River with the glass wall of memorabilia and the inlaid compass floor. When Ann Wood showed up for her interview with an anxious smile and a thumping heart in the autumn of 1941, Nicholson was already there, steadying the Cochran mood swings and honing her message.

Cochran gave in to Nicholson's pleading to be allowed to join the ATA only after she herself had flown to London and established herself on Tite Street in Chelsea. At least it would mean a friend and ally in a town where she was short of both.

Nicholson was the last woman to be cleared for action by the prickly Harry Smith in Montreal. She was loyal to Cochran to the last, declining invitations to gossip about her during the crossing to England and at the Red Cross Club in Mayfair where most American pilots congregated when on leave.

After Mary's death, Cochran wrote to her parents: 'You may be proud of her. She was a real soldier, and she went West well.' There were also letters of condolence from Pauline Gower (who had last written less than a month earlier to tell the Nicholsons how well their daughter was doing) and Sir Stafford Cripps, the Minister of Aircraft Production. Cripps signed thousands of similar letters. He knew this one was unique so far because the deceased was a woman and an American, but he had to assume there would be more like it in due course. So the wording was in the standard two-paragraph format. Mary had been doing '. . . work of the greatest importance to our war effort . . . She had proved herself a valuable officer and pilot' and would be 'greatly missed by all who knew her'. Cripps felt able to tell the parents of British pilots that their children had died in the service of their country – but not Mary's, even though this was six months after Pearl Harbor and nearly as many months since Cochran's exhilarating challenge to the airborne women of America: 'EVERY FRONT NOW OUR FRONT.'

The telegram informing Mary's parents of her death gave them three days to notify White Waltham if they did not want her to be cremated rather than buried. They did not request a burial, so five days later the cremation went ahead.

Gower failed to attend the funeral, even though Nicholson had been based at White Waltham. Sometimes, just when they most needed to be warm, the Brits could be breathtakingly chilly. Ann Wood wrote that evening:

no W.W. [White Waltham] officialdom was there – Mrs W. [Marion Wilberforce] was the first to arrive and was rather shocked to find that lacking anyone else she was the senior member so all procedure was left up to her . . . After some embarrassment and much delay a W.W. car arrived with Wendy [Audrey] Sale-Barker and three of Mary's classmates from W.W. The service was simple and cold, with many quotes from Mary Baker Eddy about strengths, light and sunshine – none of which would have helped me much . . .

It must have been a disconsolate group of young Americans who made their way back to the Red Cross Club in London for improvised funeral meats that afternoon. Mr and Mrs Nicholson would doubtless have implored them to be jolly, just as Mrs Pitman had a few months earlier, but Mr and Mrs Nicholson were stuck in Greensboro.

Ann Wood peeled away from the wake and decided to go up to the roof terrace of the Red Cross Club to sunbathe. Later she went for a bike ride in the park. Bobby Sandoz, who knew Nicholson better, found it harder to let go. 'I liked Mary,' she told me, 'and I cannot understand her crash.' After reading the official accident report she travelled to the crash site and talked to an old man who had witnessed Mary's final moments, and to the farmer whose barn had been destroyed. She became convinced that Mary had time after losing her propeller to straighten up and glide in for a relatively routine wheels-up landing next to the barn. 'The loss of her propeller wouldn't affect her ability to turn her aircraft to the side,' she said. 'It only needed fifteen degrees to avoid the barn. She was a good, cautious, thoughtful pilot, and she had plenty of time to avoid the barn and land on the field, but apparently the airplane did not change its course. And of course the whole thing burned.'

Sandoz could not stay long in Littleworth before returning to Hamble, but she knew the cockpit of a Miles Magister, and she knew Mary. She put one inside the other in the piece of sky she had studied above the burned-down barn and formed a theory that she could never quite shake – that it never occurred to Mary that she had time to save herself, so she simply closed her eyes and prepared to meet her maker. The theory was more of a judgement on Nicholson's experience, or lack of it, than on her skill. It was also a reflection of Sandoz's frustration, and of what she knew about her friend: 'She was very religious. I just know that every night, she got on her knees beside her bed and said her prayers. And if she thought she was going to die . . . you know, you search for an explanation. Well, maybe she had her eyes shut.'

*   *   *

The idea that Mary might have shut her eyes and let the barn come to her in the last few seconds of her life instead of using those seconds to make one, perhaps two, lightning, life-preserving decisions still vexed Roberta Sandoz more than sixty years later. She never said she would have used those seconds differently herself; she didn't need to. She did say, almost apologetically, that flying came easily to her. 'I just felt it in the seat of my pants,' she told me. And when the conversation moved on to Betty Keith-Jopp's inadvertent descent through cloud to the Firth of Forth, she had firm views. Keith-Jopp had been turning back onto her reciprocal course. So far so good: exactly as per standing orders. But what happened next?

'As you change your wing from normal flight [into a turn] the tendency of the aircraft is to slide down, so you must give left stick, left rudder and throttle at the same time. All it takes is more throttle so you can hold your nose on the horizon, and that's the crucial thing. Hold your nose on the horizon. The moment your nose drops you're losing altitude.' Bobby thought about it. 'I think she wasted an airplane.'

Having sat with Betty at the Indaba Hotel in Johannesburg and heard the story from the pilot's point of view, the judgement seemed harsh. But it also seemed significant for being offered at all, with such crisp supporting detail, by such a self-evidently thoughtful person, so long after the event. Betty Keith-Jopp may have erred in letting her nose drop in the cloud but she had strained every nerve and sinew and pulmonary corpuscle to survive in the minutes that followed. That made her a survivor in the most literal sense, and in the end this was the most the women of the ATA could hope for.

Many of them stated openly that they wished they could have flown in combat. 'I thought it was the only fair thing,' Maureen Dunlop mused. 'Why should only men be killed?' But men denied them the ultimate proving ground. So all the women could do to prove themselves was get on with the task in hand – delivering aircraft, day in, day out – and stay alive in the process.

Lettice Curtis worked harder than anyone to leave nothing to chance. Her description of psyching up for a difficult flight in marginal weather is illuminating, if typically detached:

> At times like this pilots become introverted and entirely wrapped up in themselves, unable to settle to anything, conversation becoming mechanical and trivial. One half of the mind would look desperately for some excuse – albeit a good one – for getting out of the trip; the other waiting to get on with it . . . On such occasions a pilot is completely and utterly alone.

On the ground, that solitude was something to be endured, but once airborne at last, especially on a clear day, it became a luxury:

> I can think of few better ways of spending a couple of hours . . . two uncommitted hours in which to let one's thoughts ramble on uninterrupted, as they did long ago during a dull sermon on a Sunday morning in church . . . yet such is the human subconscious that even with thoughts seemingly miles away, some finely-tuned monitor would sound an alert for the minutest change in background noise, be it from engine or airframe, to bring one back in a fraction of a second to the present world.

Others gave more flamboyant displays of pre-flight nerves. The two Audreys – Sale-Barker and Macmillan – specialized in what Mary de Bunsen called 'feminine vapours':

> 'My Dear,' one or the other would exclaim in the mess, 'I've got my first Hudson (or Mitchell, or whatever it might be) and I know I shall crash and I've got a pain (cold, temperature, etc).' And they would totter out, leaving a trail of handkerchiefs, lipsticks, handbags etc., which would be picked up by willing (male) hands. They would then fly whatever it was superbly to its destination, where they would be assisted out of the aeroplane and the same pantomime would take place.

(De Bunsen said she later read a description of Sale-Barker's technique for preparing for ski races, and recognised it instantly.)

There is no question that the pilots who were most constantly alert and most willing to try anything in a fix were the most likely to survive. That said, some simply ran out of luck. Margaret Fairweather, the first woman to fly a Spitfire, lost her second husband in April 1944. Captain Douglas 'Poppa' Fairweather, too large for a Spitfire and much larger than life, had been tried out as a commanding officer in Prestwick, but was found too disrespectful of rules: when the ATA tried to ban smoking in its aircraft he would start taxi flights by handing round a silver cigarette case offering 'instant dismissals'. When no-one could be found to look after his pet goat, he flew it round the country with him. When White Waltham insisted that taxi pilots use maps, he used one of Roman Britain. He was also known to leave his pocket diary open at the map pages on his knee, but never to refer to it.

Douglas Fairweather was not tall, but he weighed in at 16 stone at the start of the war and somehow kept most of his paunch despite rationing. This kept him in Ansons rather than single-seaters when he was moved from Prestwick back to White Waltham, and it was in Ansons that he specialised in getting through atrocious weather when no-one else could. His method, when unable to see the ground, was to set a compass bearing and stick to it, chain-smoking at the rate of exactly seven minutes per cigarette.

Diana Barnato once flew with Captain Fairweather from Belfast to White Waltham over continuous low cloud cover. After twenty-three cigarettes he put the last, carefully counted butt back into his cigarette case, eased the stick forward and dropped out of the cloud with White Waltham dead ahead. By 1944, most of his flying was of injured pilots to the Royal Canadian Hospital at Cliveden. On 4 April an especially urgent case was phoned through from Prestwick on an especially unpleasant day. Fairweather volunteered. For familiarity's sake he took an Anson, even though it had no radio and even though for such a special case he could have taken a Rapide with wireless navigation. In thick cloud he flew into the Irish Sea. He was mourned in the letters column of *Aeroplane* magazine for 'the rich zeal and relish with which he baited officiousness and mocked men of petty vices'. The same correspondent mentioned Captain Fairweather's wife, Margie: 'If much has been said about him and little of her it is because he was an extrovert, and to discuss him is permissible; in fact, he would have liked it. By the same mark, to discuss her would be unpardonable.'

Douglas Fairweather once said he loved Margie 'better than any dog I ever had ... or even a pig or a cat'. It was a quietly requited love. She was heavily pregnant when he died and gave birth a few days later to a daughter. She was still mourning him four months later, when she took off in a Percival Proctor from Heston bound for Hawarden, near Liverpool. She was acting as air chauffeur for a male VIP and her own sister, the Hon. Mrs Kitty Farrer – Pauline Gower's adjutant – who had a personnel problem to attend to in Scotland. Less than twenty miles from Hawarden the Proctor's engine coughed and died. Fairweather tried to restart it by switching tanks, but accident investigators found the port tank's vent pipe had been carelessly blocked by a skin-like membrane of weatherproof paint. If no air could enter the tank, no fuel could leave it.

Unflustered, Fairweather chose a field in the lower reaches of the Dee valley for a forced landing. It had been ploughed at right angles to her direction of approach, which would ordinarily have been bumpy but not deadly. The Proctor's wheels stuck in a furrow and its nose tipped forward. Kitty was thrown clear and was injured, but not fatally. The VIP, a Mr Louis Kendrick of the Ministry of Aircraft Production, broke his thumb. Margie was slammed forward, shattering her spectacles, from which shards of glass went through her eyes into her brain. The Cold Front – the grown-up with a faraway look in her eye when the ATA girls met the press at Hatfield; the first woman to fly a Spitfire – died the following day at Chester Royal Infirmary. Her reserve meant she was not widely known, but she was remembered, not least by those she had taught to fly at Glasgow Flying Club before the war. Two of them had joined the RAF and fought in the Battle of Britain. When her brother-in-law visited the crash site, he found them there in tears.

Death was not much discussed in the ATA, but it was always round the corner, or liable to happen in a split second and right in front of you, leaving no time to look away. Around lunchtime on 17 January 1943, Lettice Curtis was on her final approach to Sherburn-in-Elmet, in North Yorkshire, in one of several Hurricanes flown up there from White Waltham en route to Scotland. Visibility was good, but the Sherburn aerodrome was a mess. It had started the war as a farm, with a massive stone farmhouse that could absorb and thaw out as many pilots as pitched up there, whether from the Shetlands or the Sussex coast. But it had nothing that remotely resembled a runway. Taxi flights began and ended among chickens in the farmyard.

In late 1942 the Air Ministry approved the building of a pair of full-length concrete runways, triggering an invasion of bulldozers that turned the fields into mud baths. Meanwhile, ferry pilots had to go on landing there.

The Hurricane immediately ahead of Curtis was being piloted by Flight Captain Alan Colman (of the Colman's mustard family). His instructions from the White Waltham Maps and Signals Department were to land on the north side of the farmhouse. He did so, and ran into a broad sheet of standing water eighteen inches deep. The Hurricane cartwheeled onto its back and lay there in the water. By the time the crash crew got to Colman he had drowned in his straps. Curtis landed next to him and insisted, years later, that there was nothing anyone could do until enough people arrived to lift the tail and release the canopy. The official history of the ATA, written in 1945, stated that help arrived in 'the shortest possible time'. This may be so, but as Ann Wood noted after hearing about the accident that night, Colman died 'within sight of many a potential helping hand, so one never knows'. One never knew how death would come; nor could one ever count on others to keep it at bay.

As the war ground on it developed a terrifying momentum. Veronica Volkersz was collecting an Airspeed Oxford from Christchurch in Dorset soon after D-Day when she had to wait for an American squadron of P-47 Thunderbolts to take off for France. These were heavyweights at the best of times, even by single-engined standards. They had huge double radial Pratt & Whitney engines stuffed into their blunt noses, and semi-elliptical wings not unlike a Spitfire's that were usually enough to get them airborne. For their mission on 29 June 1944, however, each carried two 1,000-lb bombs. There was no headwind, and the runway was short, ending in houses. The Thunderbolts took off in pairs, or that was the idea. The first pair cleared the houses by a few feet, but one of the second slammed into them and blew up. Volkersz watched in horror as the third pair accelerated towards the inferno and staggered through it into the air. Then came the fourth: one made it, the other never left the ground. It ploughed through the gap left by the first crash into the next row of houses; another shattering explosion. Twenty people were dead or injured before the squadron had even regrouped above the airfield.

'What are you dicing with today?' the Hamble women would enquire dryly of each other as they headed for their taxi planes with a new day's chits. It was partly a type-check, to make sure no one else had been favoured with something new or exotic or especially fast. It was also a reference to a propaganda poem called 'Dicing With Death Under Leaden Skies' that they all felt applied not unflatteringly to them. It didn't make death itself more palatable, though; not the sudden end of a person or her physical remains. Rosemary Rees was once called to a crash site, possibly Honor Salmon's, and found that the ATA's Inspector of Accidents had got there before her and was looking unwell.

'He said, "the medics haven't done their job very well."
  I said, "there's a helmet."
  He said, "don't touch it".'

Death was a part of life even when names you knew weren't being rubbed off the Hamble blackboard. Freydis Leaf told me how she lost seven cousins during the war and how her older brother, Derek, had taken her to one side before the storm arrived and foretold it all:

He always said, when war came I must be prepared that my dear cousin Richard, who was a fighter pilot, he'd be killed within about a fortnight of getting into action. And Ronnie, his brother, who was in the artillery, he'd be killed about a month or two later. And my brother said 'I shall be killed too, you know, about a month or so after I get into action.'

At this Freydis sighed and looked away – away from the coffee table in her sitting room, and my tape recorder taking it all down. Her eyes filled and she fell silent for what seemed like a long time. 'And it did work out like that,' she said eventually.

And I remember his mother-in-law having a dream, and she said that in the dream she was in a big church and Richard and Ronald were there, standing by a bier, and they were waiting for the third crusader to come, which she felt she knew was Derek, and sure enough he did get killed then. But I'm sure they went on fighting evil, whatever it was, whatever it was.

21

Women of the World

To woo a woman more interested in aeroplanes than men took patience. No-one ever managed it with Joan Hughes or Margaret Frost. Three men thought they had succeeded with Margot Duhalde, but she tired of each of them soon after marrying them.

As for Jackie Sorour, the South African, a succession of eligible types tried their luck and their best lines on her because she was adorable to look at and maddeningly good on the dance floor. With loose black curls and a starlet's bright face, she was vaguely aware of her attraction for men even though she was shy and inexperienced with them. She was fiercely impatient whenever she thought her femininity was holding her back, but not uninterested in learning to flirt with it. At the same time she was a natural and utterly determined pilot. All of which made her a 'hot pertater' – hotter than she knew. She did fall for one of her admirers in the end – Lieutenant Reg Moggridge – because she liked the look of him and fell in love with his deliberate way of doing things. But mainly because he was as patient as a statue.

Reg first met Jackie at an army dance at Brooklands in 1940. She let him partner her but in her shyness and respect for propriety she developed neck ache making sure her cheek never touched his. He managed to get an arm round her, but only on the parquet when they had to dive for cover from a stick of bombs during the national anthem. The army provided buses home for the WAAF girls from the coastal radar station where Jackie worked before joining the ATA, watching intently for green German blobs to be called in to Fighter Command at Stanmore. She sat next to Reg on the bus and let him hold her hand in the dark. She hoped he would kiss her goodnight, but she pulled away before he took his chance.

Two years later, impelled by orders to depart for India, Reg bought Jackie a zircon ring that would fit under her flying gloves.

'You have no objections to an engagement?' he asked over lunch at his parents' house near Taunton.

'None whatever,' she answered.

Another two years, and they saw each other again. Reg decided to make his return from India a surprise. On a Friday afternoon in September 1944 he let himself into the riverside cottage in Hamble where Jackie was billeted, and sat down to wait. She had been faithful to him, deflecting advances with 'a pious pseudo-saintliness that would have made a nun of Assisi a harlot by comparison', as she put it later. But she was 300 miles away that afternoon on the north side of the Lake District, with little chance of showing up that night.

The weather over the fells and the Solway Firth beyond was bad and worsening, and Jackie's ride home was a decrepit twin-engined Mitchell bomber, a type she had not flown before. Rows of bombs, one for each operational mission flown, were painted under its nose next to a faded dancing girl. As the plane sat outside the Kirkbride operations room in driving rain, Sorour was handed her delivery chit. 'ONE LANDING ONLY', it said in red. She was to fly a new type in foul weather on its last flight before being broken up. It did not seem sensible, but Hamble personnel were invited to a dance – another dance – at a nearby American army camp that night. Sorour felt indifferent about it, but her flight engineer wanted to go.

They headed out into the rain and strapped themselves in. With her Flight Authorisation Card in her top left-hand pocket, Sorour was her own captain. Operations staff could neither ground her nor order her to take off; only advise. Advice to pilots already in their aircraft but not in wireless contact came in the form of coloured flares. Green meant it was safe to proceed; red unsafe. Sorour taxied the old bomber to the east end of the runway, hemmed in by hills, and turned to line up for take-off towards the sea. As she peered down the runway the sky darkened and a squall whipped the rain and puddles into a curtain of water. A red flare went up from the control tower.

'The dance,' hissed the engineer, and Sorour obligingly put her hand to the throttles. She took off into the storm, choosing not to notice a second flare launched as the Mitchell lumbered into the air. She levelled off almost immediately and banked to port under the clouds, hugging the coast.

To the south the weather improved, but as the Mitchell approached the Dunfold Maintenance Unit in Surrey where it was to be broken up its starboard engine failed. Sorour shouted at her engineer to feather the propeller, trimming the flaps and opening her port throttle to compensate. A quick look at her map told her they had ten miles to go, with 800 feet to lose and not enough power to go round again if she undershot on her final approach. The engineer asked if she had landed a bomber on one engine before. She said she hadn't, and he tightened his straps.

At this point a less confident pilot might have followed the instructions in the Ferry Pilot's Notes even more carefully than usual, or panicked. Sorour did neither. She realised that if she let the engineer lower the undercarriage at the recommended speed and altitude she would suddenly not have enough of either because of the increased drag. So she made him hold off until they were less than a mile from the runway, then brought the plane in crabwise, kicking the rudder pedals against a gusty crosswind and squeezing as much power out of the port engine as she could without turning the plane over. They bounced once, broke nothing and rolled slowly to a halt. As the crash wagon rushed out to meet them, Sorour noticed that the maps clutched in her hand were shaking like a flag in a stiff breeze.

An Anson dropped them at Hamble, where Jackie and her engineer went straight from the airfield to the dance and jitter-bugged till midnight. She went home without him, creeping over the threshold of Creek Cottage so as not to wake her hosts. In the sitting room she found Reg, thinner and browner than in 1942, rising from an easy chair surrounded by pipe-cleaners and maga-zines. 'I remember little of what happened in the shy haze of welcome,' she wrote. 'Except . . . that I was firmly kissed.'

The war had changed them both, but not so much that they did not want to be together. On the contrary, the cocktail of exaggerated independence and prudishness that Reg had left behind suddenly found herself 'eager to be dominated by man and marriage'. She suggested a wedding the following Easter. Reg suggested January. Jackie agreed, provided she could visit her mother in Pretoria first, and that self-imposed deadline launched her on one of the more remarkable hitchhikes of the war.

When Sorour called her mother with the news that she was getting married, her mother replied that she was suffering a ner-vous breakdown. It was not clear whether the breakdown was a result of the announcement, or even if it was genuine, but it gave Jackie grounds to request two months' compassionate leave. The request was granted, and in mid-December 1944, she left Hamble for RAF Lyneham in Wiltshire in a Spitfire with an overnight bag. 'We waved her off with quite a lot of heart-searching on our part and a great deal of aplomb on hers,' Alison King remembered. Jackie had no exit permit or air ticket; only an iron will almost completely camouflaged by coquetry, and a hopeful letter from South Africa House addressed 'To whom it may concern'.

It took her two days to persuade Lyneham that she was serious, but eventually she managed to talk her way into the co-pilot's seat of a giant four-engined Consolidated Liberator bound for Cairo (even though she had not been cleared to fly four-engined air-craft). The Liberator landed to refuel in Malta, but it developed a fault and failed to take off again. Jackie switched planes, volunteer-ing her services as a stewardess on a Cairo-bound military Dakota.

She was grounded in Egypt for three days for want of a yellow fever inoculation certificate, but eventually forged one with the help of a South African colonel who knew her vaguely from a previous life. Then she hopped another Dakota, this one bound straight for Pretoria, and arrived there three stormy days later.

She found her mother less ill than advertised, and soon had her out of her bed. She stayed for ten days, gorging on fresh milk and fruit and declining lavish inducements to cancel her return: her mother offered her a car, a flat, an aeroplane and a hand-picked selection of alternatives to Reg. None measured up. Nor did she feel at home. 'To be so suddenly engulfed in a forgotten world of rich food, naked lights and untroubled skies . . . it was too much,' she wrote. 'My destiny was with an austere island still grappling with a mortal foe.' And so, with two weeks' leave left and 6,000 miles to go, she headed north again. The third Dakota of the trip took her to Khartoum, where she dashed across the tarmac and begged her way onto a fourth, which had landed minutes before her carrying Gurkha officers from Kathmandu to Boscombe Down. There were waterspouts over the Mediterranean and a forced landing at Istres, near Marseilles, but she was back in England with six days in which to get married in Taunton and honeymoon in Brighton (with lingerie smuggled in in her slimline overnight bag from South Africa).

Jackie Sorour was Jackie Moggridge at last: a woman of the world in a world that had changed almost as much as she had. The chance to leap from Dakota to Dakota to South Africa and back was part of that change. The globe would shrink still futher when Constellations and jet-powered Comets replaced Dakotas, and the network of military air bridges that Sorour had found so useful became the basis of a civilian airline revolution after the war. But a more significant change for women who flew Spitfires, and women generally, had already occurred on the more intimate stage of the Palace of Westminster.

*　　*　　*

On 18 May 1943, Miss Irene Ward, Conservative MP for Wallsend, rose in the House of Commons to address a question to Sir Stafford Cripps, Minister of Aircraft Production. Was it his understanding, she asked, that the women pilots of the ATA received the same rate of pay as their male colleagues? The gaunt and earnest Sir Stafford (who was a vegetarian; when he visited a group of ATA women at White Waltham they fed him macaroni cheese), replied that as of the following month these women would indeed be paid the same as men of the same rank doing the same work.

Miss Ward: 'Is the Right Honourable and learned Gentleman aware how gratifying it is that this decision has been arrived at without pressure from women members of the house?'

The Minister: 'I am grateful.'

History made, the house moved on. But two days later its attention was drawn to a related subject. The board of BOAC had resigned en masse in a power struggle with the newly formed RAF Transport Command, and a new board had been nominated. Sir Archibald Sinclair, Secretary of State for Air, read out the names of his nominees. To those of Viscount Knollys, KCMG, MBE, DFC, Air Commodore A. C. Critchley, CMG, DSO, and a handful of other predictably stalwart gentlemen, the Mother of Parliaments offered little reaction. But when the last name was announced, the House suddenly bestirred itself. What began as a self-conscious 'Hear! Hear!' from the Tory backbenches grew into a generalised waving of order papers, and eventually swelled into a full-throated roar of approval that straddled the aisle and echoed – one likes to think – along the corridors of Westminster, into the Lords, across Parliament Square and down the ages.

That name was Pauline Gower's, and those few seconds on the afternoon of 18 May 1943, were her moment of triumph. She hadn't done much flying in the war, but that was because she had more to prove on the ground than in the air. What she had done was to lead a stealthy if not quite bloodless coup. Jackie Cochran made enemies by appearing to put her crusade for women before the war effort. Gower always put duty first, then merit. She almost never argued about gender. That way, any great leaps forward that she achieved for womankind could be categorised as entirely incidental. This was her genius. Under cover of war and her own brisk smile she ambushed the Establishment. Her appointment to the board of the organisation that would connect up whatever was left of the British Empire after the war was recognition that the ambush had succeeded. It would have been unimaginable before the war, and unimaginable for anyone else. She did hope that having proved equal to their task, and to men, her pilots would clear the way for a proper peacetime role for women in aviation. She had abandoned such talk, at least in public, barely a year into the war. But now her strategy of letting the flying do the talking seemed to be sweeping all before it. Anything seemed possible again.

It was suggested by one of the sketchwriters in the press gallery that afternoon that the applause for Miss Gower was started by the long-serving and honourable member for Gillingham, Sir Robert Gower. It probably was. It was also suggested, in a diary entry by Ann Wood after sharing a car journey with Sir Robert's daughter a few weeks later, that the projects to which Pauline had been devoting herself for the previous four years were not as engrossing or important as her subordinates were led to believe. This was uncharitable. Wood may still have blamed Gower for Jackie Cochran's isolation in London and Helen Richey's early return to the US; but the fact was that without Gower there would have been no women's section of the ATA; no progression from Moths to Magisters, Magisters to Hurricanes, Hurricanes to Spitfires and Lancasters and weird gas-guzzling jets; and certainly no equal pay.

The struggle with the British Treasury's rule that women were worth 20 per cent less than men had seemed one for another generation. It was, after all, 'an affront to society for a woman to ask to get equal pay for equal work', as Bobby Sandoz put it. 'The idea was that the man had a family to support and a woman alone did not.'

Even now, no-one was suggesting that any other women would get equal pay for equal work. Those working the land or in munitions factories, or building Merlin engines in Glasgow or rebuilding broken men at the Royal Canadian Hospital at Cliveden, dutifully went on giving the government their sweat, toil, tears and 20 per cent discount until peace broke out and sent most of them back home. They lacked their Pauline Gowers.

Gower had been closely involved in the manoeuvring that led to the announcement of 18 May. In a sense, the process had begun two years earlier. She had seized on her pilots' success in switching to Hurricanes to announce at a lunch for the Royal Aeronautical Society that the theory that 'the hand that rocks the cradle wrecks the crate' had been proved wrong. There was now no limit to the types of aircraft women could fly, she declared, and no-one contradicted her. In practice, it took until February 1943 for Lettice Curtis and Joan Hughes to be cleared to fly four-engined aircraft – but as soon as they were, the ATA's Director of Services and Personnel, the Hon. Ben Bathurst, urged on by Gower, asked Sir Stafford Cripps for more money for his women. At first Cripps said there was nothing he could do. Then Gower went to see him herself, and he changed his mind. It seems that she simply let him know that Irene Ward MP would shortly be raising the matter in the Commons. Armed with a credible threat of embarrassment for the government, Cripps went to the Treasury, which capitulated.

Was it part of the plan that Miss Ward would be able to congratulate the government on doing the right thing 'without pressure from women members of the house'? Presumably. But whose plan was it? Who decided to involve Miss Ward? She never claimed credit for it, but it can only have been Miss Pauline Mary de Peauly Gower.

On 22 May 1943 Ann Wood visited White Waltham and noted that Gower was 'overjoyed' at her appointment to the board of BOAC. Indeed she was, even though her new post nearly killed her: on the first of several route inspection flights that summer, her plane, a De Havilland Fortuna airliner, disintegrated while making a forced landing on a mud flat near Shannon in the west of Ireland. Miraculously Gower was unhurt.

Feeling generous, Gower gave some of her American pilots permission to go home on leave. This was, apart from anything, good people management. The Americans' lives had been upended. Many of the British women pilots could go home for their fortnightly two days off, or at least to friends. The 'cousins' were lucky if they had any. And apart from anything, there was only so much Britishness a gal could take at a stretch.

For Bobby Sandoz there was also some important family news to impart. Two days before heading home from Prestwick in a B-24 via Reykjavik, Newfoundland and New York, she was married to Peter Leveaux, a cavalry officer who had muscled in on a date she was not particularly enjoying with a test pilot in Mayfair the previous year. It was, she said, 'a pretty simplified wedding'. The groom's family was there in numbers. Emily Chapin stood in for the bride's. There was no honeymoon. Instead, the new Mrs Leveaux wrapped herself up in an oversized US Army Air Corps sheepskin coat given to her by a pitying sergeant on Atlantic ferry duty, and made the 12,000 mile trek to Evans and back. She spent four days at home in the mountains north of the Grand Coulee Dam. Mainly for practical reasons, her parents regretted that their only child hadn't married an American, but they didn't belabour her with their regret. 'My stepfather was probably afraid of crying,' Bobby said. 'My mother just wanted to hold my hand all the time.' She would not see her daughter again for another six years.

Ann Wood took a longer break. She had learned that 'he who yells loudest to the right people generally is heard' and she practically demanded a decent summer holiday. For the month of August 1943, she was Mrs Oliver Wood's prodigal daughter and the toast of Waldeboro, Maine. The strangeness of home and abundance after blockaded England – and of airborne Atlantic crossings when they were still so new – were obviously worth it. She shelved her diary writing, but her holiday snaps show a citizen of the world such as that part of the world had never seen before. In most of them she wears dark slacks, a button-down white shirt and a grin. She had been through what Waldeboro and her old flying school down on the coast at Bowdoin College had only heard about on CBS. She had seen the blackout, dived for an air raid shelter, flown the Spitfire, shaken Ike's hand and buried a comrade. She left as 'socialite' Ann Wood. Now she was First Officer. People seemed to want to reach out and touch her.

It was, she wrote to her mother on her return to England, 'a colossal holiday', and it ended in style. Weighed down with gifts and provisions, she reported to Atlantic Ferry Command in Montreal for her return to England in the second week of September. Captain Hump Moody of Illinois, aged twenty-three, was to be her pilot in a lightly laden Mitchell fitted with long-range tanks instead of bombs in its bomb bay. Harry McKinley, of New York and the Royal Canadian Air Force, was navigator. Larson Blakely of Montreal was radio operator. Wood took the co-pilot's seat; there were no others.

Hump had the choice of a straight shot to Greenland over 1,500 miles of tundra and cold sea, or a stop half-way in Goose Bay, Labrador, where the North American continent finally slips under water. He chose Goose Bay, which turned out to be the right decision. One of the reserve tanks sprang a leak which none of Hump or Harry or Larson Blakely could fix. So they stayed the night, perplexing the local wing commander, who, four years into the war, still had no agreed procedure for feeding or accommodating females.

Next morning the leaking tank was drained. At noon the Mitchell took off again and headed north by north-east for Narssarssuaq on Greenland's ice-mangled southern tip. The plan was to stay within safety limits by taking a stopping route the whole way over; they would refuel again in Iceland. But the plan did not allow for dud weather, or dud weather reports. In Goose Bay the forecast had been for clearing skies on the far side of the Labrador Sea, but they never cleared. Instead, as darkness approached, the cloud and sea mist over Greenland merged. After circling for an hour in search of a way through, Hump turned round with just enough fuel left to make it back to Labrador.

Ten minutes later Narssarssuaq radioed to say they were sending up a fighter escort to bring the Mitchell in. Hump turned the plane round again, committing himself and his crew to landing in Greenland or ditching in water that they had been told gave a healthy body about eighteen minutes' survival time. For a quarter of an hour, the Mitchell circled again, waiting for the escort. Then Greenland came on a wireless to say the escort plane had developed a problem and they were to return to Goose Bay.

At this point Hump 'hit the ceiling'. Returning to Goose Bay was out of the question. Wood started scribbling frantic notes to the radio operator to tell Greenland that if they couldn't send a plane they had better send a boat because the Mitchell would have to ditch.

Narssarssuaq said it would find another plane instead, and an hour later they saw it circling below them. Then they heard it: 'Come on chicken, tuck your wing right in behind daddy's and everything will be fine and dandy.' By this time, a second bomber had appeared off Hump's wing, also needing help. The escort led them both down to 2,000 feet and along a 30-mile fjord between rows of mountains whose glaciers could still be made out in the deepening dusk. They landed where the mountains dead-ended, 'and boys came tearing from every nook and cranny, I thought to find out how we made out', Wood recalled. 'But no – merely to look at a white woman. Many hadn't seen one for eighteen months.'

They had left Montreal on a Friday morning. On Saturday night they were guests of the Narssarssuaq US Army Air Corps Base Executive Officer for cocktails in his hut, proceeding to a series of enlisted men's messes dotted along the fjord for an impro- vised multi-venue banquet. On Sunday morning Wood attended prayers in the hospital dining room, noting afterwards that 'most of the boys including the padre thought they were seeing a mirage and would end up in the mental clinic'. Later, a boat trip was arranged. Ann and her new friends amused themselves by shooting the tops off icebergs and handing out cigarettes to Eskimos. Dinner that night was a no-holds-barred set piece: chuck steak, rehydrated potatoes, bread, butter, peas, pears and chocolate cake. Afterwards there was a movie. The boys knew every word of it and the mere appearance of the female form on-screen drew from them a gigantic ritual sigh. By this time Wood had been joined at Narssarssuaq by Grace Stevenson and Mary Ford, England-bound after leave in Oklahoma and Hollywood respectively. In the cinema they received a standing ovation. They were called at 3 a.m. for a dawn departure, three bombers thundering back along the fjord in single file, then spiralling slowly to 10,000 feet to clear the mountains and set course for London by way of Reykjavik. In all the journey took eight days; almost as long as the *Indochinois* had taken to sail from Montreal to Liverpool.

For Opal Anderson, the enthusiastically expressive Chicagoan, it took eight *weeks*. She was detained in Canada rather than Greenland (where the stopover by Wood, Ford and Stevenson turned out to be the last by women during the war as well as the first; Ford's captain afterwards accused the Narssarssuaq tower of grounding him for a day in order to see more of his personable passenger, and an investigation ensued). The reason for Anderson's inordinate delay was a lawsuit brought by her against the *New York Herald Tribune* for an article published in her absence on the women of the ATA. It called Opal an ex-stripper, and, without naming its source, gave the impression that the tittle-tattler had been none other than Pauline Gower.

Anderson was livid. At first she demanded a conspicuous retraction from Mrs Ogden Reid, the *Tribune*'s publisher. When none was printed, she sued. The affair was still unresolved on her return to London (20 lbs heavier, she claimed, then when she left). She was 'itching to get her hands on Pauline', she told Wood. But official business had called the new BOAC board member away, and the seething American was left to vent to sympathisers and scowl at any other Brits who looked as if they might have questioned her honour when her back was turned. Luckily for Gower – and probably for both of them – by the time she returned from a long series of route inspection flights there were more urgent things to worry about than slander and stripping.

22

Left Behind

Hanging from the roof of the Imperial War Museum, the doodle-bug looks oddly pitiful: blind, battered, unexploded and devised in desperation. Hanging in the sky over the English Channel – more precisely, pulsing towards London at 390 mph – it looked pitiless. With nō-one on board, it could hit a primary school or a country ditch and not know the difference. With no-one on board, you could shoot it down and still not have the satisfaction of taking a pilot out of the war.

The V1 flying bomb was powered by a ramjet and guided by gyroscopes. It could be launched from almost anywhere and could carry nearly a tonne of high explosive from German-occupied Holland to the Isle of Dogs. It was horribly advanced; so advanced, in fact, that the Allies failed to take it seriously until it was too late. The first inkling of a secret weapons programme, had anyone been paying attention, came in a British intelligence report of November 1939 that spoke of a rocket research establishment at Peenemunde on the German Baltic coast, 150 miles east of Hamburg. In a different era, Britain would launch a war on the strength of similar (albeit flimsier) intelligence, but the first Peenemunde tip-off was ignored. The next one came in mid-1943, from agents in the field. Stripped-down, ultra-streamlined photo-reconnaissance Spitfire Mark XIs (Diana Barnato's favourite type) were sent over to photograph the complex. The RAF confirmed there was something in the pictures, and destroyed it before finding out what it was.

By this time the design of the V1 had been finalised. Testing was complete, manufacture was dispersed, and hundreds of launch sites were being built across Holland and northern France. The sites showed up in more reconnaissance pictures, usually at the edge of small patches of woodland. A few were destroyed, but most were not and the Allies still had no firm idea what they were for. Then, in November 1943, a thirty-one-year-old Constance Babington Smith of the WAAF (who would go on to write Amy Johnson's biography) was poring over the top-secret photographs when she spotted something everyone else had missed: a dark cruciform object at the lower end of a set of rising rails at one of the launch sites in Normandy. It was tiny, with less than half the wingspan of a Spitfire, but it was clearly the weapon the RAF had been hunting. Judging by its size relative to a concrete storage bunker next to the rails, and the number of similar sites seen from the air, it was reckoned the Germans had stockpiled 2,000 of them.

Destroying the V1s on the ground proved almost impossible. High-altitude bombing raids usually missed the launch sites and low-level attacks ran into deathtrap corridors of anti-aircraft guns: 771 aircrew were lost in such attacks before a single V1 had been launched in anger. By the time Field Marshal Wilhelm Keitel was ready to unleash the 'buzz bomb' on southern England, the Allies had little option but to hope they could blow it out of the sky. Ground-based Bofors guns proved surprisingly effective at this, but so did the big-nosed battleaxe that was the Hawker Tempest.

Powered either by the huge 24-cylinder Napier Sabre engine or by the 18-cylinder dual radial Centaurus, Tempests packed more piston power than any other single-engined aircraft available to the RAF. Those with the Sabre engines were cooled with the aid of an enormous air scoop immediately under the propeller that made them look permanently slack-jawed, as if salivating at the prospect of an Me 109 to butcher or a lady-driven Spitfire to buzz. The Centaurus-powered version, which had given Diana 'Wamsay' so much trouble over North London in 1943, was more elegant but not much more reliable. Neither type could match the Spitfire for responsiveness or manoeuvrability; nor could they outrun the more powerful Spitfires at altitude for more than a few minutes at maximum manifold pressure. But they could lower down. Between sea level and 5,000 feet, in the thick air that the V1s breathed, nothing beat a Tempest.

Which is why, a few days after Keitel sent the first self-propelled missile in history over the Kent Downs towards Swan-scombe, Jackie Sorour was hauled off the tennis court at Hamble. There was a priority Tempest to pick up at Aston Down in Glou-cestershire and move to RAF Newchurch in Kent. She indicated she might like to dash home and change, but was overruled by the operations officer and took off for Aston Down wearing her tennis whites and shoes (though even this was more than she had once been spotted wearing by an all-male RAF crew that pulled alongside her taxi Anson in an Airspeed Oxford as she was chang-ing in mid-flight for a party). The outfit caused such a stir on her arrival that she slid into the Tempest's cockpit to cheers of 'Ride her, cowboy!'.

Jackie made a show of having to refresh her memory from her Ferry Pilot's Notes, taking a copy and jamming it up against the Tempest's windscreen as she roared into the air. She saw the doodle-bug, her first, when it was still some way out over the Channel, a black speck barely distinguishable from the French coast. She was flying south. It was flying north-east. The distance between them was shrinking at roughly 700 mph. Sorour assumed the growing dot was piloted and hoped it was friendly. She waggled her wings. When it failed to respond she turned directly towards it in the hope that the Tempest's great mouth might scare it off. She felt mildly insulted when it refused to change course, but it gave itself away when it streaked past her nose in black silhouette. She turned steeply and opened the throttle, feeling the wake of the ramjet buffet the Tempest's nose. Now London, not the coast, was on Sorour's horizon. Although her guns were empty, there were already stories of Tempests catching V1s and tipping them off course with their wings. But before she could close the gap, a ball of smoke jumped from each side of the bomb's orange exhaust nozzle. Up front, next to the warhead, the miles-to-target log had counted down to zero. The smoke was from a pair of explosive bolts, locking the tail flaps into their 'down' position. The missile dropped a wing and went into a lazy spiral dive that ended with a direct hit on an unsuspecting Surrey hamlet. Sorour circled above the burning cottages, sickened at the sight of them and vaguely aware of goose pimples on her legs. Then she forced herself to remember what she was doing, and set course for Newchurch.

This snapshot is fragile, because there were no witnesses besides Sorour herself. The scene from outside the cockpit has to be imagined, but there is no reason to doubt that it happened. Hitler had demanded an onslaught of 500 V1s a day. Keitel was launching fewer than that, but the bombardment was still almost continuous. Number 11 Group Fighter Command, tasked with destroying the buzz bombs in mid-air, was constantly demanding replacement Typhoons and Tempests for its twelve interceptor squadrons because the time between overhauls for their Sabre engines had shrunk to ten hours or less.

Given a choice of personnel for a priority delivery of a difficult aircraft, it is not surprising that Alison King, the Hamble operations officer, picked Sorour: she was a brilliant pilot. And given that she was airborne over the south coast in the first days of the offensive (when most non-operational flights were grounded) it would have been stranger not to meet a V1 than to meet one. When she did, she reacted exactly as a combat pilot would have. Had her guns been armed, she would have had as good a chance as any of the Newchurch boys of shooting down this 'macabre parody of an aircraft' in front of her, and there is no reason to doubt she would have taken it.

In March 1944, British factories produced 2,715 new aircraft, a record for the war. The average for the first half of the year was 2,400 planes a month. When ferrying of damaged aircraft to and from maintenance units was taken into account, this translated into 6,000 flights a month for the ATA, or 200 a day. This in turn created a sufficiently intense demand for pilots for the last major obstacle to women flying in the war to be quietly dismantled: the ATA started training them from scratch.

Anticipating a pilot shortage, the RAF had agreed the previous summer to release up to thirty WAAF officers for *ab initio* pilot training. Mainly to narrow the field of applicants, it was decreed that they had to be under thirty years old and over 5 foot 5 tall. They also had to be fit enough to pass the RAF aircrew medical, have a School Certificate or matriculation and get through interviews with the Ministry of Aircraft Production and the ATA. In principle, this meant that the war had finally levelled the social playing field in terms of class and background as well as gender. 'The most thrilling war work undertaken by women' was now open to anyone, regardless of whom they knew or whether they had been able to afford flying lessons before the war. Two thousand women duly applied.

In practice, a little name recognition still helped. Betty Keith-Jopp, who applied in order to escape the purgatory of Voluntary Aid Detachment work on an army base on Salisbury plain, is convinced to this day that she was accepted less as a prospective pilot than as a known quantity: she was a niece of the terrifying, one-armed Stewart Keith-Jopp. June Farquhar (5 foot 5, but only in heels) was delighted to find herself being interviewed by Kitty Farrer. They knew each other well having hunted together with the Aldenham Harriers, of whom Farrer was Master. Katie Stanley Smith, on the other hand, didn't know any of her interviewers or fellow applicants and got in, entirely, unquestionably, on merit. It was after having been accepted that she realised she needed friends.

Smith's first posting was, she said, 'the loneliest time I've ever spent'. Formerly a weather-forecaster in the WAAF, she was assigned to Hamble with instructions not to ask for ferrying work but to wait till it was offered, because the first ex-WAAF pilot to be posted there had made a nuisance of herself. She'd been too pushy, and given the *ab initios* a bad name. And as far as Smith was concerned, orders were orders. A car would pick her up every morning from her farmhouse billet outside the village and take her to Hamble aerodrome. There she would sit tight while the ATA old hands – Gore, Rees, Duhalde, Barnato and the rest – were given their chits and lifted off to Tangmere, Hornchurch, Biggin Hill and other familiar-sounding places written into history by the Battle of Britain. Then she'd be taken home again to repeat the performance the next day.

It was not a distinction of class that Smith was up against, but of experience. She was the daughter of a London lawyer; well bred and privately schooled, with a dry, quiet humour, and precisely the inner steel required to stay in one piece in this line of work. She was just new to it. Some of the others had been turning heads on the ground and 'dicing' (with death) in the air for four years now. Perhaps they were irritated that their prestige was being diluted, and by newcomers who were showing it was possible to go from ambulance driver or met officer to Spitfire pilot in less than a year with no previous experience. They may even have wearied at the thought of making another friend who could be killed by the next temperature inversion. They may simply have been overgrown schoolgirls welded into long-established cliques. If so, they were little different from the fighter pilots. If a new girl wanted some respect, she had to earn it.

A personal connection would have helped, but Katie Stanley Smith didn't have one. 'Betty Keith-Jopp was accepted completely because of her uncle,' she said. 'Betty was one of them, and she got invited out to tea and supper and a wonderful time there. But those of us who didn't have that connection were pretty much . . .' (at this point Katie – now Kay Hirsch – living among sagebrush and hummingbirds in northern Arizona, paused to choose between two versions of the Hamble story, one less idyllic than the other) '. . . we were pretty much ignored, to tell the honest truth'.

Another memory of her wartime flying, solider and ultimately more significant, sits beside her in her living room. It's a propeller tip from a Fairchild taxi plane that nearly finished her off at Castle Bromwich. She had dropped three pilots there to pick up Spitfires and was following them to their delivery destination, when her engine failed at about 300 feet. Standing Orders in case of loss of power so soon after take-off were to force land straight ahead and on no account attempt to turn back to the airfield. With no engine and so little height a crash was almost inevitable. Smith's problem was that following orders and landing straight ahead would have made a crash a certainty. 'It was all Birmingham,' she explained. 'This was a factory airfield. There was just nothing but rooftops.' So, in one of those moments when a pilot sees death one way and a chance to save herself another, and says quietly to herself that, dammit, she'd prefer the other, she put the Fairchild into a shallow turn. 'I did just make it. I thought I was going to hit the hangar roof, but I did get back on the airfield, and landed very heavy, broke the undercarriage, tipped over and broke a propeller.' She points to the half-yellow, half wood-coloured tip beside her chair. 'Somebody who came out to rescue me picked that up and handed it to me.'

Katie could easily have done a Joan Marshall, or a Mary Nicholson, or a Bridget Hill and been bumped off there and then, occasioning a difficult but practised phonecall to the Stanley Smiths of Croydon from Pauline Gower in White Waltham, and a two-paragraph letter from Sir Stafford Cripps. Instead she kept her nerve and for the few seconds in her life that nerve really counted she made all the right decisions.

When photographed in ATA uniform, Smith tended not to bother with airs or graces or awkwardness of any kind. She always looked immaculate, and somehow knowing: the quiet professional; proof that the selection procedure had been working on the day she came for interview. ('None of us could quite figure out what they were looking for,' she said. 'But I think you had to show self-confidence. You had to walk in the room like you knew what you were doing.')

She walked away from her crash landing shaken-up but unhurt and waited for another plane to take her home. While she was waiting a call came through from White Waltham and a colleague took the call. Could someone bring in a Fairchild 477? It was due for breaking up. The colleague told White Waltham not to worry; it had been broken up already. Which was almost the end of the story, except that there was still an accident investigation to be gone through. On account of violating Standing Orders, Third Officer Smith was held responsible.

Equipped with brown suede leather flying boots, leather helmets and leather gauntlets with white silk liners, Katie Stanley Smith and her fellow *ab initio* recruits signed contracts with the ATA in May 1944. Less than a month later, the women of No. 15 Ferry Pool at Hamble awoke on what was nearly the longest day of the year to learn from Central Ferry Control at Andover that there would be no flying that day regardless of the weather. As it happened, it was overcast with occasional drizzle. Some of the Hamble pilots mooched in the usual way at the aerodrome: headstands, letters, bridge, perhaps some knitting. But in the late afternoon some of the others walked through the village and down a lane which ran parallel to the Hamble River. On the water was an armada of patrol boats, corvettes and landing craft that had been gathering for weeks along the river's shady edges. Now, for the first time, they were full, laden with hundreds upon hundreds of soldiers conjured into them from the surrounding countryside. One by one they were heading out to sea.

Maureen Dunlop was among those who stayed at the aerodrome. 'We were having a coffee in the mess,' she said, 'and someone came to the door, very quietly – I can see her face now – and she said, "It's started." And we all knew.'

Preparations for the Normandy landings had been evident around Hamble since the spring. At the yacht club, a squadron of American bulldozers had arrived without warning and built an artificial harbour almost overnight for repairing landing craft. In the woods around the village temporary encampments appeared and quietly filled up with a type of soldier Hamble hadn't seen before, quite different from the fresh-looking GIs disembarking at Liverpool and Prestwick with their 'Instructions'. These were Allied veterans of the desert war, sunburned, lean, without swagger, husbanding their strength for a last big push.

It became pointless to venture into Southampton except by bicycle; day and night, the streets were blocked by convoys. At the airfields to which Hamble delivered, invasion stripes – white, black, white round each wing like ribbons – began appearing on new and newly serviced aircraft. In the operations room a new set of invasion orders arrived on Alison King's desk, this time for 'our' invasion. All were marked 'Top Secret'. So was the old set, the ones that assigned No. 15 Ferry Pool four tents and a potting shed on the edge of Salisbury plain in the event of Germans wading up the Hamble River, but that secret was already history.

'They were thrilling and nerve-tingling days,' remembered Violet Milstead, a Canadian who had made her own way to Montreal to join the ATA in 1943. They were, perhaps, especially nerve-tingling for her and the other North Americans whom Churchill had so assiduously courted. God's good time had come, he told the House of Commons, and the New World with all its power and might was stepping forth to the rescue and liberation of the old.

No-one could have been prouder to be part of the great rescue than Ann Wood. In June 1944 she was still based at Ratcliffe, but on the 5th she was given a Spitfire to deliver from Castle Bromwich to Eastleigh on the outskirts of Southampton:

> When I arrived there I was told by the pool that was to pick me up that I had to spend the night because D-Day had been postponed twice and they thought it would be any minute now. So I was locked down for the night and couldn't get home.

Ordinarily, she would have been found a bed for the night at Hamble, but being Ann Wood she had options. A friend from Cincinnati was helping to run a Red Cross rest and recuperation centre for American pilots in a nearby stately home.

> She said why didn't I spend the night with them and entertain with them if I could? So she fetched me and I spent the night with them. We had a lovely dinner. We had double summertime, and about 11 o'clock at night we're out on the lawn having our coffee, and suddenly the night was full of bombers, nothing but aircraft, black, all headed over, so we knew that D-Day was en route.

The following morning Dorothy from Cincinnati, who had access to a Jeep, formed a plan to use it to distribute strawberries. 'We're going to go up and down the line where they're waiting to get into the barges,' she told Ann. 'And that's what we did, and it was the most powerful thing that ever was.'

> There we were with nothing but strawberries to offer, and what were the boys doing? Some were reading comics, some were asleep. Some were having their hair cut or just lounging around, waiting to get aboard to go across, and they were so grateful ... and scared to death. You couldn't really talk to them much. You just offered them strawberries, and when you left you knew that that, for many, would be their last strawberry on earth.

Alison King was 'filled with a certain sadness' on D-Day. This, too, was on account of the men; the lives she had seen packed up in camouflage webbing, clambering into barges on the Hamble River, that would be ended within hours by machine guns across the Channel. But soon a different sadness would creep into the women's thoughts. It was harder to acknowledge because it was selfish, and self-effacement was the ATA's principal unwritten standing order. But as the Allies fanned out across northern France to begin their long march on Berlin, and the trainloads of wounded began returning to hospitals across the South of England, this secret sadness grew. For some of the women it was no more than a niggle. For others it was a full-blown foreboding. Their part in the great, meticulous mobilisation for D-Day may have been small, but it was a good part: well played and revolutionary in its way. It had given them the time of their lives. How long could it go on now that the boys up and down the line had had their strawberries and left? Would there ever be another part like it?

When the news that D-Day had started came quietly to the door of the Hamble mess, Maureen Dunlop knew at once that something else was finishing. 'It looked,' she said, 'as if it was the beginning of the end.'

23

Honeymoon in Belgium

Some of the ATA women were so utterly unconstrained by convention that they took their wartime flying for granted. They knew they were 'lucky'. They knew that thousands of girls would have given everything they had for the mere chance of pilot training. But they had also assumed from the outset that since they could fly, and since there was to be a war, they would, somehow, be wartime pilots.

They weren't particularly interested in the battles that Pauline Gower and Jackie Cochran had to fight to get them into their 'lovely warplanes'. They knew, if they stopped to think about it, that they were operating at the very limit of what society could tolerate, even in war. But they weren't much interested in society either, or in stopping and thinking about their place in it, and they were so used to being unusual that anything else would have been unsettling, unsatisfying – and soul-destroyingly dull.

Maureen Dunlop was one of these women, hotfoot from Argentina because a war's 'not something you hang about over'. Ann Welch was another. ('I had to be involved: and it had to be in flying. Nothing else could even be contemplated.') Veronica Volkersz, raised riding polo ponies in the foothills of the Karako-rams, was a third. Three days before war was declared – on 31 August 1939 – she was airborne over Hampshire, taking a friend on a business trip to Portsmouth. She returned to Woodley aerodrome outside London after dark to be given a furious dressing down by the chief instructor of the local flying school. In her absence, Hitler had invaded Poland and all civil aviation had been grounded.

'No news could've excited me more,' Volkersz wrote. 'Already, I could see myself flying fighter aircraft over to France.' Five years later, it seemed that the chance to do just that had come. As the Allied armies advanced across Europe they commandeered every usable airfield and built hundreds more. Churchill, in a personal note to Pop d'Erlanger in May 1944, thanked him for the ATA's first 200,000 deliveries and told him to be ready to deliver to the Continent as well. Aston Down in Gloucestershire and White Waltham had been designated ATA invasion pools. Pilots had begun learning how to parachute with life rafts dangling between their legs. Volunteers were solicited for Continental ferrying, and the first to be accepted received their inoculations. From the women's point of view there was only one problem. Air Chief Marshal Sir Trafford Leigh-Mallory, in charge of both the RAF's Second Tactical Air Force and the Ninth US Air Force, adamantly refused to let women cross the Channel, and for no better reason, apparently, than simple prejudice.

Leigh-Mallory was stubborn, humourless and ruthlessly ambitious. The younger brother of George Leigh Mallory, the superhuman mountaineer who came within a hundred yards of the summit of Mount Everest in 1924, he doubtless considered himself blessed with the same genetic reserves of strength and courage. Perhaps he was (though Montgomery considered him a 'gutless bugger').

Leigh-Mallory, who sported a very similar moustache to Hitler's, criticised Sir Hugh Dowding's tactics during the Battle of Britain and plotted afterwards, successfully, to replace him as head of Fighter Command. He was convinced that the best way to defeat the Luftwaffe was with massed fighter formations that would be able to defend themselves and destroy German bomber groups at the same time. In 1941 he was able to put his 'big wing' concept to the test, and lost four RAF aircraft for every German one shot down. He never took the fall for this disastrous strategy and instead secured for himself the most senior RAF post in Europe after D-Day by energetically cultivating British and American army top brass.

The only thing that can be said reliably in Leigh-Mallory's defence is that he was never able properly to defend his reputation. In August 1944, having been assigned the command of Allied Air Forces in South-East Asia, he and his wife were killed when their Liberator hit a mountainside above Grenoble en route to Burma.

By then, one of the women pilots had already registered her opinion of this unreconstructed mysogynist by quitting. Her name was Betty Lussier, and part of the reason for her readiness to sacrifice her job was that she had alternatives. Lussier was Canadian-born but raised on a farm in Maryland where she paid for her flying lessons by working the night shift at a nearby assembly plant, building B-26 bombers. She heard about Jackie Cochran's recruiting efforts and applied, but was rejected: at nineteen she had only 200 hours in her logbook. So she crossed the Atlantic on a freighter called the *Scebeli* in 1943 with no firm offer of a job. She joined the ATA by visiting the Ministry of Labour on her arrival and announcing that she was a pilot; they directed her to White Waltham and the business-like embrace of Pauline Gower, who deemed 200 hours more than enough.

But 2,000 hours would not have been enough for Leigh-Mallory to let her follow the invasion across Europe. When the women pilots at Hamble and White Waltham realised they were not being inoculated or briefed for Continental ferrying, Lussier called her godfather, Sir William Stephenson (who later became better known to filmgoers as *The Man Called Intrepid*). He was a friend of Winston Churchill's, but also of Lussier's father, Emile, having served with him in the Royal Canadian Air Force in the First World War. By 1943 he was supervising the operations of the Office of Strategic Service – or OSS – the forerunner to the CIA. Betty was still barely twenty-one. But she was a natural linguist, desperate to be tangled up in the war and apparently not afraid of it. He signed her up.

Lussier became the only ex-ATA woman to work for OSS. Her first task after D-Day was to convey 'Ultra' intelligence generated by the Enigma codebreakers at Bletchley Park to US combat head-quarters in Europe, inventing separate cover stories for each inter-cept so that any German mole who might gain access to it would not have to assume the Enigma ciphers had been broken. Lussier also dabbled in counterintelligence. She teamed up with Ricardo Sicre – a fellow OSS officer and veteran of the Spanish Civil War, whom she would marry – to ensnare German spies in France and turn them into double agents. One of them, a suspect who had not broken under interrogation by the French or British, revealed to Lussier that his fondest ambition was to go to Hollywood and meet Charlie Chaplin. She promised to arrange it in return for his confession, then had him arrested.

The Chaplin fan never made it to Hollywood. The women of the ATA did, however, make it to Europe. And their trailblazer was not Lussier, but the inimitable Diana Barnato.

In Hamble, Diana had shared digs with two fellow pilots. Like Diana, Anne Walker and Faith Bennett moved in elevated fighter pilot circles, living daily with the cruel paradox that the most fabulously eligible men were also the most likely to be killed. Anne was in love with Group Captain W. G. G. 'Smithy' Duncan-Smith, a Battle of Britain ace (whose son, two generations later, would become leader of the Conservative Party). Faith, a blonde and glamorous returnee from 1930s Hollywood, was seeing Air Marshal Sir William Sholto Douglas, KCB, MC, DFC. Formerly Commander-in-Chief of Fighter Command, he was by 1944 in charge of Britain's aerial defences and a regular visitor to Hamble in his staff car.

Smithy was based nearby at RAF Tangmere, and through him Diana met a blue-eyed, twenty-eight-year-old officer with light brown curls, a 'swashbuckling, springy step' and a record of inspir-ing leadership from Kent and Cyprus to the Western Desert. This was Wing Commander Derek Walker. Though not related to Anne, he too would become a frequent visitor to Hamble.

At first, Diana made Anne issue the invitations to Derek so that he would not know who was after him, but chemistry quickly removed the need for acting. On a visit to the Barnato estate at Ridgemead in the spring of 1944, Derek found Diana in her father's study. He perched on the arm of her chair and said he couldn't live without her. They were married in May, two years to the day after the funeral of her first fiancé, Humphrey Gilbert. The courtship had been brief but intense. 'Our love was very real and very deep,' Diana wrote. 'Many of my admirers had, by then, been killed in the war, so I thought I should hook him quick in case one or other of us got bumped off whilst flying.'

Most of No. 15 Ferry Pool attended the wedding at the Church of St Jude's in Englefield Green in Surrey. Diana wore a perfect sail of white silk; Derek his uniform. The reception was at Ridgemead, where several of the men fell into the lily pond and a few of the women into the swimming pool.

With no time for a proper honeymoon on account of the imminent invasion of Europe, Mr and Mrs Walker drove down to Devon after the wedding and spent three days in a hotel in Totnes. But the new bride had never let the war get in the way of japery and she was not about to start. Her husband was of the same mind: easily bored. He was on an official break from combat operations after four consecutive frontline tours, but after D-Day he was appointed personal assistant to Air Marshal Sir Arthur 'Mary' Coningham, KCB, DSO, MC, DFC, AFC. For all the initials after his name, Coningham was not from the same subspecies of commander as Leigh-Mallory. For one thing, he did not object to being called Mary (it was a contraction of 'Maori'). Having been brought up in New Zealand, he had returned to the old country to fly Sopwith Camels in the First World War, but his taste of life so far from the Imperial Metropole had infected his soul. He took the subversive view that military regulations should not be taken too seriously unless they contributed directly to the winning of the war. He also believed in the critical importance of morale, and was aware through his new assistant, Wing Commander Walker, that the women of the ATA were more than miffed at having been left in England for no logical reason while their male colleagues started flying aircraft to the advancing European battle lines. They were hurt and angry. As Diana Barnato Walker put it in her memoir (and presumably to her husband): 'For many years the women pilots had been flying – and dying – in the same aircraft types and in the same conditions as the men, yet now we were being denied these foreign trips. You can't imagine the dismay that we felt.'

By the end of September 1944, Coningham had succeeded Leigh-Mallory as head of the Second Tactical Air Force. Derek asked Diana if she would be prepared to join him on an important semi-secret mission on her next leave. He had to deliver two photo-reconnaissance Spitfire F VIIs to newly liberated Brussels to enable the RAF to take better pictures of the retreating German lines. But he was short of one pilot. Diana said she would love to help but was barred from doing so. Derek produced a letter:

Headquarters
Second Tactical Air Force
Royal Air Force

25th of September, 1944.

This is to certify that First Officer D.B. Walker, Air Transport Auxiliary, has permission to travel to Brussels and to remain there for a period of four/seven days, as from 1st October.
    She is proceeding by air and will be in uniform.

A. Coningham
Air Marshal Commanding Second Tactical Air Force

That was enough for Diana. She would be in uniform but on leave, breaking rules but also exposing them as fatuous. On 2 October, Mr and Mrs Walker, each in a Sptifire, took off from RAF Northolt and flew wingtip to wingtip over the White Cliffs of Dover. A few minutes later they crossed the cratered beaches between Boulogne and Cap Gris Nez and set course east by south-east for Brussels' Evere airport. It was Diana's first escape from Britain since her ski trip to Megève with Lorna Harmsworth at the start of the war. She wrote that she wanted to sing and 'throw the aircraft about in celebration of her freedom'. She desisted, but only because the risk of colliding with Derek was too great. Her only previous experience of formation flying had been the unsolicited and terrifying arrival alongside her of three Free French Spitfires from No. 340 Free French squadron, en route to Kenley in Surrey. The French pilots had been laughing at her red woollen pixie hat, exposed beneath the canopy because her helmet had blown away on take-off.

The free Belgians were also in party mood, and the Walkers completed their honeymoon among them. London may still have been blacked out and living on rations, but Brussels, fifteen miles from the German army, had sugar, wine, leather handbags, chocolate in its shops and lights on all night. Small wonder that 'Mary' Coningham had located his headquarters there. He had even moved his wife out to be with him. But after six days, Diana had to go home. The plan was for Derek to escort her. A thick fog had settled over much of northern Europe, but he knew the route intimately from years of combat sorties and had wireless navigation to fall back on should anything go wrong. Diana did not, but all she had to do was stay on his wing.

They took off. They had agreed that if the fog looked as bad once they were airborne as it did from the ground, they would turn back. Diana thought it looked worse, but Derek pressed on, leaving her no choice but to stay with him. He flew faster than she was used to (ATA cruising speeds were designed to save fuel) and she lost him within a few minutes.

When asked much later whether at any point on this flight she had felt completely lost, Diana said airily that if things had got that bad all she would have had to do was fly up the North Sea and turn left.

It did not seem so simple at the time. The first decision was easy enough: she could not turn back. The chances of overshooting Evere and ending up behind German lines were too great. Then there was the choice of continuing on a compass course that might or might not deliver her to RAF Northolt depending on wind and visibility over north London; or going as low as she dared and nosing around until she recognised something from her map. She chose to descend and eventually saw the hills of St Omer rising to meet her. Soon afterwards she crossed what she hoped was the French coast south of Gris Nez. If it was, seven and a half minutes on a course of 295 degrees should put her over Dungeness. She adjusted her course and began counting down. But the Channel was covered in sea fog thicker than anything so far, right down to the water. She climbed to 4,000 feet to get over it, and started finding distractions – another aircraft, which she dived to follow hoping it might be Derek's, only to find it was a Dakota flying in the opposite direction; a change from white fog to yellow fog beneath her (did that mean land?); a gap in the yellow fog just where Dungeness should have been (if she had managed to get back on the right course and allow for the right number of lost seconds after chasing the Dakota).

She stood the Spitfire on its wingtip to peer through the gap. No land. Now her brain began rewinding involuntarily to what she thought had been the French coast. If that had been east of the Cap, not south – Belgium, not France – she might already be over the North Sea rather than the English Channel, with no hope of a landfall unless she turned west. But if it had been where she thought it was and she turned west too soon, she'd fly straight down the Channel and run out of fuel somewhere over Cornwall. With one half of her mind racing, the other half hammered out a practicable compromise. After twenty-two minutes flying north-west with no sight of land she reasoned that she must have crossed the French coast further south than she thought, putting her over the Channel now rather than the North Sea. She dived to 200 feet and turned right, skimming over the water on a bearing of ten degrees.

Suddenly there was a little sheen of light ahead, a line of white in the yellow. I peered at it anxiously; and yes, it was something. Land at last? The White Cliffs of Dover, perhaps? I flew on. It was not the White Cliffs of Dover, but an east to west line of lovely sandy beach. There, right behind it, looming up beside me with a rusty grin, was the huge gasometer at Bognor.

Diana was 100 miles west of where she'd meant to be, but no longer lost. Flooded with relief, she circled the huge gas cylinder like a cat thankful for another life. Then she picked her way up the Pagham Rife River to Chichester and the approach to RAF Tangmere. The runway lights were on and green and white flares were fizzing up into the murk. Diana hung back, assuming the flares meant an entire squadron was on its way in. When nothing joined her in the circuit above the airfield she abandoned etiquette and landed. Derek's Spitfire was already parked outside the watch office. He ran out, pale, astonished and so thankful that he was almost angry. Where had she been? How the devil had she got here? The flares and lights had been for her, but it was a miracle that she'd seen them. Tangmere was the only airfield still open that afternoon in the whole of southern England.

It turned out there was no such thing as a free trip to Brussels. When the *Mail* ran a story two weeks later on 'the beautiful daughter of the millionaire racing motorist' and her belated European honeymoon, Derek had to forfeit three months' pay. But Diana had shown that French and Flemish fog did not discriminate against women any more than British fog did, and her precedent proved irreversible. By early 1945 ATA women were flying regularly to the Continent.

Diana, naturally, was one of them. She regularly smuggled cocoa from Belgium in her parachute pack, and almost collided with a Lancaster while co-piloting an Anson full of oranges to RAF Buckeberg near Hanover. After VE Day a tall and 'interestingly handsome' pilot called Zita Irwin made it to Berlin and came back with a grainy picture of herself outside the wrecked Chancellery building in the company of half a dozen Red Army soldiers. Rosemary Rees went furthest east – to Prague, which she had last visited in her own plane in a blizzard in December 1938, laden with gifts for refugees. That year, the ghost of Good King Wenceslas would have looked out on snow that was deep and crisp and might even have held out some hope of appeasement. In 1945 Rees found the place sad, grey and depressing after six winters under the Gestapo.

'But I was the first,' Diana Barnato Walker noted crisply. 'That was the point.' And it was. Had she crashed or ditched or disappeared, even 'Mary' Coningham would have been hard put to make the case for women in Europe. As it was, her survival instinct prevailed and clung on for the rest of the war; a case study in the usefulness of quick thinking and adrenalin when in a frightful fix. Diana was already the only ATA woman pilot to have been shot at by the Luftwaffe. She had not been at the controls herself, but strapped into the co-pilot's seat of a taxi Anson being flown by Jim Mollison, Amy Johnson's ex-husband, when a Messerschmitt 110 popped out of low cloud over Reading and squeezed off a few tracer rounds as it flashed past in the opposite direction. According to ATA legend, Diana's role in the encounter was to spot the swastika on the enemy tailplane and yell to Mollison, 'Jimmy, it's a Jerry!' just in time for him to pull the Anson's nose up into the cloud. In fact, from her own account, it seems that she kept quiet. If anyone did any yelling it was Jimmy.

Barnato Walker was similarly calm when it mattered in a Mitchell bomber over Cheshire, three days after Germany's surrender. It was the type of plane in which Jackie Sorour had crabbed into Dunsfold on one engine shortly after D-Day. Though smaller than a Halifax or a Lancaster, it felt heavier to fly, with two hands needed on the control column for take-off and landing and a flight engineer essential to operate the far-flung fuel cocks and undercarriage levers.

Half-way up England, somewhere over Worcestershire in

deteriorating visibility, there was a bang in the cockpit and every instrument except Diana's compass died. She could steer a course for Hawarden, her destination, but no longer had any clear idea how fast or high she was flying. Her first approach to Hawarden was too fast and too high. She went round again and landed expertly, in the circumstances, but was surprised to find her engineer – whom she knew well but not intimately – fiddling urgently with the parachute release between her breasts the moment the Mitchell touched the ground. As soon as it came to a stop he threw her out of the plane, jumped after her and set off running, dragging her behind him. He did not stop until it was safe to turn and watch the Hawarden fire engine smother the Mitchell's burning starboard engine in foam.

The millionaire racing motorist's daughter had been concentrating so hard on compensating for her defunct instruments that she had failed to notice that one of the two engines was about to explode. It was probably a good thing; had she throttled it back in a hurry the likelihood of engine failure, stall, spin and fiery death did not bear contemplating.

Diana Barnato Walker's guardian angel had been busy. She always attributed her knack for getting out of scrapes to the constant presence in her mind's eye of the melted face and clawlike hands of the dreadfully burned man who had appeared beside her Tiger Moth at Brooklands before her first solo at the start of the war, begging her not to try it. It was her way of deflecting the idea that she might have a skill, a sixth sense – or even an appetite for life – that others lacked. Yet she undoubtedly had something that she could call on when it suddenly looked as if her future might have to be measured in milliseconds. It was partly an all-or-nothing fixation; a dread of being maimed or disfigured. That was far more real than any fear of death. And it was partly a deep, unspoken conviction that in any case death 'happened to other people'. Either way, panic never quite took over, and in the space it might have filled under her red woollen pixie hat, or her helmet if it hadn't blown away, best- and worst-case scenarios would compare notes and offer up survival strategies, calmly recalibrating them as the world hurtled past beneath the cockpit. As long as she was two feet off the ground and in one piece there was always something left to try.

To wit, 30 April 1945, in Typhoon EK 347. 'Now that was interesting,' she said when reminded of it. 'That was the nearest miss. You see, the whole thing fell apart.'

Typhoon EK 347 had had a tough life, though Barnato Walker didn't know this until later. It had been used first by a detachment of New Zealand pilots and then by a Belgian squadron as an interim buzz-bomb chaser pending delivery of new Tempests. After Barnato Walker took it for a spin up the A4, it never flew again.

Like the early Tempests, Typhoons were powered by the temperamental Sabre engine and cooled by a scoop air intake below the propeller; the same scoop that had consigned Lettice Curtis to hospital the year before when it dug into a furrow in a field near Slough.

Barnato Walker was 2,000 feet over Wiltshire, en route from Lasham to RAF Kemble in Gloucestershire, when most of the underside of the plane peeled away, scoop first. Luckily the detached portion did not rip off the elevator flaps on the trailing edge of the tailplane as they flew past, leaving the Typhoon unstable but still viable.

The scoop had gone with a bang. At first, Diana had assumed engine failure and started mental preparations for a forced landing, but that was before she looked down to see nothing between her and the White Horse Hills apart from some fuel lines and electrical wiring. The next thing she noticed was the wind, a freezing, trouser-snapping tornado round her legs. At 300 mph there was not much she could do about the cold. The question was whether she could fly any slower without the Typhoon's ragged new aerodynamic profile causing it to stall. She climbed to experiment, and worked out that her new stalling speed was 230 mph, nearly three times faster than the 88 mph indicated in her Ferry

Pilot's Notes. That was too fast to lower her flaps or attempt a wheels-up landing. With so much of the underside of the plane already missing, the rest of it might disintegrate. As she put it later, 'I thought it might hurt.'

She needed an airport. Conscious that her teeth were chattering uncontrollably, she tightened her straps and flew on to Kemble. As she entered the circuit (still more than twice as fast as recommended in the Notes), her undercarriage failed to lock. For this situation the Notes advised:

> U/c [Undercarriage] Operation: Emergency: Gravity, pneu-matic assisted. Select DOWN. Press both emergency pedals forward firmly (below 200 mph). When wheels have fallen, press pneumatic assister: release to check green lights. If unsuccessful, yaw aircraft violently at 130–250 mph. Tail-wheel extends automatically.

Barnato Walker followed the instructions as best she could, but at over 230 mph. At that speed the yawing felt especially violent, but three green lights came on. She made several low passes over the airfield to alert the ground crew to a potential problem. They registered that she was flying too fast to land and switched on a red light on the watch office roof to indicate that she should go away and come back slower. Rosemary Rees was also there, waiting to take an Anson-load of pilots back to Hamble. Eventually someone suggested that a fire truck get ready. A few spectators gathered. Diana climbed again to check her stalling speed once more and give herself a moment to think clearly about landing with no floor at over 200 mph. There was no guarantee she would make it. In fact, she found out later, there was an over-whelming probability that she wouldn't. Twenty-six Typhoons including hers were lost to structural failure in the course of the war. Twenty-five of their pilots died.

In the end she made survival look easy. She came in very low to make sure she didn't waste a yard of runway. 'I landed without flaps, keeping the speed just above 230, squeezed the brakes on for a second touchdown, then took them off again quickly so I wouldn't turn over.' At the far end of the runway she applied full brake, turned smartly and taxied to dispersal in search of a cup of tea. No-one offered. The duty airman came out and chided her gently for bringing only half an aeroplane. He gave her a snag sheet to fill out so that no-one else would try to fly it.

The Anson was ticking over. As Diana climbed in, Rees paid her the compliment of asking what the devil had taken her so long, and then rolled her eyes at the audacity of the line-shoot when she tried to explain. It was time to go home.

24

Better To Have Lived

'I would say that every woman should learn to fly,' Pauline Gower had told *Woman's Journal* in 1942, when her own women flyers were proving themselves capable of anything. 'Psychologically, it is the best antidote to the manifold neuroses which beset modern women.'

By 'neuroses' Gower seems to have meant whatever had been holding women back in the prewar world where men still thought they could assign women their roles and temper their ambitions. The brute imperatives of war had already taken a good swipe at these neuroses, she continued. 'But with the return of peace my advice to all women will still be – "Learn to fly" . . . I feel confident that when this war is finally won, aviation will be considered as a normal and satisfying career for young girls leaving school as well as for older women.'

How right she was, and how wrong. Aviation would offer women a career – as air stewardesses. Some of the ATA women found work as pilots, but only those with still-untapped reserves of the bloody-minded tenacity that made them ATA women in the first place. Meanwhile, the swing back to patriarchy became unstoppable. So did the swing forward to the cult of the laconic ex-RAF, 110 per cent male airline captain. Gower, as a BOAC board member, saw it coming as clearly as anyone. In 1944, the brave new world of international air travel was carved up at a Chicago conference attended by fifty-four nations. Once Nazi

Germany and Japan had been dealt with there would be dozens of new airlines and hundreds of new routes – but thousands upon thousands of military pilots angling for work and striding in and out of interviews with combat records almost as impressive as their sense of entitlement.

In March 1945, Gower was interviewed in London by the *Daily Sketch*. She received hundreds of letters every month, she said, from land girls, girl guides, secretaries and housewives, all asking how they could get jobs in flying come the peace. 'Well,' she told them, 'my answer is a brutally frank one. You can't!'

If that seemed unfair, it seemed much more so to those who had been through the wringer of six years' continuous service flying more than a hundred aircraft types, many of which RAF recruits had been leery of trying until embarrassed into doing so by the sight of an ATA girl climbing out of one. Among the men who worked with that tight cadre of veterans, overt chauvinism had long since been ridiculous. 'It came down to men and women becoming just people,' Rosemary Rees would write. 'All those pretty little barriers that are put up in peacetime melt away and life becomes a grim struggle of tired, grey people all doing whatever it is they can do.'

The war was supposed to have gone a good way towards demolishing class and national barriers as well as gender ones, at least according to Pinewood. *The Way Ahead* was the way taken by David Niven and his men when they managed to forget they came into the war from parallel social worlds. *The Way to the Stars* was the way shown by British and American pilots when at last they stopped giving into mutual bafflement and started speaking the parts of the English language that they had in common.

The final measure of the barriers that Pauline Gower's girls demolished came a month into the post-war era. It was thirty-two days, to be precise, after General MacArthur received Japan's unconditional surrender on the foredeck of the USS *Missouri*, that Veronica Volkersz, the girl from Srinagar and Windsor, was handed a ferry chit by Flight Captain William Cuthbert of No. 2

Ferry Pool at Whitchurch to which she had been posted from Hamble. Throughout the war, Whitchurch had been an all-male pool. Its men tried to observe a 'no fraternising' rule for a few days when women were first foisted on them, but Volkersz and two others thawed them out by beating them at bridge.

Too late to help with any war except the Cold one to come, Whitchurch had started ferrying some of the RAF's first jets. After a couple of weeks there, Volkersz asked if she could fly one. Cuthbert waited until his commanding officer and second-in-command were unavoidably elsewhere, then quietly instructed Flight Captain Volkersz – who held the same rank as he did, after all – to take Meteor III EE 386 from the Gloster Meteor plant at Morton Vallence to RAF 124 Squadron at Molesworth.

She was offered no conversion course, no cockpit inspection, no helpful hints, no comment. Just a new four by five inch card to be inserted in her ringbound Ferry Pilot's Notes in alphabetical order between Martinet and Oxford, to be glanced at on her way out to dispersal.

METEOR III
engine: 2 Derwent jet engines

FLYING PARTICULARS
Static Run-up: 16,500 r.p.m plus 100 or minus 200
Jet tube temperature: 690 degrees C max
Oil pressure: Normal 35 lbs. Minimum 30 lbs
Oil temperature: 80 degrees C max. O degrees C minimum

Take-Off:
Booster pumps: ON
R.P.M.: 16,500
Jet temp: 600 degrees C max
Elev. and Rud.: Neutral
Flaps: quarter
Safety speed: 130 mph
Note: Open throttles fully before releasing breaks. Unstick
   120 mph.

It is worth pausing to digest what was happening. A pilot (who happened to be one of around twenty women still flying operationally outside Russia) was climbing into a brand-new jet fighter, the shape and high-pitched scream of the future, with orders to take off, fly across England and land in one piece after as much instruction as she might get nowadays renting a car from Avis.

Inside the cockpit, the main piece of evidence that aeroplanes were changing was the rev counter. Flight Captain Volkersz had to have her two Derwents spinning at 16,500 times a minute – compared with about 2,700 for a Spitfire – before she even released the brakes. There would be no pistons, plugs or propellers; just Frank Whittle's invisible compressors, sheathed in smooth aluminium. Volkersz wound them up, took her feet off the brakes and 'seemed to hurtle away like a shot from a gun'.

The Meteor drank 160 gallons of fuel per engine per hour, more than ten times as much as the Airspeed Oxford that jettisoned Amy Johnson when she ran out. (Was it any wonder that the post-war West developed a peculiar fixation with the Middle East?) The Notes said both tanks should be full before takeoff. Flight Captain Volkersz's were not. She had just enough for a twenty-five-minute hop at 270 mph with a reserve for one overshoot on landing, but only one. So she kept things simple: took off to the west, turned at once, set course for Molesworth, streaked across England's green and pleasant hips and was on the ground again by lunchtime. 'It was really no different from any other delivery,' she would tell people when asked about it. Except that she was the first British woman to fly a jet, and possibly only the second in the world after the German test pilot Hanna Reitsch. She would have liked to mark the occasion by bumping into a friend and shooting a line, but friends were already scarce a month after VJ Day, and anyway, the officers of RAF Molesworth were at lunch. She handed her chit to the watch officer, climbed into the waiting Anson and flew back to Whitchurch.

*　　*　　*

Volkersz had been assigned to Whitchurch not for special training but because Hamble had closed down. 'For all the women, as far as they knew, it would mean going back to marriage and jobs, and paying for flying,' Alison King wrote glumly. 'It seemed a terrible waste of such hard-earned experience.' But time, which had seemed to crawl through the lean and deadly years between Dunkirk and D-Day, was now racing. Peace was rearranging lives as jarringly as war had. Mussolini was shot by Italian Communists. Hitler dispatched himself and Eva Braun. (Reitsch, his favourite pilot, accepted a cyanide pill from her beloved Führer in the bunker, but didn't use it – at least not at once. She lived until 1979, and there is evidence that she took it then.) Roosevelt was already gone. Churchill had been humiliated in the polls by Labour in July. And on 6 August Hiroshima was obliterated.

Compared with which, the memo from an assistant secretary at the Ministry of Aircraft Production to the Secretary of the Board of BOAC on 2 June 1945, on 'methods which will permit the gradual contraction of [the ATA] and its ultimate winding up' was less than momentous.

Still, winding up was hard to do. Lettice Curtis's mother had died during the war, and her family home had 'broken up'. She had not found love, not that she had looked particularly hard for it. Neither did she sense that finding work was going to be straightforward. In short, 'to those of us who had nothing to go back to and nowhere particular to go . . . the end of the war was about as climacteric an experience as the outbreak'.

Ann Wood was just as driven as Curtis, but more adept as a mover and a shaker. In April 1945 she wrote to her mother in phlegmatic mood: '[I] will be really sorry when I have to stop flying the world's loveliest aeroplanes . . . but all good things must end.' By the time the end came she had resolved to stay in England if she could. The country of powdered eggs and puny moustaches had got under her freckled skin, and she pinned her hopes on landing a job as assistant to the air attaché at the US Embassy. His name was Tony Satterthwaite. He was a friend, and generally 'pro-women'. Even better, he had his own Spitfire that often needed ferrying. There was only one problem, he told Ann apologetically as Washington writhed through the summer in the bureaucratic frenzy entailed by switching from warring behemoth to peacetime superpower: the State Department was dubious about the appointment, on account of her being a woman.

'Winding up' was effected in as gentlemanly and civilised a manner as possible. The ATA organisation simply shrank back to its original two pools at White Waltham and Whitchurch, and then to White Waltham alone. Pilots who wanted to stay on to the bitter end were accommodated if possible. Those who left received a note of thanks from Pop d'Erlanger and a Certificate of Service. They were also allowed to buy their uniform at a steep discount. Those who stayed felt the pace of work slacken steadily. Weekends were weekends; long, empty invitations to fret about the future. When the weather closed in there was no pressure to fly, and when it cleared most of the ferrying was to storage depots in Scotland or Wales – or breakers' yards. Margaret Frost found these depressing. 'This is a beautiful aeroplane and should not be broken up,' she wrote on the fuselage of one Spitfire that she was assigned to deliver to its final, oily resting place.

On 29 September, 12,000 members of the public paid to attend a pageant at White Waltham organised to raise money for the families of the 170 dead ATA ferry pilots, and to show off the planes they flew. Lord Beaverbrook was guest of honour. He chipped in £5,000 of his own towards the new benevolent fund and thanked from his heart a group of aviators who 'were soldiers fighting in the struggle just as completely as if they had been engaged on the battle front'. He concluded with a plea for generosity to ensure 'now and in the years to come, the education and the upbringing of the orphans of the men who were too old to fly and fight, but not too old to fall'.

He made no mention of the women. Many of them were not there in any case. Jackie Moggridge, recently married to Reg, had broken a cardinal ATA rule in not telling Pauline Gower as soon as she became pregnant; but after seven months she could conceal it no longer and had quit to go and live in Taunton, near her in-laws. Ann Welch, Bobby Leveaux (née Sandoz) and Katie Hirsch (née Stanley Smith) were likewise spoken for. Jadwiga Pilsudska was at Liverpool University studying architecture. Betty Lussier was in Spain being romanced by Ricardo Sicre, her partner in espionage, through whom she would become friends with the movie star Ava Gardner and with whom she had four sons. Emily Chapin and Helen Richey were long gone. They had accepted Jackie Cochran's standing offer of a place among the WASPs. Helen Harrison was home in Canada. Opal Anderson was back in Chicago with her boy, now six years old. Maureen Dunlop and her sister, Joan, who had spent the war as a nurse, had been reunited with their parents on the tarmac at Buenos Aires International Airport. Margot Duhalde was, at last, in France.

At least the weather rose to the occasion for the pageant at White Waltham. In glorious autumn sunshine, Alex Henshaw, the Castle Bromwich test pilot, who knew the ATA as well as any outsider, roared in over the Shottesbrooke church spire in an overpowered Seafire F4 and strained every neck on the ground with the kind of solo display not seen in these parts since 1940. Lettice Curtis was there, and remembered the occasion as 'bitter-sweet', the end of flying for many of the pilots present, the end of the best years of her life. But the organisers did her the honour of asking her to bring in the biggest plane on show that day, a Consolidated Liberator. A film crew caught her climbing out of it, and caught her smiling.

A month later, Lettice delivered her last plane for the ATA, a Tempest from Langley to Aston Down. The next day, she emptied her locker at White Waltham, said goodbye to friends, and left. 'Already the days filled with flying were assuming a dreamlike quality,' she wrote. 'It was almost as if they had never been.' Already, Pop d'Erlanger had relinquished command of his valiant invention to one W. D Kemp, Officer in Charge of Winding Up. Already, those who had left were finding the privations of peace harder to endure than those of war. Rationing was still in force, jobs were rarer than butter, and of those who were still single only the wealthiest could afford to ignore the question of how to make ends meet once their ATA pay stopped. Small wonder that a few clung on to the very end.

At around 4.30 on the afternoon of Friday, 30 November, six months after VE Day and six years after Pauline Gower started recruiting women flyers for the ATA, three of those women were in a tiny gaggle of spectators on the roof of the White Waltham watch office, looking west towards the darkening horizon. 'The sun went down in a blaze of crimson and gold,' one of those present wrote. As it did, a lone Anson appeared and circled the airfield once, and landed. A handful of men climbed out, walked across the dispersal area to the watch office and handed in their parachutes. They joined the spectators at the flagpole at the entrance to the aerodrome. Ann Wood, Diana Barnato Walker and Audrey Sale-Barker were among them. Audrey stepped forward and lowered the ATA flag in the fast-fading light.

The story could, in deference to the war, end there. But the Spitfire women were not known for their deference, nor for giving up flying when there was the slightest chance of carrying on. A fairer place to end would be Bandar Abbas, a desolate port-oasis on the north shore of the Persian Gulf.

Epilogue

It is 1953. The Iron Curtain has long since fallen across Europe. Eisenhower is in the White House, Queen Elizabeth II is on the throne, and in her honour Edmund Hillary and Sherpa Tensing have stood at last on top of the mountain that did for Trafford Leigh-Mallory's brother. Britain has lost an empire, and her former colonies and mandates are fighting new wars of their own. For these, they are building new air forces. Israel has bought dozens of Spitfires from England and has extracted sterling service from them in the first Arab-Israeli war, but is upgrading to jets for the second. To help fund the upgrade it is selling thirty used Spitfires to Burma. The town of Bandar Abbas, in Iran, is on the air route there.

Seasonal rains have turned Bandar's dirt streets into river beds. Between the town and the brilliant waters of the Strait of Hormuz there is a dun-coloured airstrip, thoroughly water-logged. But the moisture is invisible from the air, held in salty suspension under a deceptively smooth layer of topsoil. When four Spitfire Mark IXs, newly painted in the blue, white and yellow livery of the republic of Burma, roar in off the Gulf in echelon formation at 200 feet, the lead plane sees no warning sign. While the others pull up to form a neat holding pattern, it lines up, lowers its wheels and floats in to land. The undercarriage skims the topsoil for a second, but as soon as the pilot feels the wheels touch they start to sink. Instead of rolling, the Spitfire digs in. When the pilot touches the brakes it pitches violently forward, burying its propeller in the mud. The second pilot sees the crash, fears the worst and dives for the airstrip, landing as an urgent shout comes over the headset: 'Don't use your brakes! Don't taxi!' The second aircraft lists heavily, but shudders to a halt undamaged. Out of it into the scalding Persian sun climbs Jackie Moggridge – née Sorour; former flying instructor and wartime ferry pilot.

Moggridge is four days' flying time from her husband, Reg, and daughter, Joy, and now she is marooned on the airstrip with two Spitfires and an ex-fighter pilot called Gordon Levett. They have been thrown together by this strange flight back to the future for six months already, after a chance meeting in Prestwick. She had tried and failed to become the first woman through the sound barrier: the Air Ministry complimented her on her 'spirit' but then fobbed her off with regrets. At Prestwick she had been freelancing on a charter flight from Weston-super-Mare when she bumped into an old friend from the ATA, just in from Newfoundland on a Stratocruiser. He told her about a small ad he had seen for ferrying Spitfires to Burma.

By the autumn of 1953 Moggridge is on her fifth flight. Each one has been a major undertaking, with drop tanks, oxygen masks and detailed briefings on how to avoid the Syrian and Iraqi air forces, and what to do if forced down. (The answer was to say that you took off from Cyprus and hope for the best.) She has become a minor celebrity in the hotels and nightclubs of Nicosia, and the mechanics at Lydda airport outside Tel Aviv love her for her tight scarlet jeans. She knows the RAF bases from Karachi to Rangoon, and they know her and make exceptions to their men-only messing rules. She has been yanked out of housebound drudgery in Taunton and hurled back into the skies, and not just any skies but incandescent blue ones, with mauve dawns and pink sunsets; the land of the Bible beneath her and Gordon Levett on her wing.

Levett is miraculously unhurt after crash-landing at Bandar Abbas. Scrambling out of his Spitfire, he dashes across the mud to Jackie's and uses her headset to tell the two others circling above to go on to Sharjah, and order him a new propeller. They make a low pass, whistling goodbye with their superchargers, then head south into the heat haze.

Moggridge and Levett spend six days in Bandar, pretending to be married in order to qualify for the only guest room in town. In the mornings they borrow a Jeep to drive out and inspect the runway. They bicker about logistics so as not to have to talk about each other. In the evenings they dine with the Iranian Oil Company representative, who has an Indian cook and beer. Sunsets are early. The evenings are long. They smoke on a balcony looking out towards the Gulf, and retire one at a time to their separate beds. On the seventh day Levett judges brusquely that the runway can be made safe enough for Moggridge to take off from, and she agrees. With the help of the Iranian Oil Company's resident engineer he assembles a team of labourers to prepare a hard central strip by shovelling gravel onto it and rolling up and down it in a truck. There is still a risk that her Spitfire might stick in the mud and flip onto its back. The truck will therefore have to stay with her on take-off for a long as possible, carrying sand, shovels, ropes, axes and a makeshift fire crew. Levett selects volunteers and briefs them in more detail before leading a small convoy out to the waiting aircraft.

Jackie climbs in, tightens her straps and pulls on her helmet. Gordon steps onto the wing to remind her she will need maximum power before releasing her brakes, then full right rudder to counteract the swing. She nods, and looks up at him. He leans forward to kiss her, but it's awkward – her helmet, his footing on the sloping wing.

'Call me on the R/T after you take off,' he says.

The Spitfire does seem to stick at first, shaking and accelerating sluggishly despite the bellow of its engine at full throttle. Out of the corner of her eye Jackie can see the truck keeping up for longer than it should, but then it slips behind her wing. She feels her tail come up and kicks the rudder pedal to stay on course. Momentarily her nose dips, then it rears up again as the wheels spring clear of the gravel and the shaking stops and the wings and engine are unleashed to hurl their tiny, blinking cargo into the clear blue sky.

Jackie Moggridge never did kiss Gordon Levett. She flew six Spitfires to Burma, then went home to Somerset to be with Reg and Joy. In 1957 she became Britain's first woman airline captain, though more often than not she was mistaken for a stewardess as she boarded her aircraft. In 1994 she flew a Spitfire again. It was a machine she had delivered from Castle Bromwich to Selsey on the Sussex coast half a century earlier, and when she died in 2003 her ashes were scattered over the English countryside from the wings of the same plane.

Freydis Leaf and Veronica Volkersz also flew fighters to Asia; Tempests to Pakistan in 1948, by which time Volkersz's brief marriage to a Dutch airman had failed. She was the first Englishwoman to have flown a jet, but was still barred from the officers' mess at RAF Langley where that 5,000-mile delivery flight began, and at Karachi, where it ended. 'We thought we had proved ourselves in the war,' she wrote, 'but some people have conveniently short memories.' Freydis bore no grudges, except against Hitler for the early deaths of so many in her family. She became a champion air racer, married and moved to Africa to run a farm, then took up micro-lighting on her return to England.

The race to be the first woman through the sound barrier came down to a contest between Jackie Cochran and the daughter of the President of France. Cochran won. She did it over Rogers Dry Lake in California in 1953 in a Canadian Air Force F-86 Sabre jet, with clearances secured from the Department of Defense by her good friend General Charles 'Chuck' Yeager. Her grand vision of a women's air force for the United States was snuffed out by Congress in 1944, but she never dwelt on setbacks. She covered the end of the war in the Pacific as a magazine reporter, attended the Nuremberg trials and claimed some of the credit for persuading Eisenhower to run for President.

The first supersonic British woman was – who else? – Diana Barnato Walker. In 1963 she persuaded the Air Ministry to let her loose over the North Sea in an English Electric Lightning which made her, for a while, the fastest woman in the world. In the same week she was diagnosed with cancer, but she had no-one close with whom to celebrate her record or talk to about her illness. Her husband, Derek Walker, had crashed and died in a Mustang on his way to a job interview eighteen months after their wedding. She had a son and a long relationship with Whitney Strait, the businessman and aviator, but never married again.

One wet autumn day while researching this book I visited Lettice Curtis in her retirement home near White Waltham before lunch, and Diana for tea. Lettice was terrifying, as usual. I tried to learn from the mistakes of my previous visit and keep my questions short, well sourced and to the point. She still considered most of them ridiculous, and made it clear she'd rather be downstairs having coffee with the widow of the man who had led the Dambusters. Diana was, as usual, charm itself. She served Victoria sponge and sherry with the tea, and offered supper as the evening closed in. I declined in order to make the most of my time in her drawing room, where Bentley-owner magazines adorn the coffee table and her scrapbooks fill a long shelf next to the window. The star of the scrapbooks, in swimsuits, ballgowns, frocks by Schiaparelli and uniforms by Austin Reed, was a radiant, irresistible young woman who lived each day as if it was her last, which many of them nearly were. The owner of the scrapbooks is not so young now, but still somehow irresistible.

As I was getting ready to leave she went over to her bookshelves, from one of which hangs a group portrait of the pilots of No. 15 Ferry Pool at Hamble. 'There's a tough bunch of babies,' she murmured, more to herself than me. And toughness, in the end, defined them. It is what Lettice and Diana had in common, even if they showed it differently. It is what Jackie Cochran and Pauline Gower had in common, even if they found they couldn't work together under the pressures of war. Could they have done so in peace? We will never know. Pauline Gower died in 1947, two years after marrying and two days after giving birth to twins.

By then the former Dorothy Bragg had married David Beatty and given him an heir. It was a difficult pregnancy and a difficult marriage. Despite her new position as a countess, or perhaps because of it, certain members of the British ruling class still considered her both fascinating and available. She met Anthony Eden, then Shadow Foreign Secretary, at a weekend house party at Ditchley Park in the late 1940s. They fell in love. Beatty tolerated their affair at first, possibly hoping for political advancement, then he threatened to expose it.

The relationship was already an open secret in high society. Had it become an open scandal it would have ruled out Eden's progression to Prime Minister. The Suez Crisis, not to mention world history, might have turned out very differently. In the event, Churchill persuaded Beatty to withdraw his threat on condition that Eden stop seeing his wife. The affair ended quietly and Dorothy, divorced from Beatty in 1950, went on to marry Abe Hewitt, a millionaire horse-breeder and attorney who had helped draft the New Deal for Franklin Roosevelt. She had three more sons, took up scuba diving aged seventy-seven and died in 2006.

Her friend and mine, Ann Wood, died a few months earlier after becoming Pan Am's first female vice president and de facto custodian, via the new miracle of email, of the Cochran pilots' collective memory. Her early dismay at English fecklessness had long since been replaced by deep affection. In 1946 she told an audience at D'Youville College, her alma mater in upstate New York, that she would 'always deem it the greatest privilege of my life to have served the British Government in its hour of need and to have come to know the English people so intimately'. She was a towering figure in aviation and in life, whose only complaint as it drew to a close was that George Bush had ruined her retirement.

Mary de Bunsen was lucky to have a retirement at all. Laid low by pneumonia and the hole in her heart – diagnosed as an interatrial septal defect – she flew to Philadelphia in 1954 for pioneering surgery in which she was given a one in ten chance of surviving. She did survive, retiring to a two-room former army hut at the foot of the South Downs to write her memoirs (the chapter on her coronary crisis is proudly entitled 'Not Beyond Salvage').

By the time of de Bunsen's operation, Margot Duhalde had joined the Free French, served in Morocco as their only female pilot and returned to Chile where for thirty years she worked as an air traffic controller in Punta Arenas, Patagonian gateway to the Antarctic. From the British government she received nothing more effusive in the way of thanks than her Certificate of Service with the ATA. From President Jacques Chirac of France she received a personal letter in June 2006, appointing her Commander of the Order of the Legion of Honour and thanking her for putting her life 'in the service of the land of your ancestors'.

Joan Hughes, the second woman cleared to fly four-engined aircraft, received an MBE after the war – and an acquittal in 1968 from the Buckinghamshire Quarter Sessions at Aylesbury, after facing seven charges there of endangering people and property while flying under a motorway bridge during the filming of *Thunderbirds*. Shortly before her death in 1993 she told her old friend Alex Henshaw, the former Castle Bromwich test pilot: 'I have had a wonderful life and would not change a thing.'

Most of the surviving ATA women are now those who joined late in the war. Of these, the truly miraculous survivor is Betty Keith-Jopp. After sinking to the seabed off St Monans in her Barracuda and being hauled to safety by John Morris of the *Providence*, she was taken to the nearest RAF station, at Crail, across the Firth of Forth from Edinburgh. There she was laid in a heated cradle specially designed to thaw out frozen pilots. Like Captain Morris, she was ordered not to speak to anyone about her accident, but news of her escape spread quickly. On her return to Prestwick she found herself constantly approached by well-wishers who had heard a little and wanted to know more.

Betty was thankful to be alive, but mortified to have lost an aeroplane. To prove herself and repay the ATA for her training, she continued flying. Her logbook shows four more Barracuda flights from Prestwick in the weeks after the accident. But her nerves were shredded. 'You think nothing will ever happen to you,' she said. 'But once it does you know it can, and probably will again.'

Ordinarily she would have been expected to appear in person before the Accidents Committee. No-one invited her to do so and to this day she does not know for certain why. But she suspects her Uncle Stewart, minus arm, eye and sundry other body parts, took it upon himself to represent her. If so, his intentions may have been noble but he made little attempt to fight her corner. When she left the ATA in August 1945, she was sent her personal file and with it the official Accident Report. 'Pilot to blame', it said. Remembering this as we wait for lunch to arrive at the Indaba, she looks momentarily helpless; more embarrassed than angry. 'I was shattered,' she says. 'I so wanted to be *useful*.'

Acknowledgements

My thanks are due, first, to the Spitfire women themselves, and in particular to Diana Barnato Walker, Freydis Sharland, Lettice Curtis, Margaret Frost and Maureen du Popp in England; Ann Wood-Kelly, Dorothy Hewitt, Roberta Leveaux, Kay Hirsch and Betty Lussier in the United States; Betty Keith-Jopp in South Africa; Margot Duhalde in Chile; and Jadwiga Pilsudska in Poland. Ann was not only a mine of anecdote but also, before her death, tireless in putting me in touch with her fellow American pilots. Eric Viles, Ed Heering and Sir Peter Mursell were, likewise, generous with their recollections and collections. For their help providing access to scrapbooks, logbooks, letters and photographs I am also indebted to Paul Jarvis, Ted Stirgwolt and many of the pilots' relatives, including Lord James Douglas-Hamilton, Michael Fahie, Jan Welch, Sharon Hirsch, Ann Shukman, Caroline Roos, Joanna Pitman, Frances Guthrie and Mary Walton, niece and namesake of Mary Nicholson.

Christopher Kelly was a constant source of encouragement and alerted me to the existence of Gerard d'Erlanger's magnificent photo album. Minnie Churchill kindly showed it to me. Walter Kahn, Jennifer Gordon, Roy Fisher, Jo Loosemore, Lady Mary Teviot, John Austin and Mike Rowland all offered valuable leads or hunted them down, or both. Xavier Rey went far beyond the call of duty in matters of translation and diplomacy. Richard Poad put the Maidenhead Heritage Trust's fine collection of ATA documents at my disposal and was unfailingly generous with both his time and advice. In Denton, Texas, Dawn Letson made available a treasure trove of papers, painstakingly assembled.

My colleagues at *The Times* tolerated my absences with alarmingly good grace but I am grateful nonetheless, and especially to Tim Hames, Anne Spackman and Robert Thomson. This book would not have been started but for the enthusiasm of Bill Hamilton at AM

Heath and Richard Johnson at HarperCollins. It would not be comprehensible but for the genius of Katie Johnson. It would not have had any pictures but for Melanie Haselden. There would have been nowhere to write it without the shed built for the purpose by Jim Whittell, and it would never have been finished but for the extraordinary and undeserved patience shown me by Bruno, Louis and Karen.

A Note on Sources

My interviews with many of the pilots in this book yielded more detail and anecdote, more vividly recalled, than I dared hope. That said, no account of this kind would be possible without drawing extensively on the pilots' own writings. Lettice Curtis rightly regards her magnum opus, *The Forgotten Pilots* (Foulis, 1971), as the closest thing there is to a full-length official history of the ATA. It supersedes the livelier but slight *Brief Glory* (ATA Association, reprinted 2001), written immediately after the war by E. C. Cheeseman, and I have relied on it for detail on the decision to recruit women, their training and their progress to operational aircraft. Curtis is reluctant to acknowledge that different women had very different experiences of wartime flying, but proof of this is provided by Diana Barnato Walker's superbly racy *Spreading My Wings* (Patrick Stephens, 1994), Jackie Moggridge's *Woman Pilot* (Pan, 1959) and *The Sky and I* (W. H. Allen, 1956), by Veronica Volkersz. Pauline Gower's *Women With Wings* (John Long, 1938) and *ATA Girl* (Frederick Muller, 1983), by Rosemary du Cros (née Rees) show what fun could be had in pre-war Europe with an aeroplane and a reasonable allowance, while Ann Welch's *Happy to Fly* (John Murray, 1983) chronicles the adventures of someone who would surely have commanded the SAS had she been born male. *Mount Up With Wings* (Hutchinson, 1960), by Mary de Bunsen, stands apart as a thoughtful, moving and often hilarious autobiography by an extraordinarily courageous woman who happened also to be an obsessive flyer and natural writer. *Golden Wings* (Pearson, 1956), by former Operations Officer Alison King, is a fond and sometimes wistful 'view from the ground'.

In 1953 Jackie Cochran published her remarkable rags-to-riches story as *The Stars at Noon* (Little, Brown). In 1987 she left the writing to Maryann Bucknum Brinley, whose updated version is titled, with suitable caution, *Jackie Cochran: The Greatest Woman Pilot in Aviation*

History (Bantam). Ann Wood Kelly would not have disagreed, though her wonderful unpublished diaries cut through the hyperbole to which Cochran was prone. *Sisters in Arms* (Pen & Sword, 2006), by Helena Page Schrader, is tough on Cochran but a meticulous and useful study of the differences between the ATA and the WASP.

Midge Gillies's *Queen of the Skies* (Phoenix, 2004) is now the definitive biography of Amy Johnson, though Constance Babington Smith's earlier *Amy Johnson* (Collins, 1967) still complements it. I used Jonathan Glancey's *Spitfire – the Biography* (Atlantic, 2006) and *Spitfire, Flying Legend* (Osprey Aviation, 1996) by John Dibbs and Tony Holmes as substitutes for the costly alternative of flying the real thing. Audrey Sale-Barker's papers, archived by her nephew, James Douglas-Hamilton, include in her lipstick and Fleet Street's breathless prose the story of her ill-fated trip to South Africa, while Douglas-Hamilton's own history of *The Air Battle for Malta* (Wrens Park, 2000) describes in taut detail the background to the ATA's finest hour, loading Spitfires onto the USS *Wasp*. The theory that the war was won by damming the Columbia River is set out in Marc Reisner's *Cadillac Desert* (Penguin, 1987); the more complete theory that it took prodigious quantities of aluminium but also pilots, blood, toil, tears and sweat is all there in Winston Churchill's essential *The Second World War* (Cassell, 1949).

The best newspaper cuttings collections on the ATA are held by the Maidenhead Heritage Association, the ATA Association and Texas Women's University. The Imperial War Museum's archives and *The Times'* electronic archive also proved invaluable.

Each of the 139 women ATA pilots who survived the war could have written their memoirs. This account inevitably relies on those who did and those I was able to interview. As a result, some may still not have received the recognition they deserve, but I hope they would agree that their collective story is worth retelling, however imperfectly, for those who thought Spitfires were only ever flown by men.

Index

P.S.

Ideas,
interviews
& features . . .

About the author

About the book

Read on

Blown out of the Sky

Travis Elborough talks to Giles Whittell

You mention being aware that your grand-mother's neighbour, Margaret Frost, had flown Spitfires in the war, which must have been fairly unusual when you were growing up, but I wondered if you could say a little bit about when you became interested in these extraordinary women and how you came to write the book.

I'd known about them since literally being a kid, but because of that I suspect I took it for granted. I certainly didn't think it was as extraordinary as I do now. It really was just one of those things. 'Maggie flew Spitfires in the war.' That was that. And she and my grandparents were very much of the generation that didn't brag. Obviously there were two reasons people didn't talk about the war. Firstly, if there was even the slightest chance it might be considered bragging and, secondly, that it was a trauma they didn't want to revisit. In this instance, it was more of the former than the latter.

It was really the coincidence of marrying someone who had grown up next to a female pilot – Ann Wood – who had done exactly the same thing. But she had grown up in Massachusetts. Given that there was a total of just twenty-five American women who came over, the chance of that was extremely remote. I didn't instantly leap to write the book because my wife knew one of them and so did I, but it didn't hurt.

The idea for a book was actually born one summer when Ann's son happened to mention a fantastic ATA photo album

2

that Gerard d'Erlanger had put together and that had been passed on to his daughter, Minnie Churchill. Ann wanted to put the pictures up on her website. I thought it would make a nice magazine article. I wrote that in November 2005 and it all started from there.

Given the ever present dangers and the remarkable obstacles some of these women had to overcome to fly for the ATA in the first place, what's noticeable in your book is the considerable reticence of so many of those involved. The formidable (forbidding even) Lettice Curtis, for instance, seems to have been especially unwilling to discuss her experiences. Were there any occasions when this kind of self-effacement presented particular difficulties for you?
With Lettice it was a real problem. It would have been wonderful to have a real conversation with Lettice and I didn't. Arguably she's the greatest character of those pilots who are still alive. She probably had the most remarkable wartime record. But she just didn't want to talk about it. Every question was preposterous. 'How do you expect me to remember?' etc., etc. And to be fair, she is in her nineties. She'd also broken her leg. So there were plenty of factors associated with old age that could have accounted for this. But, in fact, what's interesting about her is that she's always been like this. It's not, in her case, to do with old age at all. On one of my attempts ▶

❛They were self-consciously, deliberately different from the rest of their sex. Only a tiny minority of women could fly or were even inclined to.❜

Author photograph by John Atwell

LIFE
at a Glance

BORN

Oxford 1966

EDUCATED

Cambridge University

CAREER

Ski bum and travel writer (*Lambada Country*, *Extreme Continental*) until joining *The Times*, first as LA Correspondent, then Moscow Correspondent, feature writer and now leader writer

LIVES

In London with wife and three sons

Q and A *(continued)*

◀ to interview her, Freydis Sharland, another ATA pilot, had accompanied me. They don't live too far from one another and Freydis has kept an eye on Lettice over the years. On our way out, Freydis turned to me and said, 'She's mellowed.' I thought, you're joking. She was a really intimidating person to try to interview.

You're very good at conveying both the personalities of the pilots and the stiff upper lip atmosphere of the times. I have to confess though, I kept being struck by how buttoned up, and quite emotionally odd, alien almost, some of these women seem today...

The first thing we must remember, obviously, is that everything happened at such an extreme, atypical time. The world was at war, so in a sense all norms were off. But it was definitely the case that these women constituted a group that fitted no pattern. They were self-consciously, deliberately different from the rest of their sex. Only a tiny minority of women could fly or were even inclined to. We do hear a lot about those who did. But nonetheless it was a highly unusual thing to do. Then there's the social component. I may, perhaps, have rather unfairly typecast them as posh, or top drawer. But it is extremely difficult to imagine nowadays the social structure of Britain back then. It was far more stratified and nuanced. Even those with cut-glass accents and family money regarded themselves as poor and certainly many rungs below aristocratic.

So, I think that bred a whole set of

neuroses or attitudes that they shared. Going back to them not fitting any norms, they were doing work that was completely atypical for their sex and that broke new boundaries. But to a woman they rejected traditional feminism. I have no beef with feminism, but I think one of the amusing things about them was that they represented a get-on-with-it ethos rather than any sense of a gender war. That wasn't what it was about at all.

Picking up that point, the critic Erica Wagner wrote that she was glad a man had written this book because it might make it 'easier for these courageous women's stories to take their place among all the heroic stories of that war (and all wars) rather than remaining, somehow, of "special interest"'. Did you yourself, though, ever question if you were the right gender?
No. I guess because it was never an issue as far as they were concerned. Not one of my interviewees ever said, isn't it funny that you've come to see me to talk about this, rather than a woman? What distinguished me from any of the people who had spoken to these pilots before was that I was a generalist, not an aviation specialist. I make no great claims for the book, but it is different from the rest of the subgenre because it is written for general readers. I've unashamedly picked the best stories at the expense of comprehensiveness or technical detail. And I have had one or two letters on that score from aviation buffs. ▶

> ❝ What distinguished me from any of the people who had spoken to these pilots before was that I was a generalist, not an aviation specialist. I've unashamedly picked the best stories at the expense of comprehensiveness or technical detail. ❞

Q and A *(continued)*

◄ **The tragic death of Amy Johnson is perhaps one of the stories in your book that is more familiar to the public at large. You make it plain that Johnson desperately wanted to head the ATA. Reading your account of her life, I couldn't help feeling, however, that she wouldn't have made a very good job of it. What do you think?**

No, I agree. Pauline Gower set the bar very high. I think Gower was an extraordinary woman. She had her critics but very few. She seems to have been pretty highly strung but to have worn it lightly. She was a formidable organizer and even more of a remarkable agitator. Again not in the feminist political sense; more of a lobbyist really. Whereas Amy Johnson, despite herself, would have been a prima donna. It would always have been about her. In that respect she was not unlike Jackie Cochran. Pauline Gower and Jackie Cochran never saw eye to eye but I got a real sense that Gower got the measure of her. She was quite clear what she was dealing with and was able to work around her while letting Cochran do her own thing. I don't believe that Amy Johnson could have been that politically savvy.

If we consider the lower casualty rates of women ATA flyers and the high esteem in which RAF men like Sir Peter Mursell held Lettice Curtis, could it be argued that the war effort was hindered by the lack of female combat pilots?

We can posit the idea. In practice there could never have been very many of them; there simply weren't enough women pilots. But if you had taken the cream of those who flew for the ATA, they would have managed in combat. I don't think there's any doubt about that. I remember asking one of them, Maureen Dunlop, if she would have flown in combat if she'd been able to. She replied, 'Yes, of course. Why should men have been the only ones to get killed?' She believed absolutely that if she'd been ordered into combat she would have just climbed aboard and done it. And if that moment had come when she was blown out of the sky she would have taken that too.

Amidst all this heroism, something you do reveal that seems quite shocking – and certainly shocked Ann Wood at the time – is that many of the RAF top brass were clearly on the fiddle. It's not quite the image of the RAF that has come down to us, is it?
I did love Ann's diaries for that reason. The sheer honesty, the clarity of what she saw. Whether it was representative of the bigger picture or not, I don't know. There is really only one example in the book; there's a major general who tries to get re-billeted in order to qualify for a petrol allowance. But the fact is that Ann came over, so gung ho to help, an Anglophile instinctively, and then was so appalled by the officers' sense of entitlement.

Of course there is a huge scholarly literature on life on the home front, but I suspect general readers are largely unaware of the sleaze that accompanied the war effort. This fascinated Ann and she tried to scribble down all the details she came across, especially in London. As she records, ▶

Q and A *(continued)*

◀ it was a seething metropolis of ne'er-do-wells as well as heroes.

Some of these women trekked halfway across the world in order to fly for the ATA, and yet the British don't seem especially grateful, do they?
I do think at the time the prevailing attitude in London was that we were too busy to thank anyone for anything. We were in a fight for our very souls and there was a certain expectation that the colonies and dominions would come to our aid, which explains but I don't think excuses this haughty attitude. Dorothy Hewitt, who, sadly, has died since I interviewed her, was the one who described Gerard d'Erlanger's lecture on ill-mannered Americans. Sixty years on, it still rankled. And yet, according to Minnie Churchill, d'Erlanger's daughter, he loved Americans. But that's it in a nutshell: here you have a well-bred, affluent Brit, who in principle loves America, but appears to have a blind spot when they arrive to help. His overriding priority is that they behave themselves – and in his defence some American men had, apparently, come over to fly for the ATA before and they'd turned out to be rather bad pilots and had gone home leaving a few broken hearts and a large unpaid bar bill.

I have to say, given the omnipresent threat of death, I was rather surprised by the lack of roistering, as it were.
There definitely was some roistering. Some of it I excised from the book at the suggestion of

my copy editor, but Helen Harrison, Ann Wood's companion on the boat going over, was by all accounts a thoroughgoing nymphomaniac. At least two people told me that she wanted to have sex – and she was using that phrase in the 1940s – with every officer in the American army. Her mission, coming over, was simply to bed a lot of the boys. According to Ann, she certainly succeeded in sleeping with most of the ship's crew during their crossing!

So there was some roistering. The Americans seem to have been less inhibited than the Brits, though Diana Barnator Walker didn't do too badly. In her case, I think the trappings of romance always accompanied her escapades but she never let her chaperones cramp her style.

Most of them, though, were jolly hockey sticks, knee socks, head girl types who took their work extremely seriously. Crucially, for Pauline Gower and many others, flying was a wonderful alternative to having to worry about men at all. In those days, if you weren't the belle of the ball, marriage was such a minefield. There was the potentially awful business of getting stuck with the wrong bloke and having to stay with him.

The end of the war was evidently as climactic for some as its outbreak, and it's obvious that many talented women pilots found it difficult or nigh on impossible to find jobs in aviation come peacetime. What, ultimately, do you think, then, was their legacy?
There was almost no legacy. What they left ▶

6 Perhaps if they had been suffragettes and chained themselves to the undercarriage of the planes they wanted to fly at the end of the war, things might have been different but that was never their style. 9

Q and A *(continued)*

◀ was a sort of a shadow of an impression that women had flown among the few who knew. Militarily and then in civil aviation they were completely eclipsed. I got a wonderful phone message from a commercial airline captain called Sally someone who flew 747s for Virgin Atlantic. She said she'd really enjoyed the book but only had one thing to say – *plus ça change*. And that was in 2007, and you only have to listen to the voices of those who still welcome us aboard.

It's extraordinary that the really important point that they made, namely that women could fly big planes as well as little planes just as proficiently as men, was not more widely appreciated. It was Rosemary Reece who put it best. She was challenged on whether she could fly a four-engine bomber, and said, hang on, the idea's not for me to carry it but it to carry me.

Perhaps if they had been suffragettes and chained themselves to the undercarriage of the planes they wanted to fly at the end of the war, things might have been different but that was never their style. ■

A Writer's Life

When do you write?
Early morning, late at night and whenever deadlines become unendurable.

Where do you write?
In a specially built shed at the bottom of the garden, at the kitchen table when that gets too cold, and at a desk with an oblique view of a thundering four-lane highway at *The Times*.

Why do you write?
For the same reason that I was a big hand-raiser at school: to tell people what I think I know.

Pen or computer?
For books, pen then computer.

Silence or music?
Silence.

What started you writing?
The Eastern European revolutions of 1989 served as inspiration; Bruce Chatwin's *What Am I Doing Here?* served as style guide.

How do you start a book?
As cinematically as possible, with whichever scene leaps most vividly from the early pages of my notes.

And finish?
Briskly, on the basis that it's better to leave the reader wanting more than yawning. ▶

A Writer's Life *(continued)*

◄ **Do you have any writing rituals or superstitions?**
I drink mainly instant coffee from a favourite floral teacup, and try to know how the next sentence will begin before getting up to make it.

Which living writer do you most admire?
Aaron Sorkin.

What or who inspires you?
Mountains, and half-empty flights to faraway places.

What's your guilty reading pleasure or favourite trashy read?
The property section of the *Evening Standard*. ■

Of Pilots and Politics

By Giles Whittell

ONE OF THE MORE sobering moments in the research for *Spitfire Women* came as the sun began to set over the dry hills of northern Arizona, and Kay Hirsch suddenly stopped talking. We had been deep in conversation about her wartime flying for perhaps four hours – first in a hotel coffee shop, then in the living room of her home on the outskirts of Prescott. She had made soup and sandwiches for lunch, and tea at tea-time. We had talked about her recruitment by the ATA from the Women's Auxiliary Air Force, her training and her feelings of isolation on first being assigned to the all-women's ferry pool at Hamble, where most of the pilots were vastly more experienced than she and not especially friendly.

This question of group dynamics was a delicate one. Kay wanted to be truthful, but didn't want a writer whom she scarcely knew to seize on her memories of loneliness and use them to distort the record instead of setting it straight. I had the impression that after some initial doubts prompted by previous interviews that she had regretted giving, Kay had decided to trust me. I was wrong.

'I don't know why I'm telling you all this,' she said sternly, after a long pause. 'You're not going to muck it all up, are you?'

All non-fiction involves cherry-picking other people's stories. It can be a strangely brutal process, especially if the stories are also precious memories, shut away for generations for fear that they may be ▶

13

Of Pilots and Politics *(continued)*

◄ misused or misunderstood – and many of the Spitfire Women were as fearful in this respect as they were fearless in the air. So I did my best not to 'muck it all up', but was still nervous on publication. Never mind the general reader; what would the pilots think?

Mercifully, they seemed to approve. Kay wrote, on an old-fashioned aerogramme, to say she was pleased the book was out even if she wished I'd made clear that only 17 of 2,000 applicants for '*ab initio*' flight training actually became ferry pilots (and I'm glad to have the chance to make that clear here). The irrepressible Margot Duhalde emailed a brisk thumbs-up from Santiago, where I'd drunk some exceptionally good Chilean Air Force cabernet sauvignon with her at the Air Force country club. But the most gratifying response was from a pilot they both remembered well, not least because her story was so hard to forget. It came in the form of a radio interview. The pilot was Betty Keith-Jopp, and the interview was with BBC Radio Scotland, after a producer had read in the book about Betty's extraordinary escape from the bottom of the Firth of Forth, and had phoned her at her home in Port Elizabeth, South Africa, to hear it in her own voice.

Of all the ATA women I interviewed, Betty was the most nervous. This was partly because of an instinct to defer to pilots who attained higher ranks in the ATA (like Kay, she joined late in the war) and partly because she was still mortified at having lost a plane in the process of saving herself. But she had steeled herself to describe it all to me, and she

did it again for Radio Scotland, prefacing her account with extraordinarily generous praise for the book.

That interview seems to have started something. Among the listeners was Nigel Griffiths, MP for Edinburgh South and a keen private pilot. Nigel read the book over the Christmas holiday and phoned me afterwards bubbling over with admiration for what the women had achieved. Towards the end of our conversation I mentioned that few of them had received any official recognition beyond a standard certificate of service. Twenty thousand surviving land girls, by contrast, had received a belated but warmly appreciated campaign badge from the Government the previous year.

Nigel knew all this already, and intended to do something about it. He first sought cross-party support (from Gerald Howarth of the Conservatives and Lembit Opik, the Liberal Democrat, both fellow pilots), then emailed Gordon Brown. The Prime Minister's decisiveness in matters of state was being questioned on all sides at the time, but there was no hint of it in the matter of the veterans of the ATA. His support for Nigel's idea for a 'badge of honour' was instant and unequivocal, and on 20 February he confirmed his approval at Prime Minister's Questions.

The following day *The Times* published a front-page picture of Lettice Curtis climbing into a Spitfire. Her own book on the ATA, as it happens, is titled *The Forgotten Pilots*. If at last they have been unforgotten, it has been a privilege to help. ∎

If You Loved This, You Might Like …

They Fought in the Fields: The Women's Land Army
Nicola Tyrer

Land Girls
Angela Huth

Bombers and Mash: The Domestic Front, 1939–45
Raynes Minns

We Are at War: The Diaries of Five Ordinary People in Extraordinary Times
Simon Garfield

Betty's Wartime Diary 1939–1945
Betty Armitage

Fighter Boys: Saving Britain 1940
Patrick Bishop

Women's War: At Home in World War II
Stewart Ross

Our Longest Days: A People's History of the Second World War
The Writers of Mass Observation and Sandra Koa Wing

Spitfire: Portrait of a Legend
Leo McKinstry

Have You Read?

Other books by Giles Whittell

Extreme Continental: Blowing Hot and Cold through Central Asia

Following in the footsteps of the Edwardian writer Stephen Graham, Whittell undertook a journey from the Caspian Sea to Siberia in the wake of the break-up of the Soviet Union. Travel writing at its finest, *Extreme Continental* offers a lively and immensely entertaining portrait of a region that up until then had been barred to westerners for decades.

Lambada Country: A Ride across Eastern Europe

When the Iron Curtain fell, Whittell grabbed a touring bike and set off with his notebook and minimal luggage to discover life in Eastern Europe before consumerism swept the last vestiges of Communism away.